Trafficking of Women and Children

Trafficking of
Women and Children

Article 7 of the Rome Statute

Joshua Nathan Aston

OXFORD
UNIVERSITY PRESS

OXFORD
UNIVERSITY PRESS

Oxford University Press is a department of the University of Oxford.
It furthers the University's objective of excellence in research, scholarship,
and education by publishing worldwide. Oxford is a registered trademark of
Oxford University Press in the UK and in certain other countries

Published in India by
Oxford University Press
YMCA Library Building, 1 Jai Singh Road, New Delhi 110 001, India

ISBN-13: 978-0-19-946817-1
ISBN-10: 0-19-946817-6

Typeset in Adobe Jenson Pro 11/14
by The Graphics Solution, New Delhi 110 092
Printed in India by Replika Press Pvt. Ltd

I expose slavery in this country, because to expose it is to kill it.
Slavery is one of those monsters of darkness to whom
the light of truth is death.

—Frederick Douglass in
Narrative of the Life of Frederick Douglass

Contents

List of Tables and Figures   ix

Foreword by Talia Fisher   xi

Preface   xiii

List of Abbreviations   xvii

List of Laws, Statutes, Regulations, and Conventions   xxi

Introduction: Trafficking and the Rome Statute   1

1. Trafficking of Women and Children: Basic Concepts   10

2. The Legal Prohibition   51

3. Establishing an Effective Legal Response   91

4. International Institutions vis-à-vis Crimes against Humanity   134

5. The Feasibility of Prosecution of Crimes against Humanity
   by the International Criminal Court   176

6. Enforcement Mechanism of the International
   Criminal Court   197

Conclusion and Suggestions   220

Appendices   225

Index   263

About the Author   276

Tables and Figures

Tables

1.1 Difference between Trafficking in Human Beings
   and Smuggling of Migrants   14
1.2 Comparison of Drug and Human Trafficking   16

2.1 Annual Profits from All Trafficked Forced Labourers
   (in USD)   85
2.2 Estimate of the Total Cost of Coercion (in USD)   86

3.1 Comparison of the UN Trafficking Protocol and the CoE
   Trafficking Convention   93

Figures

2.1 Education Level of the Victims of Human Trafficking   87

3.1 Three-P Strategy   123

Foreword

Trafficking in persons is a grave violation of human rights, affecting thousands of individuals worldwide, targeting mainly women and children. Almost every country in the world is implicated in human trafficking, whether as a country of origin, transit, or destination. Efforts to combat human trafficking include the adoption by the United Nations of various protocols and conventions, the most notable of which are the Palermo protocols. These protocols—aimed at human trafficking, generally, and at the trafficking of women and children, specifically—have been widely ratified. Joshua Nathan Aston's book *Trafficking of Women and Children: Article 7 of the Rome Statute* makes a significant contribution to the field by aptly articulating how the provisions of the Rome Statute and the creation of the International Criminal Court (ICC) can be further invoked to prevent trafficking of women and children, sexual slavery, and forced prostitution. The book also highlights additional legal mechanisms and responses to human trafficking, examines the efficacy of various law enforcement agencies, and analyses derivative issues, such as the legalization of prostitution.

Aston's book is extremely informative and well written. It aptly identifies the nature, causes, and consequences of trafficking, and highlights ICC's capacity to prosecute human trafficking cases under Article 7 of the Rome Statute. The book covers all aspects associated with trafficking, especially of women and children, while deeply delving into the human crime perspective, surveying international and regional legal responses to combat this crime, and presenting the victim protection aspect as provided under the Trafficking in Persons Protocol. The challenges and shortcomings of the ICC are also portrayed, using the test case of President Omar al-Bashir, sitting head of Sudan, who was indicted in cases of crimes against humanity.

I truly appreciate Aston's excellent scholarship and his fresh outlook on the crime against humanity perspective in the fight against human trafficking. His book makes a very valuable contribution to the field, and provides a useful tool for both scholars and practitioners. Law enforcement personnel, human rights activists, civil society groups, researchers, and anyone interested in the topic will immensely benefit from this book. I would like to congratulate Joshua Nathan Aston for his notable accomplishment.

Talia Fisher
Professor of Law
Buchmann Faculty of Law
Tel Aviv University, Israel

Preface

The main aim of this book is to identify the extent of the human trafficking trade and the law-enforcement measures with a focus on Article 7 of the Rome Statute and crimes against humanity. The book also focuses on the feasibility of application of the ICC in prosecuting cases of crime against humanity with a special reference to trafficking and possible alternative measures, suggestions, and recommendations for effectively dealing with human trafficking and thereby combating it.

The increasing dominance and widespread scope of trafficking of women and children into sexual servitude represents a major breakdown of international law. Bilateral and multilateral treaties and UN conventions and protocols have, at best, served symbolic purposes and produced minimal results. The strategies to combat sex trafficking are based solely on national competencies that are neither uniform nor universal. These discrepancies have negative implications, which are corresponded by the lack of effective enforcement mechanisms and the lack of political will to respond uncompromisingly to the problem. This book focuses on the countries that have ratified the ICC statute.

The ICC statute is a legally binding treaty that came into force on 1 July 2002. Till date, it has been ratified by 124 countries. It established a permanent criminal court to punish the most serious types of crimes concerning the international community, namely genocide, war crimes, crimes against humanity, and crimes of aggression. The ICC statute includes trafficking of persons as a crime against humanity, which is defined under Article 7 of the ICC statute to include 'enslavement', 'sexual slavery', 'enforced prostitution', and 'any other form of sexual violence of comparable gravity'.[1] Further, the statute defines 'enslavement' to mean 'the exercise of any or all of the powers attaching to the right of ownership over a person and includes the exercise of such power in the course of trafficking in persons, in particular women and children'. The ICC has a complementary jurisdiction over these crimes, which means it may prosecute only when countries are unwilling or unable to investigate or prosecute. Indeed, there are many challenges that the ICC faces in prosecuting sex trafficking and the alternative approaches adopted to combat this atrocity. Despite the challenges faced by the ICC, when compared with alternative approaches, prosecution by the ICC constitutes the most appropriate legal response.

The actual scope of trafficking into sexual slavery is unknown. There is no centralized database from which an accurate determination of the scale of this global problem can be made. The database of human trafficking trends established by the United Nations Office on Drugs and Crime (UNODC) is available, though this information is incomplete and non-exhaustive. This lack of information is partly due to the hidden nature of trafficking that makes it difficult to detect. According to the data collected by the US State Department in 2010, an estimated 800,000 to 900,000 men, women, and children are trafficked across

---

[1] 'The International Criminal Court (ICC) Becomes a Reality: When Will the Court Prosecute the First Trafficking in Persons Case', available at http://196.12.39.132/theprotectionproject/sites/default/files/file/law%20lib/icc.pdf (accessed on 12 December 2013).

international borders each year; of these approximately 70 per cent are women and girls, and up to 50 per cent are minors. The data also illustrates that the majority of transnational victims are trafficked into commercial sexual exploitation. As mentioned earlier, these figures, however, always run a risk of becoming a 'guesstimate'.

Other reasons that prevent the collection of accurate information on trafficking are factors such as differences in the methods of collecting data, legal systems and their enforcement levels between nations, conceptual confusion between trafficking and smuggling, and international and transnational trafficking. The available information, thus, is fragmented, thereby making it difficult to conduct a comparative analysis in order to devise effective counter-measures and to assess progress in combating this problem.

With reference to the available data, this book attempts to answer various questions: has the ICC been able to prosecute cases of human trafficking as being a crime against humanity by setting Article 7 of the Rome Statute in motion, and if it has succeeded in doing so, to what extent can this widespread menace be curbed? What would be the limitations faced by the ICC in doing so? Is it time for the United Nations to introduce a special convention on crimes against humanity just like the way it has done for genocide and war crimes?

The book further delves into the role of international law and other related laws, such as international humanitarian law and human rights law, to deal with the rapidly growing transnational network of this form of organized crime.

Though this book is an individual work, I could have never reached the heights or explored the depths without the help, support, guidance, and efforts of several people. I would like to express my gratitude and sincere thanks to Dr V.N. Paranjape, General Manager-Legal, Power Grid Corporation of India, Government of India, New Delhi, under whose able guidance I was privileged to complete my book. He has always been a philosopher, friend, and mentor to me.

I must also thank Dr Talia Fisher, the director of Taubenschlag Institute of Criminal Law, Tel Aviv University, Tel Aviv, Israel, for her unremitting concern and help which enabled me in developing the right attitude towards the subject.

I thank Professor Richard Vogler, who is senior lecturer, University of Sussex, Brighton, UK. He, with his indomitable energy and versatility, gave me insight into the field of international criminal law.

I am also grateful to Professor Bimal Patel, who teaches Public International Law and is Director/Vice Chancellor of Gujarat National Law University, India, for his support and continuous encouragement.

Learning resources at Symbiosis International University Law School, Pune; Faculty of Law, Tel Aviv University, Israel; and Gujarat National Law University, Gandhinagar, Gujarat, were a great boon throughout my academic career.

I thank the Ministry of Foreign Affairs, Cultural and Scientific Affairs Department, Government of Israel, for awarding me the Israeli Government Scholarship for 2012–13, which enabled me to pursue my research at Tel Aviv University, Israel.

My sincere thanks to the Chancellor and members of the management of the University of Sussex for awarding me the Chancellor's International Scholarship for pursuing my LLM at the University of Sussex, Brighton, UK, in 2007.

I thank the Sir Ratan Tata Trust and Symbiosis for awarding me a grant which enabled me to attend the global conference Justice for All? The International Criminal Court—A Conference: A Ten Year Review, organized by the Faculty of Arts and Social Sciences and the Australian Human Rights Centre of the Faculty of Law, University of New South Wales, Sydney, Australia, in February 2012.

My mother, father, and brother—I thank for their unconditional encouragement. The good in me comes from my parents and I could not have completed this book without everything they sacrificed to raise me, educate me, and facilitate this mission.

Abbreviations

ACES	Advisory Committee of Experts on Slavery
AI	Amnesty International
AIDS	acquired immune deficiency syndrome
AU	African Union
AWHRC	Asian Women Human Rights Council
CARA	Central Adoption Resource Authority
CAT	International Convention against Torture and Other Cruel, Inhuman or Degrading Treatment or Punishment
CATC	Coalition against Trafficking of Children
CATW	Coalition against Trafficking of Women
CCAA	China Centre of Adoptions Affairs
CCPA	Child Care Protection Act
CCPR	Covenant on Civil and Political Rights

CDA	child development agency
CDB	child debt bondage
CDW	child domestic worker
CEACR	Committee of Experts on the Application of Conventions and Recommendations
CEDAW	Convention on All Forms of Racial Discrimination against Women
CESCR	Covenant on Economic, Social and Cultural Rights
CGIL	Italian General Confederation of Labour
CIRPEE	Center on Risk, Economic Policies and Employment
CIS	Commonwealth of Independent States
CLMS	child labour monitoring system
CLS	child labour survey
CLU	child labour unit
CoE	Council of Europe
CONEPTI	National Committee for the Progressive Elimination of Child Labour
CSEC	commercial sexual exploitation of children
DVD	digital video disk
ECCC	Law on the Establishment of the Extraordinary Chambers in the Courts of Cambodia
ECOSOC	Economic and Social Council
ECPAT	End Child Prostitution in Asian Tourism
EDU	European Drug Unit
EP	European Parliament
EU	European Union
EUROPOL	European Police
GAATC	Global Allegiance against Trafficking in Children
GAATW	Global Alliance against Traffic in Women
HIV	human immune virus
HRC	human rights committee
HRW	human rights watch
ICA	inter-country adoption
ICAID	child abuse image database
ICC	International Criminal Court

ICCPR	International Covenant on Civil and Political Rights
ICESCR	International Covenant on Economic, Social and Cultural Rights
ICJ	International Court of Justice
ICTR	International Criminal Tribunal for Rwanda
ICTY	International Criminal Tribunal for Former Yugoslavia
ILC	International Law Commission
ILO	International Labour Organization
INTERPOL	International Criminal Police Organization
IOM	International Organization for Migration
NATO	North Atlantic Treaty Organization
NGO	non-governmental organization
OC	organized crime
OHCHR	Office of the High Commissioner for Human Rights
OJ	official journal
OSCE	Organization for Security and Cooperation in Europe
SCSL	Statute of the Special Court for Sierra Leone
STD	sexually transmitted disease
THB	trafficking in human beings
TVPA	Trafficking Victims Protection Act
UDHR	Universal Declaration of Human Rights
UN	United Nations
UN.GIFT	United Nations Global Initiative to Fight Human Trafficking
UNDOJ	United Nations Department of Justice
UNDP	United Nations Development Programme
UNHRC	United Nations Human Rights Council
UNICEF	United Nations Children's Fund
UNIFEM	United Nations Development Fund for Women
UNODC	United Nations Office on Drugs and Crime
UNTOC	United Nations Convention against Transnational Organized Crime
VAC	violence against children

VCA	Voluntary Coordinating Association
VOT	victim of trafficking
WHO	World Health Organization
WMA	World Medical Association

Laws, Statutes, Regulations, and Conventions

Charter of the United Nations, 1945
Prevention of Immoral Trafficking Act (PITA) India, 1986
Rome Statute of the International Criminal Court (ICC), 1998
Statute of the International Criminal Tribunal for Rwanda (ICTR),
    1994
UN Economic and Social Council, Supplementary Convention on the
    Abolition of Slavery, the Slave Trade, and Institutions and Practices
    Similar to Slavery, 1956
UN General Assembly, Advancement of Women: Traffic in Women
    and Girls, 1996
UN General Assembly, Convention against Torture and Other
    Cruel, Inhuman or Degrading Treatment or Punishment (Torture
    Convention), 1984
UN General Assembly, Convention on the Elimination of All Forms
    of Discrimination against Women, 1979

UN General Assembly, Convention on the Rights of a Child, 1989

UN General Assembly, Declaration on the Elimination of Violence against Women, 1993

UN General Assembly, International Covenant on Civil and Political Rights (ICCPR), 1966

UN General Assembly, International Covenant on Economic, Social and Cultural Rights, (ICESCR), 1966

UN General Assembly, Optional Protocol to the Convention on the Rights of the Child, Sale of Children, Child Prostitution and Child Pornography, 2000

UN General Assembly, Protocol to Prevent, Suppress and Punish Trafficking in Persons, Especially Women and Children, Supplementing the United Nations Convention against Transnational Organized Crime (Palermo protocols), 2000

UN General Assembly, United Nations Convention against Transnational Organized Crime, 2000

Introduction: Trafficking and the Rome Statute

'Trafficking in persons' means the recruitment, transportation, harbouring or receipt of persons, by means of the threat or use of force or other forms of coercion, of abduction, of fraud, of deception, of the abuse of power or of a position of vulnerability or of the giving or receiving of payments or benefits to achieve the consent of a person having control over another person, for the purpose of exploitation.

—Trafficking Protocol, 2000

Human trafficking is a form of modern-day slavery. It was condemned in the early twentieth century by almost all developed nations but sadly, its presence has been haunting us until date.

Trafficking of women and children for sexual exploitation is an international, organized, criminal phenomenon that has grave consequences for the safety, welfare, and human rights of its

victims.[1] Human trafficking has been assuming a dangerous proportion, threatening the fabric of our society. It is estimated that the total
number of prostituted children around the world at any given time is
10 million, with about 1 million being forced into prostitution every
year.[2] According to the 2009 EUROPOL report, females under eighteen years of age comprise one-third of those forced into prostitution
in a number of countries.[3] Children as young as ten years of age have
been victimized, and the evidence indicates that the age of children
trafficked for sexual servitude is gradually declining.

Most of the women are recruited into sexual slavery by deceit, involving false advertisements and agencies offering employment or opportunities for education and matchmaking services. In addition, there are
cases of women contributing to the sexual exploitation of other women
and children that are vital to evaluate, considering women are seen to be
taking up top-level positions in these cases, facilitating trafficking from
their country of origin and community. Once recruited in the trade,
their passports and other travel documents are confiscated and they
are forced to work as prostitutes to pay off the debts that traffickers
incurred in purchasing them and in paying for their travel and living
expenses. This is followed by a process where the victims are 'broken
in' or sex-tested in order to assess their sexual performance. Violence
is a common means to control these victims. When compared to the
profit generated, the risks for traffickers are generally minimal; hence,
trafficking is a low-risk, high-profit crime.

Thus, human trafficking, along with the other two major transnational crimes—drugs trafficking and arms trafficking—poses a threat to
the legal framework, integrity, and security of nations. Organized crime
syndicates mobilize people to in turn smuggle more people for working

[1] INTERPOL (International Criminal Police Organization), 'Trafficking
in Women for Sexual Exploitation', available at http://www.interpol.int/pub-
lic/THB/Women/Default.asp (accessed on 15 December 2013).

[2] The Body, 'Child Prostitution a Global Problem', available at http://
www.thebody.com/cdc/news_updates-archive/apr22_02/child_prpstitu-
tion.html (accessed on 15 December 2013).

[3] The Body, 'Child Prostitution'.

as migrant workers, who are then exploited as forced labours and slaves, and the women victims are forced into prostitution. They are also used for trafficking drugs and arms, thereby weakening the economic and legal structure of countries.

Thus, human trafficking—a threat to human dignity, rights, and liberty—needs to be prevented and eradicated through proper enforcement of laws, internationally as well as nationally, by identifying the flaws and deficiencies in the existing laws, taking corrective measures, and adopting policies for effectively implementing cooperation and coordination among countries. A strong legal response to human trafficking, identifying the deficiencies in laws and resolving the problems faced in dealing with human trafficking, is a priority now and needs to be addressed immediately.

The law needs to have a 'victim-centred' approach—a solution given by the Palermo protocol in overcoming problems and weaknesses in effectively dealing with human trafficking victims as well as the traffickers. This three-P strategy of the Palermo protocol includes prevention, protection, and prosecution, followed by the three-R approach—rescue, rehabilitation, and reintegration.[4] Apart from this, international organizations such as the United Nations, UNODC, United Nations Global Initiative to Fight Human Trafficking (UN. GIFT), and the International Criminal Court (ICC) have undertaken various measures towards the prevention, protection, and prosecution of cases of trafficking. Two very important legal instruments—the UN Trafficking Protocol and the Council of Europe (CoE) Trafficking Convention—have also been enforced to prevent and combat human trafficking, albeit with different methods of working.[5] Some of the

---

[4] United Nations Human Rights, 'Protocol to Prevent, Suppress and Punish Trafficking in Persons Especially Women and Children, supplementing the United Nations Convention against Transnational Organized Crime', available at http://www.ohchr.org/EN/ProfessionalInterest/Pages/ProtocolTraffickingInPersons.aspx (accessed on 30 May 2016).

[5] V. Roth, *Defining Human Trafficking and Identifying its Victims: A Study on the Impact and Future Challenges of International, European and Finnish Legal Responses to Prostitution-Related Trafficking in Human Beings* (Boston: Martinus Nijhoff Publishers, 2012).

most important and crucial international human rights instruments adopted by the United Nations also refer to the prevention in trafficking of persons along with measures to abolish slavery and related practices.

In this context, Article 7 of the Rome Statute and its role in the prosecution of trafficking cases as a crime against humanity by the ICC is of utmost importance since it deals with the characterization of crime against humanity and various statutes and the laws enforced to curb these forced crimes. With its focus on enslavement, sexual slavery, enforced prostitution, and other forms of sexual violence of comparable gravity, the jurisdiction of the ICC and its applicability to trafficking crimes as crimes against humanity is a major focus of this book. Even though Article 7 of the Rome Statute defines crimes against humanity, which helps in the prosecution of trafficking cases, the ICC faces many challenges and has limitations in effectively prosecuting these cases.[6] Despite being the universal authority to prosecute cases of international crimes, such as those specified by the Rome Statute, the ICC has not been able to deliver many successful judgements in such cases. Besides Article 7 of the Rome Statute, many charters and statutes have also been enforced to identify and prosecute crimes against humanity with a focus on human trafficking; the most important ones are the Nuremberg Charter and its Article 6(c), Article 5 of International Criminal Tribunal for Former Yugoslavia (ICTY), and Article 3 of International Criminal Tribunal for Rwanda (ICTR). These charters and statutes justify the nature of conduct of acts or crimes with reference to the specific clauses adopted by these charters to constitute such crimes as crimes against humanity and violation of human rights. Reference to them as crimes against humanity must ensure that these were conducted as a widespread or systematic attack directed against a civilian population and committed with the use of force or coercion.

---

[6] Leigh Howard, 'The International Criminal Court—Limitations upon Prosecuting Crimes against Humanity', *Global Affairs*, no. 11 (2008), available at http://www.globalaffairs.es/en/the-international-criminal-court-%E2%80%93-limitations-upon-prosecuting-crimes-against-humanity/ (accessed on 15 March 2014).

Trafficking of women and children into sexual servitude has been proscribed since the beginning of the twentieth century by a plethora of international legal instruments, regional treaties, bilateral and multilateral agreements, and national laws. In spite of these powerful legislations, international law has failed to curb the menace of human trafficking. These legislations have best served a symbolic purpose and produced minimal results. International law undoubtedly condemns slavery and related practices[7] and it is well established that the prohibition of these practices has attained the status of customary international law.

An insight into the statistics of human trafficking provided by these international organizations that have enacted various protocols and conventions and enforced laws for preventing human trafficking, gives a perspective on the effectiveness of the measures taken by the United Nations.[8] A regional outlook on the extent of the human trafficking crime and the laws enforced to combat the trafficking of humans in these regions—namely South Asia, the Middle East and Central Asia, the African region, Europe, Latin America, and the Caribbean region—gives a clear picture:[9] a strong legal response is very much required to combat this rapidly growing organized crime against humanity. Various legislations and legal frameworks enacted and enforced across the world at the domestic, regional, and national levels in accordance with the international standards are still striving to prevent it. In spite of the international conventions and protocols

---

[7] Human Rights Watch, 1993, 'A Modern Form of Slavery: Trafficking of Burmese Women and Girls into Brothels in Thailand', Asia Watch and Women's Rights Project, available at https://www.ssatp.org/sites/ssatp/files/publications/HTML/Gender-RG/Source%20%20documents/Issue%20and%20Strategy%20Papers/trafficking/ISTRFK2%20UNIFEMtrafficking%20fact%20sheet.pdf (accessed on 4 July 2016).

[8] UNODC, 'Human Trafficking and Migrant Smuggling', available at http://www.unodc.org/unodc/human-trafficking/ (accessed on 18 August 2014).

[9] South Asia Regional Conference Compendium, *Responding to Trafficking for Sexual Exploitation in South Asia* (New Delhi: UNODC and UN.GIFT, 2007).

for combating the crime, there are countries that do not have any legislation of their own and have thus become the hub of trafficking. Hence, enforcement of a strong legislation at the domestic level by countries would act as an effective measure to deal with the crime of trafficking and further exploitation of trafficked people in the form of forced labour, slavery, sexual servitude, and forced prostitution. The role of international human rights law, international labour law, and international criminal law has been much helpful in preventing this hideous act of trafficking of persons.[10]

However, the law-enforcement measures may confront a variety of practical challenges in their efforts towards detecting the crime, identifying the trafficked victims, investigating the offences, and contributing to the successful prosecution of the offenders. One of the challenges is that trafficking is often misunderstood and confused with human smuggling and the two terms are often used interchangeably. While they are closely related, they have some prominent distinctions as well. The scope of human trafficking into sexual slavery is very broad, while the actual scope of trafficking into slavery is unknown.

Another challenge is the absence of a centralized database from which an accurate determination of the scale of human trafficking can be readily available. This makes it very difficult to measure the extent of human trafficking. While there is a database on human trafficking trends established by the UNODC, the information available is incomplete and non-exhaustive.[11] Even other international agencies dealing with this organized crime involving women and children as trafficked persons do not provide the actual gravity of the crime that leads to sexual slavery and forced prostitution.

Then there are crime groups that are well funded and mostly backed by influential multinational criminal networks which are highly sophisticated and comprise local, national, regional, and international 'crime syndicates'.

---

[10] UNODC, *Combating Trafficking in Persons: A Handbook for Parliamentarians* (United Nations Publications, 2009).

[11] UNODC, *Global Programme against Trafficking in Human Beings—Toolkit to Combat Trafficking in Persons* (United Nations Publication, 2006).

There is also a challenge with regard to the application of these law-enforcement measures at the national level. Although, the UN Convention on the Elimination of All Forms of Discrimination against Women (CEDAW), 1979 states that the parties are obliged to eliminate discrimination and must take all appropriate measures to suppress all forms of trafficking in women,[12] it does not explain what these measures might be. So, while Thailand ratified CEDAW in 1985, it had reservations on Articles 7, 9, 19, 11, 15, 16, and 29, from which some reservations were recently withdrawn. This shows that there is no uniformity of law among nations to tackle this issue.

The misinterpretation of the term 'trafficking' in different countries has been a major problem in the effective implementation of the legislations in combating the crime. The confusion created thereby has affected the proper implementation of anti-trafficking laws in various countries, due to which the trafficking victims are often considered illegal migrants.[13] Many countries have also enforced legislations to combat trafficking, keeping in mind only women and children, but the persons who are also trafficked and exploited for forced labour and slavery are neglected. A lack of cooperation between the nations in effective implementation of anti-trafficking laws and proper coordination in dealing with the prosecution of the traffickers and protecting the victims is a hindrance in effective implementation of laws. This lack of cooperation is due to the distrust among the various countries and the fear of losing documents or evidences, which thus compromises the protection of the victims (an aspect that would be explored in the chapters of this book).

In the light of the nature, scope, and consequences of human trafficking as well as the problems integral to the existing legal countermeasures, this book explores a combination of doctrinal as well as a non-doctrinal analysis of relevant laws, jurisprudence, and various cases pertaining to human trafficking. It does so in order to establish

[12] Articles 2(e) and 6, Convention on the Elimination for All Forms of Discrimination against Women.

[13] UNODC and UN.GIFT, *Human Trafficking: An Overview* (New York: United Nations Publications, 2008).

that this atrocity is a crime against humanity and its prosecution by the ICC constitutes the most pragmatic, appropriate, and potentially the most effective legal response to this widespread global problem.

The ICC statute is a legally binding treaty that came into force on 1 July 2002. As on 4 March 2016, 124 countries were a party to the statute.[14] The ICC, with its headquarters in The Hague, is a permanent criminal court established to punish the most serious types of crimes concerning the international community, namely genocide, war crimes, crimes against humanity, and crimes of aggression. Crimes against humanity are defined under Article 4 of the ICC statute to include 'enslavement', 'sexual slavery', 'enforced prostitution', and 'any other form of sexual violence of comparable gravity'. The ICC statute further defines 'enslavement' to mean 'the exercise of any or all of the powers attaching to the right of ownership over a person and includes the exercise of such power in the course of trafficking in persons, in particular women and children'. The ICC has complementary jurisdiction over these crimes, which means it may prosecute only when the countries are unwilling or unable to investigate or prosecute. Indeed, there are many challenges that the ICC faces in prosecuting human trafficking cases. Despite these, when compared with alternative approaches adopted to combat this atrocity, prosecution by the ICC constitutes the most pragmatic and appropriate legal response to this widespread menace.

The author believes that the increasing dominance and widespread scope of trafficking of women and children into sexual servitude represents a major breakdown of international law. As stated earlier, bilateral and multilateral treaties and UN conventions and protocols have at best served symbolic purpose and produced minimal results. The author opines that the strategies to combat sex trafficking are based solely on national competencies, which are neither uniform nor universal. These discrepancies have negative implications, which are corresponded by lack of effective enforcement mechanisms and a

---

[14] United Nations, 'State Parties to the Rome Statute of the International Criminal Court' (Netherlands: International Criminal Court, The Hague), U.N.Doc. A/CONF.183/9; with time-to-time amendments.

corresponding lack of political will to respond uncompromisingly to the problem.

The following chapter explains the basic concepts of trafficking, gives an overview of the differences that exist between human trafficking and human smuggling, highlights the role of the organized crime, and gives an overview of how the ICC and Article 7 of the Rome Statute can help in prosecuting human trafficking crimes.

1 Trafficking of Women and Children

Basic Concepts

Over the last three decades, trafficking in human beings has become a major global concern. International organizations, governments, and civil societies have increasingly focused their attention on trafficking and on effective measures to prevent it. Related issues such as prostitution, child labour, slavery, irregular migration, and transnational organized crimes have been subject to immense political discussions and ambitious legal regulations at the international, national, and regional levels.[1]

'Human trafficking affects us all, whether we live in countries of origin, transit or destination. Preventing and combating it requires a comprehensive international approach. We must act together to stop

[1] United Nations Office for Drugs and Crime, 'Responding to Trafficking for Sexual Exploitation in South Asia', Regional UN.GIFT Meeting, New Delhi, 10–11 October 2007.

this crime in our midst that deprives countless victims of their liberty, dignity and human rights.'[2] It is said that 'having control over who touches one's body, and how, lies at the core of human dignity and autonomy.'[3] Protection of human dignity is an indispensable underpinning principle and indeed the very raison d'être of international humanitarian law and human rights law; indeed, in modern times, it has become of such paramount importance as to permeate the whole body of international law. The aforementioned statements are highly authoritative, given the fact that they were made by distinguished judicial authorities—the UN Deputy Secretary-General and the judges of the Supreme Court of Canada. It can be derived thus that the increasing prevalence and wide scope of trafficking of women and children into sexual slavery, which is an absolute violation of human dignity and autonomy among other fundamental rights, represents a major failure of international law.

Human trafficking is modern-day slavery, something that was condemned in the early twentieth century by almost all the developed nations, and the misery of which has, unfortunately, been haunting us ever since. The problem of illegally trafficked women and children for sexual servitude remains poorly defined in terms of scope. Both the raw numbers of such incidents as well as when and where these occur are yet to be fully identified with any degree of guarantee. Further, the operational structures of the organized crime syndicates—responsible for the majority of the trade—remain undercover and thus there is inadequate knowledge about the range and paradigm of trafficking flow. This is in spite of the fact that there are organizations such as UNODC offers practical help to states by not only assisting in drafting laws and creating comprehensive national anti-trafficking strategies but also supporting with the resources to implement them.[4]

---

[2] Speech delivered by UN Deputy Secretary-General Asha-Rose Migiro to the International Conference on Trafficking in Women and Girls, United Nations Headquarters, New York, 5 March 2007.

[3] *R.* v *Ewanchuk*, (1999) 1 SCR 330 (Can), para 28.

[4] UNODC, 'Human Trafficking', available at http://www.unodc.org/unodc/en/human-trafficking/what-is-human-trafficking.html (accessed on 12 October 2013).

Human Trafficking versus Human Smuggling

Before we examine the nature and scope of trafficking, it is important to distinguish between the terms 'human smuggling' and 'human trafficking', which are often used interchangeably even though they refer to specifically different criminal acts. Delineating the two involves taking a closer look at the subtle differences between them. Although, legally, the phenomenon of human trafficking and smuggling are clearly outlined, the situation is not always very clear in reality. Since trafficking often happens within the context of large-scale migration, there are several possibilities for abuse. Individuals may start as paying clients of human smugglers, but some of the migrants, especially women and children, become victims of trafficking.

Human trafficking refers to the recruitment, transportation, transfer, harbouring, or receipt of persons, by means of coercion, abduction, fraud, deception, abuse of power or of a position, vulnerability, or of the giving or receiving of payments or benefits to achieve the consent of a person having control over another person for the purpose of exploitation.[5]

From this definition, it may be derived that trafficking involves the treatment of victims as merely articles of commerce to be traded for financial gain. Victims are purchased and sold within and across borders by traffickers who exercise a type of ownership over them that is intrinsic to slavery. They are then exploited by force—physical and/or psychological.

Based on the aforementioned definition given in the Trafficking in Persons Protocol, it is evident that trafficking in persons has three constituent elements:

1. the act (what is done?): recruitment, transportation, transfer, harbouring, or receipt of persons;

---

[5] United Nations Human Rights, 'Protocol to Prevent, Suppress and Punish Trafficking in Persons Especially Women and Children, Supplementing the United Nations Convention against Transnational Organized Crime', Article 3, available at http://www.ohchr.org/EN/ProfessionalInterest/Pages/ProtocolTraffickingInPersons.aspx (accessed on 30 May 2016).

2. the means (how is it done?): threat or use of force, coercion, abduction, fraud, deception, abuse of power or vulnerability, or giving payments or benefits to a person in whose control the victim is;
3. the purpose (why is it done?): for exploitation, which includes exploiting for prostitution, sexual exploitation, forced labour, slavery or similar practices, and the removal of organs.[6]

On the other hand, human smuggling is a synonym for illegal immigration. It is defined as 'the facilitation, transportation, attempted transportation or illegal entry of a person(s) across an international border, in violation of one or more countries [*sic*] law, either clandestinely or through deception, such as the use of fraudulent documents'.[7] It involves an exchange of money for the illegal entry into a state of which a person is neither a citizen nor a permanent resident.[8] Migrants voluntarily seek out the services of the smugglers and engage in a relationship of general cooperation with them. Once they are in the destination country, smuggled migrants are usually left to fend for themselves and are not necessarily exploited.

Thus trafficking involves the violation of human rights whereas smuggling involves the violation of political/diplomatic interests of the state by permeating its borders. Another crucial point of difference between the two is that human smuggling often takes place across national borders whereas human trafficking can even occur within national borders.[9]

Sometimes, there is a gender dimension to the distinction between smuggling and trafficking: those who are smuggled are often assumed

---

[6] International Criminal Court (ICC), 'Rome Statute of the International Criminal Court', Article 9, available at https://www.icc-cpi.int/nr/rdonlyres/ ea9aeff7-5752-4f84-be94-0a655eb30e16/0/rome_statute_english.pdf (accessed on 17 May 2016).

[7] US Department of State, 'Fact Sheet: Distinctions between Human Smuggling and Human Trafficking 2006', 1 January 2006, available at http:// www.state.gov/m/ds/hstcenter/90434.htm (accessed on 20 October 2013).

[8] INTERPOL, 'People Smuggling', available at http://www.interpol.int/ Crime-areas/Trafficking-in-human-beings/People-smuggling (accessed on 2 May 2016).

[9] US Department of State, 'Fact Sheet'.

to be mostly men, whereas victims of trafficking are more commonly assumed to be women and children.

. In some cases, however, victims of trafficking are also smuggled across national borders depending on the methods used by the traffickers to bring them into a country. This overlap causes confusion about when individuals are victims of trafficking. It is important to know this difference clearly, because victims of trafficking need to be dealt with care, protection, and sympathy. Most of the times a victim of human trafficking is misunderstood as a victim of human smuggling, and treated with stringent laws, such as laws relating to deportation, thereby causing grave injustice to the sufferer.

Table 1.1 lists down the key differences between trafficking of human beings and smuggling of migrants.

Table 1.1   Difference between Trafficking in Human Beings and Smuggling of Migrants[10]

Basis of Differentiation	Trafficking in Human Beings	Smuggling of Migrants
Classification	Classified as a crime against a person	Classified as breach of national sovereignty
Consent	Person has not consented to be smuggled or has initially consented but the consent is considered irrelevant due to the illicit means by which it is taken	Person has consented to be smuggled
Exploitation	Ongoing exploitation in order to generate illicit profits for the traffickers	Person free after being transported; no exploitation
Movement of the victim	Does not need to entail the physical movement of a person across international borders	Always transnational

[10] US Department of State, 'Fact Sheet'.

Scope of Trafficking into Sexual Slavery

An increased supply and demand over recent years have created a flourishing business for traffickers. Traffickers choose to trade in human beings because there is low start-up cost, high profit, minimal risk, and, of course, human trafficking is in high demand. For organized crime groups, trafficking of human beings has an added advantage over trafficking of drugs: they can be sold repeatedly. (For a comparison of drug trafficking and human trafficking, see Table 1.2.) Due to the repetitive nature of the transactions, analyses of the magnitude of human trafficking can inevitably be based only on estimates. Owing to this lack of reliable and validated data, it may be concluded that the enormous interest and concern for trafficking in human beings is running ahead of the theoretical understanding and factual evidence, thus hampering the efforts to counter trafficking and causing unintended side effects.

For example, instances of trafficking leading to sexual slavery are unknown. There is no centralized database allowing for an accurate determination of the scale of this global problem. There is a database on human trafficking trends established by the UNODC, but the information available is incomplete and non-exhaustive. Similarly, the INTERPOL Child Abuse Image Database (ICAID), which although has been linked with the rescue of nearly 400 children, is also incomplete.

The lack of information is partly due to the concealed nature of trafficking, which makes it difficult to detect. Differences in data-collection methods, legal systems, and enforcement levels in various countries; conceptual confusion between trafficking and smuggling; and the differences in regulation in internal and transnational trafficking have prevented the collection of accurate information. The available information is disjointed, thereby making it difficult to conduct a comparative analysis and devise effective counter-measures as well as to assess the progress of combating this problem.

The UNODC reports that human trafficking follows a general paradigm: victims are recruited in the country of origin, transferred

Table 1.2   Comparison of Drug Trafficking and Human Trafficking[11]

Basis of Comparison	Drug Trafficking	Human Trafficking
Perpetrator	Many large-scale organizations, some smaller ones. Mostly males; women's role limited to courier-criminals, guerrillas, insurgents, and terrorists.	Full range of traffickers from small-scale entrepreneurs to major organizations. Many female perpetrators, functioning as heads of organization as well as recruiters. Some high-status individuals as well as guerrillas, insurgents, and terrorists.
Commodity	Marijuana, heroin, cocaine, opium, synthetic drugs. One-time production and selling.	Men and women for sexual and labour exploitation. Children for adoption, beggary, pornography, and even to work as child soldiers. Trade in body parts. Many bought and resold. A continuous source of profit.
Region	All parts of the world, but prominent in Latin America, USA, EU, Africa, Middle East, Asia.	All parts of the world. Particularly prominent in crime groups from Asia, former socialist countries, Balkans, Mexico, and Nigeria.
Risk	High profit but some risk.	High profit but low risk.

through transit regions and then exploited in the destination country'.[12]

Human trafficking is a ruthless and fast-growing business with an estimated net worth between USD 7 and USD 12 billion. The

[11] Louise Shelley, *Human Trafficking: A Global Perspective* (New York: Cambridge University Press, 2010), 89.

[12] UNODC, *Trafficking in Persons: Global Patterns*, Chapter 2, Global Patterns, 57, available at http://www.unodc.org/pdf/traffickinginpersons_report_2006ver2.pdf (accessed on 20 May 2016).

INTERPOL, however, puts this figure at USD 32 billion.[13] Several sources identify it as the third largest moneymaking venture in the world after arms trafficking and drugs trafficking.[14] The core business of international criminal organizations, human trafficking is carried out with virtual impunity.

The Role of Organized Crime

In the present time, organized crime has spread its roots further, including not only drug trafficking, human trafficking, and smuggling but also money laundering, corruption, and other criminal activities that are categorized as white-collar crimes. The growth of organized crime groups has been manifold in the last few years.

As these crimes become more difficult to trace due to a change in the course of their activities, international agencies find it challenging to tackle organized crime and to curb its activities. Discussion is still on regarding the effective actions and measures that need to be taken against organized crime groups. It has been observed after considerable study that organized crime groups are now working in a different manner and have changed their organizational structure, which has posed great difficulty in actually understanding organized crime and taking proper actions against the groups. Now, it has become very hard to understand due to its unclear definition.[15]

Recent studies state that these crime groups have been impacted by rapid globalization and changes in the financial markets across

[13] At the time of writing this book, these figures were sourced from various database and reports of the International Labour Organization (ILO), United Nations, and INTERPOL. However, since this organized crime business is increasing continuously, it is evident that the figures keep changing, rather increasing.

[14] INTERPOL, 'Trafficking in Human Beings', available at http://www. interpol.int/Crime-areas/Trafficking-in-human-beings/Trafficking-in-human-beings (accessed on 20 October 2013).

[15] H. Abadinsky, *Organized Crime* (Wadsworth Publishing, 10th edition, 2012); Michael D. Lyman and Gary W. Potter, *Organized Crime* (Prentice Hall, 2007).

the world.[16] This, along with factors like advanced technologies and increased communication techniques, has facilitated the development and spread of such groups. Professionals with specific skill-sets and expertise are hired, taking into account new market trends, so that profits can be earned on a larger scale. Therefore, the members of these groups are experts in the use of latest technologies and opportunities in accomplishing organized crimes.

Organized crime groups have been observed to target money laundering and fraud in financial institutions and banks across the world, especially in the European Union nations, to accomplish their mission. Such crimes involve corruption at various levels, whereby the employees of these banks and financial institutions also play a vital role. These crime groups hire professionals for providing suggestion and guidance for this purpose.[17] Often, these professionals are hired as full-time and permanent employees of the enterprise or group; this way, they are believed to be more faithful and trustworthy to the crime groups. They play an important role in the management of money laundering activities and corruption. Such professionals create an equilibrium between their criminal activities and law enforcement by the authorities with the help of their skills in managing corrupt activities. While earlier they were often observed to use violence and cruelty, with globalization and technological advancement as well as communication facilities and the increased measures in the enforcement of laws against such crimes, these groups have been forced to change their tactics and their organizational structure. They are well connected with other organized crime groups across the borders, thus being very adaptive to the constantly, rapidly changing global environment.

[16] Examples of such studies include Kristin Kvigne, 'Transnational Organized Crime—Impact from Source to Destination', The Vienna Forum to Fight Human Trafficking 13–15 February 2008, UN.GIFT, available at http://www.ungift.org/docs/ungift/pdf/vf/backgroundpapers/Kristin_Kvigne.pdf (accessed on 30 May 2016); Abadinsky, *Organized Crime*; Lyman and Potter, *Organized Crime*.

[17] M.E. Beare, *Critical Reflections on Transnational Organized Crime, Money Laundering and Corruption* (University of Toronto Press, Scholarly Publishing Division, 1st edition, 2003).

Transnational crime groups work in an organized manner, more or less like a corporation or a company, for dealing with the varied worldwide markets. They have a more systematic approach, with structured organizations having different levels of working, such as for marketing, production, and operation. These have been observed to be mostly decentralized, giving up on the erstwhile rigid organizational structure; further, this flexibility helps reduce the risk of being targeted and caught by law-enforcement measures, chances of which are high in a rigid and centralized structure.[18] With minimal procedures and smaller groups, they work quickly to accomplish their illegal activities in cooperation with the other groups according to the demands and requirements of their operations and of market competition. These organized groups have also been observed to have recruited small groups and executives from outside the main group to carry out and accomplish tasks in coordination with the central or principal organization located in the origin country from where the crime is being facilitated or directed. This increased distance between the leaders of the main group and the ground-level workers has made it difficult to trace the source and to link the crime to the leaders of the group. Further, this structure has provided an insulation to such crime groups against law enforcers. People who are involved at the ground level and perform the actual activities are either not aware of the original organization and/or its activities, or know only a part of it—these executives only work as small units of a broader network around the world. This kind of an organizational structure is often observed in drug dealings.

In view of such a structure, organized crime groups have to work with mutual understanding and in agreement, especially taking into account the political situation and law enforcement in countries across the borders. These groups are also seen to be majorly opting for for less risk and only major opportunities, often entailing mutual agreements done for entering into the new global markets.[19]

[18] S.L. Mallory, *Understanding Organized Crime (Criminal Justice Illuminated)* (Jones & Bartlett Publishers, 1st edition, 2007).
[19] Mallory, *Understanding Organized Crime*.

At the lower level markets, dominance of the crime groups is ensured through violence, commonly seen in drug trafficking and prostitution in the eastern European countries. However, at the higher level, dominance is gained through cooperation among the organized crime groups, especially those who have already established their roots in that area or locality and have full knowledge of the legal problems that might be faced.[20]

Such agreements and tactics have been observed to exist between the Columbian crime associations and the local Polish crime groups that deal with drug trafficking in the European markets. However, these agreements are also associated with conflicts among the crime groups, violence, weaker organization structures, change in market trends, lesser resources, demands, and high risk of law enforcement.

Recent studies on organized crimes state that the development of a complex structure of the organized crime groups has made it very difficult for the stakeholders of international agencies and law keepers to understand the actual definition of organized crime.[21] Since it is an international problem and a national threat, every country is now required to find its own solutions to tackle the problems and crimes in their individual countries by altering or making strict legislations; however, it is also important that such tactics and solutions should be sought in cooperation with other countries. Stricter laws in each country will help in this mission. This will help get a better solution to fight organized crime in a better and greater way, and stamp out the crime from its roots.

Since human trafficking is an organized crime, it is carried out by organized crime syndicates of such organized criminal associations where they work with an objective or a mission of accomplishing crimes and several other illegal activities related to human trafficking. These organized criminal groups follow a mafia culture and hence it

[20] UNODC, *Trafficking in Persons to Europe for Sexual Exploitation* (United Nations Publications, 2010).
[21] Abadinsky, *Organized Crime*.

becomes difficult to prove their illegal activities and accuse them of human trafficking.[22]

To tackle the mafia culture prevalent in such crimes, many countries have enforced laws. A particular example can be cited Italy, which, in 1982, enacted and enforced a law against such crimes.[23] This law was enacted in view of the major three association crimes—common association crime, drug-trafficking association crime, and mafia-type association crime. Among these, two—common association crime and drug-trafficking association crime—are interrelated, while mafia-type association crime is a graver offence. Mafia-type association crime is done through systematic exploitation of the economic and political environment of a country or a region by coercion, threat, or force, controlling the economic activities and gaining illegal profits and benefits. The law against this enacted by Italy has also laid down penalties that include a minimum of four years' imprisonment, which can be increased to fifteen years for ordinary members and twenty-two years for the leaders of the mafia group. Further, the penalty stated by this law also defines the specific crime committed by and within the association, to be punished separately.[24] Again, the mafia-type association could also be a drug-trafficking association crime, in which case the

---

[22] Abadinsky, *Organized Crime*; Lyman and Potter, *Organized Crime*; UNODC, United Nations Convention against Transnational Organized Crime and the Protocols Thereto, Article 2(a), available at https://www.unodc.org/documents/middleeastandnorthafrica/organised-crime/united_nations_convention_against_transnational_organized_crime_and_the_protocols_thereto.pdf (accessed on 30 May 2016); A. Lavorgna and A. Sergi, 'Types of Organized Crimes in Italy: The Multifaceted Spectrum of Italian Criminal Associations and their Different Attitudes in the Financial Crisis and in the Use of Internet Technologies', *International Journal of Law, Crime and Justice* (2003), available at http://dx.doi.org/10.1016/j.ijlcj.2013.11.002 (accessed on 30 May 2016).

[23] Center for Study of Democracy, 'Antimafia: The Italian Experience in Fighting Organized Crime', Policy Brief No. 31, October 2011.

[24] Center for Study, 'Antimafia'.

penalty and punishments are increased for such crimes committed in cooperation.

Trafficking into sexual slavery is carried out by powerful, well-funded, well-organized, and influential multinational criminal networks that are highly sophisticated and comprise local, national, regional, and international 'crime syndicates'. These networks use established global routes to transport victims and they are linked to international mafia cartels and supported by financers and brothel operators in the destination country. The crime groups are also backed by corrupt government officials including politicians, law-enforcement officers, immigration officials, and members of the judiciary who accept bribes in the form of money, sexual favours, and political support. In some countries, particularly in the Asian continent, government officials are the traffickers and brothel owners. Depending on the size and sophistication, organized crime groups involved in trafficking are also usually involved in other criminal activities such as profit laundering, human smuggling, smuggling of weapons or drugs, and counterfeiting of money, passports, and any other valuable items that bear security features. The versatility of these groups is a result of their business-like approach, which enables them to engage in as many areas of profit as possible and make use of legitimate company structures to secretively conduct their criminal activities. This is evidenced in their frequent use of travel and employment agencies. The crime groups are governed by the rationale of risk reduction while maximizing economic results. They are able to react easily, quickly, and appropriately to any change in the market, including changes in the law and law enforcement.[25]

According to Anna Diamantopolou, European Commissioner for Employment and Social Service, 'these multinational criminal networks know their business inside out and respond to changes in the market with a speed unmatched by even the most competitive corporations. Their expertise and their ability to exploit the market

[25] ICC, 'Rome Statute of the International Criminal Court', Article 24, available at https://www.icc-cpi.int/nr/rdonlyres/ea9aeff7-5752-4f84-be94-0a655eb30e16/0/rome_statute_english.pdf (accessed on 30 May 2016).

are surpassed only by their disregard for human life.' The bottom line is 'profit'.[26]

According to a EUROPOL report, the money paid to purchase a trafficked victim can be recovered through her sexual exploitation within two to three days.[27]

The Birth of the First Permanent International Criminal Court

Human trafficking is a thriving trade all over the world—it has earned billions of dollars of wealth at the cost of millions of men, women, and children who have been victims of this shameful trade. These people are exploited and are deprived of their rights and freedom. Owing to their miserably poor living conditions, these victims are exploited by traffickers, who use them like commodities and later throw them away.[28]

To curb this heinous crime, international laws have been made functional with the help of international organizations such as the United Nations and the ICC. Today, every country in the world is affected by trafficking as a country of origin, transit, or destination. The UNODC, as the guardian of the United Nations Convention against Transnational Organized Crime (UNTOC) and the protocols thereto, assists states in their efforts to implement the Protocol to Prevent, Suppress and Punish Trafficking in Persons (Trafficking in Persons Protocol).[29] After the ICC being operational, seventy-four countries of the world consented on the Rome Statute to deal with

[26] Anna Diamantopolou (European Commissioner for Employment and Social Service), 'Trafficking of Women', Second Conference on Women in Democracy, Vilnius, 15 June 2001.

[27] EUROPOL, 'Organised Crime Report—Public Version', Council of the European Union, 13788/1/05 REV 1 CRIMORG 117, 2005.

[28] J.N. Aston and V.N. Paranjape, 'Abolishment of Human Trafficking: A Distant Dream', *Social Science Research Network*, available at http://papers.ssrn.com/sol3/papers.cfm?abstract_id=2112455 (accessed on 28 July 2014).

[29] UNODC, 'Human Trafficking'.

and have universal jurisdiction on the most serious crimes which are of concern to humanity.[30] Article 7 of the Rome Statute was constituted to deal with crimes against humanity, including enslavement, sexual slavery, enforced prostitution, and any other form of sexual violence of comparable gravity.[31]

The Rome Statute: Effectiveness to Deal with Human Trafficking

In 2002, the Rome Statute of the ICC came into force for combating human trafficking, which was growing day by day. It was enacted with reference to trafficking in persons, which is considered as a crime against humanity under the enslavement provision of the statute. To further ensure that a proper mechanism is in place to combat the crime, in 2003, the Protocol to Prevent, Suppress and Punish Trafficking in Persons, Especially Women and Children, Supplementing the United Nations Convention against Transnational Organized Crime (Palermo protocol) came into force as part of the UN convention against organized crime.

Article 7(1) of the Rome Statute enumerates acts which 'when committed as part of a widespread or systematic attack directed against any civil population', with knowledge of the attack, constitute a 'crime against humanity' (for details, see Appendix A1).[32] Article 7(1)(c), the 'enslavement' provision, is further elaborately defined under Article 7(2)(c) as the 'exercise of any or all the powers attaching to the right of ownership over a person and includes the exercise of such power in the course of trafficking in persons, in particular

---

[30] J. Doria, 'The Legal Regime of the International Criminal Court', *International Humanitarian Law Series*, no. 19 (2009).

[31] M.Y. Mattar, 'The International Criminal Court (ICC) Becomes a Reality: When Will the Court Prosecute The First Trafficking in Persons Case?', The Protection Project, 9 June 2002, available at http://www.protectionproject.org/wp-content/uploads/2010/09/icc.pdf (accessed on 30 May 2016).

[32] ICC, 'Rome Statute', Article 7(1).

women and children.'[33] The Elements of Crimes to the Rome Statute see (Appendix A2) explicates that exercising 'any or all of the powers attaching to the right of ownership over one or more persons' includes, but is not limited to, 'purchasing, selling, lending or bartering such a person or persons, or by imposing on them a similar deprivation of liberty.'[34]

Article 7(1)(c) of the Rome Statute has included 'trafficking in persons, in particular women and children', and also in the Elements of Crimes, but the definition of trafficking is not accurate and not properly expressed in the statute, except the 'attaching to the right of ownership over one or more persons' and/or 'by imposing on them a similar deprivations of liberty.'[35] The lack of a precise definition of 'trafficking' in the Rome Statute has created doubts in the potential prosecution of traffickers, with trafficking emerging as a form of modern-day slavery. In the Rome Statute as well, trafficking has been included under the enslavement provision. Here, a reference can be made to the Supplementary Convention on the Abolition of Slavery, the Slave Trade, and Institutions and Practices Similar to Slavery in the Elements of Crime of the Rome Statute, which states that 'deprivation of liberty may, in some circumstances, include exacting forced labour or otherwise, reducing a person to servile status as defined in the Supplementary Convention on the Abolition of Slavery, the Slave Trade, and Institutions and Practices Similar to Slavery of 1956 [hereinafter The Supplementary Convention on the Abolition of Slavery, 1956]. It is also understood that the conduct described in this element includes trafficking in persons, in particular women and children.'[36]

The phrase 'right of ownership over a person' in the statute also raises questions if Article 7 is applicable to human trafficking. Another major concern is whether Article 7 of the statute is applicable to only

---

[33] ICC, 'Rome Statute', Article 7(2)(c).

[34] ICC, 'Rome Statute', Article 9.

[35] J. Kim, 'Prosecuting Human Trafficking As a Crime against Humanity under The Rome Statute', *Columbia Law School Gender and Sexuality Online*, 6 March, 2011.

[36] ICC, 'Rome Statute', Article 9.

major or severe forms of human trafficking or all forms of human trafficking, as mentioned in the Palermo protocol.[37]

Jurisdiction of the ICC: Implications

The ICC statute includes trafficking in persons as a crime against humanity, defined under Article 7 of the Rome Statute, including 'enslavement', 'sexual slavery', 'enforced prostitution', and 'any other form of sexual violence of comparable gravity'.

The ICC statute follows Article 7 of the Supplementary Convention on the Abolition of Slavery, where slavery has been defined as 'the status or condition of a person over whom any or all of the powers attaching to the right of ownership are exercised'. Hence, the ICC statute clearly recognizes trafficking in persons as a 'crime against humanity'. It is subject to prosecution 'when committed as part of a widespread or systematic attack directed against any civilian population, with knowledge of that act'.[38]

To be eligible as a crime against humanity, a crime should be an organized one or should be committed against a considerable number of people who could be the victims of the crime. Even though a crime should be widespread or systematic as per the ICC statute, a single crime is sufficient to be considered as one against humanity.[39] Thus, ICC could prosecute cases of trafficking in persons, sexual slavery, and forced prostitution under the statute.

Furthermore, under Article 7 of the Rome Statute, the ICC can also prosecute cases of crimes of trafficking of persons for the purposes of labour servitude, which may include subjecting the trafficked person to conditions of involuntary servitude, restricting such persons' movement, physical restraint, or subjecting them to forced or compulsory

[37]   ICC, 'Rome Statute', Article 9.
[38]   W. Duncan, 'The Hague Conference on Private International Law and its Current Programme of Work Concerning the International Protection of Children and Other Aspects of Family Law', *Yearbook of Private International Law* II (2000): 41.
[39]   International Criminal Tribunal for the Former Yugoslavia (ICTY)

labour or services.[40] This also includes women and children being forced into sexual slavery and prostitution.

The ICC can prosecute any crime against humanity that comes under Article 7 of the Rome Statute, irrespective of the time when the crime was committed, wherein the statute states: 'The crimes within the jurisdiction of the Court shall not be subject to any statute of limitation.'[41] While the ICC can prosecute a person who has committed such a crime under Article 7 of Rome Statute, it also states that '[n]o person shall be criminally responsible under this Statute for conduct prior to the entry into force of the Statute' and '[i]n the event of a change in the law applicable to a given case prior to a final judgement, the law more favourable to the person being investigated, prosecuted or convicted shall apply.'[42]

The ICC has specified human trafficking for sexual slavery or sexual enslavement by defining enslavement as an exercise of power of the right to ownership over a person, which has established enslavement as crimes against humanity, including all forms of slavery—from sexual slavery to labour servitude. Thus, the ICC provides a widespread base for the prosecution of cases related to human trafficking under the crimes against humanity.

The Nature of Recruitment, Scams, Sale, Trade, and Exploitation of the Prosecutrix (Victim)

Human beings are recruited into sexual slavery by trickery and deception, often involving false advertisements offering high-paying employment or education opportunities; matchmaking services; mail order bride agencies; or even a relative, a boyfriend, or a friend of a friend. Sometimes, victims are abducted from orphanages. In case of women, once they are recruited into the trade, their identification documents are confiscated and they are told that they must work as

---

[40] V.E. Munro, *Demanding Sex: Critical Reflections on the Regulation of Prostitution* (England: Aldershot, 2008).

[41] ICC, 'Rome Statute', Article 29.

[42] ICC, 'Rome Statute', Article 24.

prostitutes to pay off the debt incurred in purchasing them and in paying for their travel and living expenses. This is followed by an initiation process where the victims are 'broken in' or sex-tested to assess their sexual performance. This would involve repeated sexual torture, usually in front of other victims, until the women are turned into uncomplaining prostitutes. Violence is a tactic commonly employed to control victims.[43]

Once broken in, the victims are forced to work in red light areas, massage parlours, brothels, and strip clubs, and are coerced to blend in with those engaged in prostitution by choice. It is important not to confuse prostitution with sexual slavery as they represent two very different circumstances: prostitution involves genuine consent on the part of the women to perform sexual acts in exchange for money; whereas sexual slavery involves forced sexual exploitation of the victim. In some cases the victims are already working as prostitutes when they are recruited and are aware that they would be working in the sex industry, but are unaware of the conditions and violence that would accompany their work. Trafficking victims are subjected to repeated violence and rape (including gang rape); victims are required to serve between ten and thirty men in one night and cannot refuse a customer or a demand, including a demand for unprotected intercourse with a client willing to pay more. Victims are not remunerated for their services and usually live where they work, locked in rooms, under constant guard due to the fear of extreme violence and threats by the clients. They are deprived of food and water and are blackmailed by threats of violence towards the members of their family or threats to report the forced exploitation as sexual promiscuity to everyone back home. Victims are also told that if they escape, they will be prosecuted and deported by the authorities. These victims are not free to leave nor can they easily escape. They are often resold and sometimes transported to other countries. The EUROPOL reports that women can be resold up to seven times, often to prevent them from becoming acquainted with

---

[43] A. Gentleman, 'Children's Domestic Labour Resists India's Legal Efforts', *International Herald Tribune*, 18 February 2009.

their surroundings.[44] Many victims are auctioned off on the Internet through sex websites, escort services, and virtual brothels. Victims that are too ill or are considered too old are simply discarded. This is the only way these women can escape victimization.

Trafficking of Children into Sexual Slavery

Various studies and commentators have put women and children in a single group but the law against trafficking in women and children must differentiate the two classes and treat them as two separate categories. For instance, although there are arguments both for and against the boundaries of forced adult prostitution, there are no such arguments that prostitution of a child is not coercive and an evil act. Unmistakeably, by international law, a person under eighteen years of age is a child and has not reached the age of consent (only a child above that age can consent).[45] By the definition of the UN protocol (2000), a case where a seventeen-year-old young woman agrees to choose to be a prostitute and follows the trafficker to another country or city for the purpose of prostitution or engaging in a high-paying engagement does not exculpate the trafficker from criminal liability for the charge of child trafficking. Therefore, coercion and duress are not the necessary components of trafficking in children. Furthermore, it should be noted that parental consent is irrelevant in the defence to a charge of trafficking in children. The UN protocol defines child trafficking as 'the recruitment, transportation, transfer and harbouring or receipt of a child for the purpose of exploitation shall be considered "trafficking in persons" even if this

---

[44] R. Chaikin, *Trafficking and the Global Sex Industry* (MD Lexington Books, 2009).

[45] United Nations Human Rights Council (UNHRC), 'Protocol to Prevent, Suppress and Punish Trafficking in Persons Especially Women and Children, supplementing the United Nations Convention against Transnational Organized Crime', Article 3(d), available at http://www.ohchr.org/EN/ProfessionalInterest/Pages/ProtocolTraffickingInPersons.aspx (accessed on 30 May 2016).

does not involve any of the means set out in Sub Para "a" (coercion, fraud, deception, and so on) of this article.[46]

In international child trafficking, the form of labour in which the child will be engaged is irrelevant. The only requirement in such a case, at the time of trafficking, is that the child be transported out of his or her country. Once again, his or her consent or that of parent(s) or guardian(s) is irrelevant. Children under eighteen years cannot give a valid consent and thus any recruitment, transportation, transfer, and harbouring or receipt of a child for the purpose of exploitation is a form of trafficking regardless of the means used.

It is estimated that the total number of prostituted children around the world at any given time is 10 million, with about 1 million children being forced into prostitution each year. According to Willis and Levy, females under eighteen years comprise one-third of those forced into prostitution in a number of countries.[47] Children as young as ten years have been victimized, and evidence indicates that the age of children trafficked for sexual slavery is falling. The reason behind this phenomenon is the belief that sexual intercourse with a child, particularly a virgin, will decrease the likelihood of contracting sexually transmitted diseases (STDs).[48] This is despite the fact that 50–90 per cent of children rescued from a brothel in Africa were found to be infected with human immune virus (HIV).

Children get trapped in sexual servitude in ways similar to adult women, although the Internet is increasingly the point of recruitment. The Internet is the initial point of contact used to entice children into a more direct contact such as a telephone conversation or physical meetings. Children are targeted also because they are easy prey and less able to escape exploitation.[49]

[46] UNHRC, 'Protocol'.

[47] Brian M. Willis and Barry S. Levy, 'Child Prostitution: Global Health Burden, Research Needs, and Interventions', National Institutes of Health, 20 April 2002, available at http://www.ncbi.nlm.nih.gov/pubmed/11978356; see also Julia O'Connell Davidson, *Children in the Global Sex Trade* (Polity, 2005).

[48] Davidson, *Children in the Global Sex Trade*.

[49] Davidson, *Children in the Global Sex Trade*.

The Child Trade Paradigm: A Review

Every country follows a unique established paradigm for child trade. Trading in children involves different facilitators, such as lawyers, doctors, midwives, orphanage employees, birth registrars, so-called spotters who look for pregnant women or single mothers, and even visa, passport, and border-control officials. In some countries where corruption is a serious problem, police officers and judges are also seen to be close-eyed about it, passing unjustified judgements. In a number of cases, intermediaries in the receiving countries have further placed the children for adoption. Typically, intermediaries work individually or in small groups and do not know intermediaries in the other stages of the process. Likewise, some adoptive parents know that illegal or unethical methods have been used in the adoption process, but regardless of it, they genuinely believe that a child from a poor family gets a better and materially secured life in a foreign country.[50]

Chances of abuse, however, abound in such cases, owing to the multiple methods of placing the children for adoption as well as the numerous individuals involved in the process. According to United Nations Children's Fund's (UNICEF's) Child Trafficking Specialist Daja Wenke, the various means to obtain and forward children to adoption vary.[51] In any case, traffickers are extremely able—they use extremely clever methods, change their tactics to avoid the risk of being caught, and are dynamic and work in secrecy. This again makes trafficking techniques or manners partially unknown and difficult to trace. Traffickers who traffic women can also traffic children or they can start

---

[50] Leonard Territo and George Kirkham, *International Sex Trafficking of Women & Children* (Looseleaf Law Publications. Inc., 2009).

[51] UNICEF, *Risks and Realities of Child Trafficking and Exploitation in Central Asia*, 2009, available at http://www.unicef.org/protection/Child_trafficking_in_central_asia_FINAL_23_03.pdf (accessed on 30 May 2016); Council of the Baltic Sea States Child Centre, 'Children Trafficked for Exploitation in Begging and Criminality: A Challenge for Law Enforcement and Child Protection', a CBSS Project in Lithuania, Poland, Norway, and Sweden, available online at http://www.childcentre.info/public/Childtrafficking_begging_crime.pdf (accessed on 30 May 2016).

facilitating trafficking for sexual exploitation and might later change it to some other form of exploitation. They have money to recruit top specialists who are better than the police or other institutions investigating their practice. Wenke explains that the evidence from cases and reports shows that child traders are usually not connected with organized crime, but work in groups of approximately three-to-four persons.[52] Some of them work in cooperation with people from private as well as government offices. Moreover, since the nature of trading in children is often transnational, these traffickers even have links in the ruling government.[53]

The same people who traffic women, drugs, and guns are involved in trading in children for adoption—for them it does not matter what they are trading in, as long as they are able to earn high profits. For the same reason, the people they traffic can be sold into anything; they do not care what the end destination is. Wenke acknowledges that since adoption offers very high profits, it is a significant business for them. Criminals who trade in children for adoption use the same channels like human traffickers, for example, in obtaining illegal documents and organizing transportation. There are no statistics available because this is a clandestine activity, but the general trend is that trafficking and trading in humans is increasing and the methods are becoming increasingly cruel.[54]

Regarding adoption, it has to be remembered that not all or even majority of the agencies worldwide are involved in illegal adoption-related activities. Although, neither are there any official statistics available, nor do we have accurate estimate of the figures, but according to an unofficial estimate, 15 to 25 per cent of agencies in the sending countries are found to use illegal and unethical practices.[55] Regardless of this, we cannot say that since most of the adoptions are successful

[52] Bridget Anderson and Julia O'Connell Davidson, *Trafficking—A Demand Led Problem?* (Sweden: Save the Children Sweden, Sida, and Ministry for Foreign Affairs, 2009).

[53] Anderson and Davidson, *Trafficking*.

[54] Gentleman, 'Children's Domestic Labour'.

[55] Gentleman, 'Children's Domestic Labour'.

and legal, it is enough to approve the adoption processes as they are occurring in the present scenario. Worldwide, noticeably, a great deal of efforts have been made to ensure adoptive parents' suitability to care for a foreign-born child, but in relation to this, little has been done to effectively ensure that the child is legally obtained for adoption, or if it has been done, there have not been any immediate results.

However, this should not mean that less effort should be made to ensure parents' suitability. But, a great deal of efforts should also be made to ensure a transparent method in the adoption of a child. This is to ensure further that the child should not face any problem when s/he arrives to the point of proving that s/he is the legal child of adoptive parents/custodian. This should be as per the laws of the sending country and needs to be monitored in a better way.

While older children might be, for example, bought or lured by offering shelter, food, and toys,[56] infants are often bought, kidnapped, stolen, or taken with the help of a hospital or institution staff. As infants usually live in a more sheltered environment, such as their homes, day care, or hospital, it might demand planning and the criminals would be required to disguise themselves as helpers at hospitals, institutional staff, or vehicle drivers.

Women are trafficked to sell off their children. The so-called mail-order brides are ordered from other countries, often from Asia to Europe, with the hidden intention of getting them pregnant and obtaining their children for sale. Anecdotal evidence from social services in some of these countries also shows that women with their (already existing) children are ordered for marriage and the new husbands adopt their children with the real purpose being to sexually abuse the children.[57]

There is sufficient evidence from parts of Europe such as Bulgaria and Romania that women, especially young Romanian women, are trafficked to Greece, where they stay in private flats or maternity clinics waiting for delivery. However, the purpose is to get them to relinquish

---

[56] Chaikin, *Trafficking and the Global Sex Industry*.

[57] End Child Prostitution in Asian Tourism (ECPAT), 'Frequently Asked Questions About CSEC', available at www.ecpat.net/eng/csec/faq/faq12.asp (accessed on 22 December 2013).

their babies who are then sold for adoption. Some of these women are below eighteen years of age. It is difficult to say how many of these women voluntarily agree to move abroad in order to conceive a baby for adoption. Some women knowingly promise to deliver and sell their children; some, however, do not. The traffickers might convince them that the only available choice for a pregnant, unmarried, especially indigenous, woman is to deliver the baby in secrecy and give it away for adoption. In many cases women are deceived: they are promised a certain sum of money as payment for their child, but receive only a small portion of it, if at all. In addition, these women are often expected to pay for travel expenses, arrangements for forged visas, other documents, and illegal border-crossings. They might be also charged for the expenses for the child they give birth to, including the hospital fees as well as rent for the flat where they are made to stay prior to delivery. After paying up for these expenses, the price that they receive from the selling of the child is much smaller than anticipated. Although women might be aware of what is going to happen ultimately, other elements of trafficking still exist. The awareness and willingness of women to get into such a pact might be relative, but it also depends on the situation she is in when she is taken in; there are various methods of coercion, some not even evident at the first instance.[58] In countries where selling one's child is a crime, for example in Bulgaria, women who are forced to sell their babies are afraid to go to police in fear of being prosecuted. The sentences might be harsher for the mothers than for the traffickers.[59]

Infants who are sold for adoption are likely to bring more profits than almost any other illegal trade. Child traders typically get USD 500 to USD 10,000 per child, while the charge of a woman sold for prostitutions is likely to be at least half less, and the price for a child for work only 10 to 30 per cent of this rate. Selling a child to adoption gives profits only once, while women can be sold several times, so the traffickers or employers earn regularly from it. On the other hand, trading in children for adoption enables them to gain bigger

---

[58] Munro, *Demanding Sex.*
[59] Munro, *Demanding Sex.*

sums of money faster and constant effort is not required. In a nutshell, trading in children for adoption—whether internationally or in the domestic market—is more labour-demanding and more complicated but it also brings considerably higher profits. Then again, the financial profits that inter-country adoption brings to the country of origin tempt the traffickers to facilitate adoption even under questionable circumstances—dubious, illegal, and fake circumstances, which the child traders create so that they are not caught and are able to accomplish the crime without any hassles, even with the high risk involved. For the legal system of inter-country transfer, the countries of origin have to devise measures to facilitate keeping these children within the country—they would need to strengthen or altogether create and fund the concerned institutions to care for the children.[60] Acting on such measures would result in double the cost, since the money that would have been received from international adoption is not financing these improvements.

Regardless of their obligations to the Hague Convention on the Civil Aspects of International Child Abduction, often the reality is that there is no political will and no money to invest in the improvements being made in the country of origin. However, corruption in these sending countries aids the trading: the direct monetary benefit that government officials gain from the trade might keep them from tightening the regulations for adoption. In addition, it is very difficult to draw a line between legal and illegal methods of transnational adoption, for example, in case of payments made in order to induce birth-parents to relinquish their child for adoption or payments for parents who would have relinquished their child even without a payment.[61]

Also, adoptive parents may contribute to illegalities—in the mildest cases they offer to pay more to the orphanage or adoption agencies and in the worst cases, when adoption is not proceeded through the official channels, a child may end up with abusive parents, such as paedophiles. This is not just the case with undeveloped countries,

---

[60] Duncan, 'The Hague Conference', 41.
[61] Duncan, 'The Hague Conference', 48.

but even developed countries lack adequate monitoring of adoption agencies.[62]

On the other hand, trading in children is possible because the long-term causes of the problem cannot be attributed quickly. Child trade generally takes place in undeveloped or developing countries. Since these countries face various problems pertaining to economic crisis, besides having serious problems of gender discrimination, lack of proper education facilities, social exclusion of the community, a weak system of protection, and a weak legal system, child trade and child trafficking thrive in these countries. If the root causes of poverty would be diminished, it would be likely that the parents would be able to raise their children instead of giving or selling them for adoption. However, in the short term, these changes are unrealistic. Elizabeth Bartholet from Harvard University explains that there should be alternatives for thousands of children without parental care at the times of crises and that it is simply not enough to protect the children who are prone to abuse, but the absence of carers should be addressed.[63] Any kind of abuse should be prevented while permanent placement for children should be secured.

Causes of Sex Trafficking

There are more than 30 million slaves in the world today—more than at any other point in human history.[64] The various wars in Asia, Africa, Eastern Europe, the Middle East, and South America as well as many national disasters that took place in many regions of the world from the 1960s through the 1990s created several orphans and orphan-

---

[62] W. Zalisk, 'Russian Organized Crime, Trafficking in Women, and Government's Response', available at http://www.policeconsultant.com/index6.htm (accessed on 23 December 2012).

[63] E. Bartholet, 'International Adoption: Thoughts on the Human Rights Issues', *Buffalo Human Rights Law Review*, no. 13(2009): 9, available at http://www.law.harvard.edu/faculty/bartholet (accessed on 5 December 2012).

[64] 'Slavery—Real Stories', available at http://www.notforsalecampaign.org/about/slavery/ (accessed on 12 October 2011).

ages in Indonesia, Cambodia, India, Africa, the Middle East, and other regions.[65] These orphanages brought about adoption hysteria, and consequently the child predators found orphanages and orphan-concentration areas to be places that could readily contain the available population for trafficking in children. In Southeast Asia, especially in Thailand, there are so many orphans, which the orphanages cannot handle at all. Some of these orphans roam on the streets and are very easy prey to the traffickers and sex tourists who flood Southeast Asia for the sole purpose of sexually abusing these minors.

These wars and national disasters thus created new opportunities for the emergence of transnational human smuggling and trafficking in human beings, in addition to the opportunities already present in the parts of the world that are traditionally poor regions.

Another causal factor of trafficking in women and children is globalization. The idea of shared political policies, culture, trade, and regional treaties that will eliminate the demand for visas at the borders of, for example, Economic Cooperation of West African States Nations, European Union, NATO, and so on, made the trafficking of women and children across international borders very easy, especially among states which were parties to the treaty.

So, trafficking into sexual slavery is caused by various socio-economic and political factors that often reinforce one another. The first is globalization, entailing the opening up of markets and borders,

---

[65] See also Alexis A. Aronowitz, *Human Trafficking, Human Misery: The Global Trade in Human Beings* (Connecticut: Greenwood Publishing Group, 2009); Jerry W. Hollingsworth, *The Social Problems of Children in Sub-Saharan Africa* (Newcastle, UK: Cambridge Scholars Publishing, 2013); Suzanne Kaplan, *Children in Africa With Experiences of Massive Trauma: A Research Review* (Sida, 2005); The National Multi-Sectoral Orphans and Vulnerable Children Task Force, *Orphans, Children Affected by HIV and Other Vulnerable Children in Cambodia: A Situation and Response Assessment 2007* (June 2008); Hafiza Zehra Kavak, *Report on World's Orphan* (Istanbul: IHH Humanitarian and Social Researches Centre, July 2014); K. Bales, 'Expendable People: Slavery in the Age of Globalization', *Journal of International Affairs* 53, no. 2(2000); Obi N.I. Ebbe, Dilip K. Das, *Global Trafficking in Women and Children* (CRC Press, 2007), 35.

resulting in the improvement of infrastructure, thereby increasing the mobility of people. Globalization has also brought advancements in communication and information that have extended the reach of criminals and have increased the efficiency with which they are able to operate, while maintaining the desired level of anonymity.[66] The availability of new media such as Polaroid film, digital video disk (DVD) recording, interactive DVDs, camcorders, computer scanners, CU-SeeMe transmission (live video and audio transmission), and computer cameras have all made the production and reproduction of pornography very easy. The Internet, email, message boards, live video and chat rooms, pornographic websites, peer-to-peer networks, and file-swapping programmes, have meanwhile made the advertisement of brothels and the distribution of pornographic material quick and easy. The sale of sex over the Internet is now a highly competitive market and, as a result, Internet pornography has become rougher, more violent, and degrading. Images of women being raped and tortured or children being assaulted are readily available at the click of a button. Clients use the Internet to book sex tours and sexual encounters with women anywhere in the world. They post reviews of women's sexual performance and communicate with pimps about their appearance or performance with anonymity.[67]

Traditional values and cultural practices that accord a lower social status to women are also factors known to encourage the search for opportunities abroad. Some women and children leave their home countries to escape violence and other human-rights violations. Many countries of origin of trafficked victims have a high rate of violence against women and children. In other countries, prostitution is a culturally embedded tradition. Most South Asian men are regular, if not frequent, patrons of brothels and the number of men who lose their virginity to prostitutes is so large as to render it a rite of passage. Economic instability, gender inequality, poverty, and unemployment, coupled with a belief that more and better opportunities exist abroad

---

[66] L. Shelley, *Human Trafficking: A Global Perspective* (Cambridge University Press, 1st edition, 2010).

[67] Munro, *Demanding Sex.*

represent the strongest motivators for responding to fraudulent advertisements, which ultimately lead to trafficking. The same economic
conditions draw criminals into the trade, which offers substantial
economic advantages.[68]

Natural disasters, armed conflict, breakdown of law and order, and
political instability, including government corruption, are also conditions characteristic of countries of origin and destination. In fact,
evidence reveals a correlation between military presence and sexual
exploitation of women. The use of 'comfort stations' as facilities for
sexual slavery by Japanese military personnel during World War II is
evidence that this is not a new phenomenon. Weak law enforcement
and a high level of organized crime in the country of origin and/or
destination as well as an increase in the demand for sexual services are
the other factors which have contributed to the incidence of trafficking
into sexual slavery.

Consequences of Human Trafficking

Human trafficking is a global trade involving and affecting men,
women, and children, especially women and children, in more than
130 countries across the world.[69]

While a lot of attention has been given to drug trade and its consequences, scholars and mass media still need to analyse the subject of
human trafficking. Although there are similarities between these two
forms of organized crimes, there are also distinctions in terms of demographic decline, depression of wages, humiliation of women, and several
forms of gender-based victimization.[70]

Victims of trafficking face severe physical and psychological
consequences that deprive them of the basic human rights and
their independence. The consequences are economic and cultural in

[68] V.M. Moghadam, 'The "Feminization of Poverty" and Women's
Human Rights', *Brown Journal of World Affairs* 5, no. 1 (1998).

[69] United Nations Office on Drugs and Crime, *Trafficking in Persons:
Global Patterns* (Vienna: 2006).

[70] Gentleman, 'Children's Domestic Labour'.

nature, besides having social, political, and demographic implications as well. The victims suffer physically, psychologically, and emotionally due to sexual abuse, physical violence, and rapes.

Although, due to its secretive nature, it is difficult to find out the exact consequences of trafficking on its victims,[71] various studies are being conducted by institutions such as the United Nations.[72] Some of the consequences are elaborated in the following sections.

Social Consequences of Human Trafficking

The social consequences of human trafficking are undeniable. The crime mostly affects the poor, disabled, and socially isolated people. Trafficking involves physical abuse (such as beatings, exploitation, and torture), psychological abuse following emotional stress, forced use of substances, and unhygienic working and living conditions,[73] as well as political and economic impact on the society as a whole.

Traffickers lure young girls and boys through employment agencies and marriage bureaus, offering them jobs in foreign countries. They target and contact them mostly through friends and family members and ask these victims or their families for a good amount of money in return for providing jobs or fixing marriage alliances. In this way, the families and communities from poor economic background fall prey to the traffickers and pay them the money. Later, when they realize the plight of their family members or friends who have been already trafficked, they go through a lot of mental agony. Often, the traffickers

---

[71] See, for example, http://www.trafficking.org/learn/statistics.aspx (accessed on 7 May 2016); Bruce A. Forster, 'Human Trafficking: A Transnational Organized Criminal Activity', *American International Journal of Contemporary Research* 3, no. 1 (2013), available at http://www.aijcrnet.com/journals/Vol_3_No_1_January_2013/1.pdf (accessed on 7 May 2016).

[72] United Nations Office on Drugs and Crime and UN.GIFT, 'An Introduction to Human Trafficking: Vulnerability, Impact and Action', background paper, 2008.

[73] United Nations Office on Drugs and Crime, *Toolkit to Combat Trafficking in Persons* (United Nations Publications, Sale No. E.06.V.11).

pressurize these victims and their families to help them in trafficking of persons and blackmail them that their role in trafficking and smuggling will be reported to the authorities. With a sense of guilt and the fear of being caught, the victims help out the traffickers; once stuck, it is difficult to get out of the network.

Trafficked individuals have very limited future opportunities in their life. Trafficked children are deprived of the opportunities of getting educated in the formative years and thereby suffer from psychological scars that never heal. Teenagers and women who are trafficked for both sexual and labour exploitation are often deprived of the opportunity of marriage or of having children. Families who have lost children and youth to traffickers may be permanently traumatized, affecting the health of the family and solidarity of the community. Thus, the damaging effects of human trafficking are not only seen on individuals but also on the families, communities, and, in turn, countries of origin. The importation of trafficked women into the community, such as what occurred in the Balkans after the arrival of UN Peacekeepers, has many unforeseen repercussions.[74] Sexual services become more frequently available in commercial markets, affecting the quality of relations in the family, especially impacting marriages. Many victims who survive sexual trafficking suffer permanent psychological damage: post-trauma stress, painful flashbacks, anxiety, fear, insomnia, depression, shame, sleeping disorders, and panic attacks.

Women and girls suffer secondary victimization (defined as victim-blaming) even if they are rescued from those who originally exploited them. They may be treated badly, which is common even in advanced nations: they are deprived of leading a normal life, and face abusive behaviour and ill-treatment from the society and family

---

[74] The arrival of the UN Peacekeepers in the Balkan region has been seen to have increased human trafficking, sex trafficking, child trafficking, and prostitution in the region. For reference, see Louise Shelley, *Human Trafficking: A Global Perspective* (New York: Cambridge University Press, 2010), 89; Aronowitz, *Human Trafficking, Human Misery*, 139; UNICRI, 'Trafficking, Slavery and Peacekeeping: The Need for a Comprehensive Training Program', a conference report, 9–10 May 2002.

members, which worsens their emotional, mental, and psychological stability.[75]

Even if the victims are provided with assistance after their return to their country of origin, they find it difficult to cope with the regime and are afraid of participating in development programmes or even accepting help from them, fearing the same physical and psychological abuse that they have been through.

Political Consequences of Human Trafficking

The political consequences of human trafficking are diverse. Trafficking undermines democracy and its principles, thus puncturing the legal framework and the governance structure of a nation. It also poses a direct threat to national security as it sometimes transports terrorists along with the labour force.

Apart from impacting individuals, human trafficking also influences the domestic and foreign policies of countries. Since it involves movement of human beings across the borders of different countries, governments have been compelled to bring in and enforce stricter laws and policies to abate this organized crime, especially the laws involving migration.[76]

Trafficking is now being seen as a more profitable business than human smuggling. The countries of destination are developing profitable and beneficial markets for traffickers despite the enforcement of various policies and laws in the countries of origin to curb the illegal movement of human beings across the borders. Traffickers are becoming more sophisticated day by day in their methods of doing business and overcoming the barriers of stricter laws created by these countries.

Trafficking represents a new form of authoritarianism in which individuals are subjected to coercion and control outside the state.

[75] Aronowitz, *Human Trafficking, Human Misery*.

[76] United Nations, 'Convention on the Elimination of All Forms of Discrimination against Women', available at http://www.un.org/women-watch/daw/cedaw/cedaw.htm (accessed on 12 August 2014).

This authoritarianism is not a result of state ideologies such as fascism, communism, or authoritarianism of an individual dictator. Rather, it is a consequence of growth of an illicit economy and the rise of powerful transnational crime groups linked to but not part of the state. So, while democratic societies have made enormous efforts to develop labour, health, and occupational standards and policies to ensure protection of workers at their workplace, the rise of human trafficking contradicts the values and interests of these societies by denying the workers a healthy labour environment. Illegal immigrants trafficked for sexual exploitation or labour are now pervasive throughout most of the developed world including USA and Canada. These victims (individuals) are subject to a lot of torture which falls outside the purview of both civil and criminal justice systems, further undermining the quality of democracy.[77] Thus, growth of human trafficking, failure of government policies, and children forced to beg on streets reveal the failure of democracy to protect the principles of the society from the increasing violations committed by the traffickers.

Demographic Consequences of Human Trafficking

Most of the victims of trafficking fall prey to human trafficking due to their dreams and wishes of a good economic condition, stability, better living conditions, and hence become vulnerable to fake employment offers. Besides, political instability and military forces of the country, armed conflicts, war, and natural disasters also add to the causes of human trafficking.

It has been observed that various social or cultural practices also help human trafficking to spread and survive. Many people, due to poverty, hand over their children to friends or relatives who have a sound economic condition. They also give away their children in return of money and with a hope that their children will lead a good life away from poverty. The deterioration and displacement of population further increase the susceptibility to trafficking and exploitation. These

[77] United Nations, 'Convention on the Elimination of All Forms of Discrimination against Women.'

kinds of conditions and situations of countries and their populations greatly affect the demographic profile of the country of origin as well as the destination country. The opportunities of employment of the destination country lure the migrants' and victims' families from the developing countries who tend to fall prey to trafficking either knowingly or unaware of the fact that they are being trafficked for exploitation by fake employment offers and opportunities.[78]

Such displacements of populations from one country to another with the help of the organized crime groups have considerably changed the demography of the countries of origin as well as the countries of destination.

Further, it has been observed that human trafficking has devastating and catastrophic consequences in many parts of the world as it deprives societies of women of child-bearing age. This situation is acute in many former socialist states, which were already facing demographic crises and were epicentres of sex trafficking. Countries like Russia and Ukraine have lost many women to sex trafficking due to which women from these post-soviet states do not give birth to children in their own countries, since they are trafficked abroad. Many of these women would never return, and in case they do return, they may not be in a good enough physical state to be mothers because they would have undergone unbearable traumas and psychological hammering. In this way, human trafficking and related crimes indeed change the demographics.

Health-Related Consequences of Human Trafficking

Since human trafficking is of an nature and involves exploitation of individuals, it has serious health-related consequences for the victims. Many victims are trafficked specifically for their physical characteristics and structures suitable for specific working conditions. Such victims'

---

[78] K. Bales, 'What Predicts Human Trafficking', *International Journal of Comparative and Applied Criminal Justice* 31, no. 2 (2007): 269–79, available at http://www.humansecuritygateway.com/documents/FTS_What PredictsHumanTrafficking.pdf (accessed on 10 December 2013).

physical attributes are exploited and they are left with ailments like lung diseases, damages to their eyes, or impaired growth.

Health-related consequences in case of women and children trafficked for the purpose of sexual exploitation are far more serious. These victims are treated violently, and are forced into sexual acts. Trafficked women who are compelled into such forceful sexual activities are often scarred for life with problems like headaches, fatigue, loss of weight, chest pain, stomach pain, back, pelvic and vaginal pain, and various other problems such as ear-, skin-, eye-, and teeth-related problems. Their infections and sickness are never treated, and they are continuously and consistently exploited sexually.[79]

Trafficking victims either die, fall sick, or seriously injure themselves as a result of the hazardous work conditions in which they labour. For many who are impaired, there is no effective treatment as they are psychologically damaged for life, suffering frequent nightmares and flashbacks, and often developing suicidal tendencies. The constant abuse and ill-treatment they have suffered makes it impossible for them to return to normal conditions. For example, hundreds of victims die annually due to dehydration while attempting to cross the deserts from Mexico to USA. Others die in transit, as they are kept in poor conditions and transported in overcrowded buses or unseaworthy vessels.

Many of the victims suffer from HIV or other Sexually Transmitted Diseases (STDs) and have no resources nor any possibility to protect themselves in their sexual encounters. Lack of knowledge and necessary information about HIV and other STDs have aggravated the spread of these diseases. The traffickers and the clients generally have a misconception that sexual intercourse with a virgin cures the disease and younger girls are not affected by diseases. This has increased their demand and thus young girls and children have become vulnerable to trafficking. But the studies have revealed that since these young girls are subjected to longer periods of time in brothels, they are more

---

[79] C. Zimmerman et al. *Stolen Smiles: A Summary Report on the Physical and Psychological Health Consequences of Women and Adolescents Trafficked in Europe* (London: London School of Hygiene and Tropical Medicine, 2006).

vulnerable to HIV/AIDS. To make situations worse, in the trafficking culture, the lives of these young girls infected with HIV/AIDS are cheaper than the cost of their medication. Often, several sex trafficking victims are killed by their clients, their numbers being unknown.

Children who are forced to beg suffer from injuries that cannot be cured. Many-a-times the traffickers themselves break the limbs of the children so that when they are sent for begging: beggars with broken limbs would attract more sympathy from the public.[80] Handicapped children are forced to beg in the heat of the sun, without any food, and die of dehydration and other illnesses. Broken limbs may result in crippled life forever. Further, children are also subjected to sexual abuse and exploitation, hunger, and malnutrition. The consequences may lead to stunted growth, reproductive problems at a later stage in life, fatigue, and lower resistance to various communicable diseases. They may have behavioural problems such as becoming anti-social, aggressiveness, addiction, and sexualized behaviour. They may also have delayed developmental processes, problems in learning, poor verbal skills, and poor memory.[81]

Trafficking of women and children into sexual slavery causes an increase in the incidence of cancer, STDs, and communicable diseases, all of which pose serious health threats to the society at large. Many victims become drug addicts and develop serious psychological and mental problems because of the permanent damage to their reproductive organs, often leading to death or suicide. Sexually exploited women might need to have abortions. Pregnant women are forced to work until the day they go into labour. Thus, many babies are born with STDs such as syphilis, are HIV positive, and suffer from drug withdrawal.[82]

---

[80] C. Zimmerman, M. Hossain, and C. Watts, 'Human Trafficking and Health: A Conceptual Model to Inform Policy, Intervention and Research', *Social Science and Medicine* 73, no. 2 (2011): 327–35.

[81] Zimmerman, Hossain, and Watts, 'Human Trafficking and Health'.

[82] C. Zimmerman, *Health Risks and Consequences of Trafficked Women in Europe: Conceptual Models, Qualitative and Quantitative Findings* (London: London School of Hygiene and Tropical Medicine, 2007).

The devastated mental health and well-being of the victims of human trafficking are consequences of severe sexual exploitation, abuse, and trauma. This gives rise to persistent anxiety, fear, and insecurity. The psychological effects on the victims include post-traumatic stress disorder, depression, disorientation, memory loss, isolation, extreme sadness, hopelessness, and suicidal feelings. The victims are also seen to have low levels of concentration, anger and tend to remain withdrawn.[83]

Thus, human trafficking has become a serious concern for national security and, as such, has become a priority on the international human rights agenda and on the political agenda of many states.

***

It may be concluded that trafficking in human beings is a complex crime and the translation of anti-trafficking laws into practice is challenging. The law enforcement may confront a variety of practical challenges in their efforts to detect trafficking, identify the trafficked victims, investigate the offences, and contribute to the successful prosecution of the offenders.

Human trafficking, as it is discussed, affects everyone. A proper approach on an international basis towards combating it is the need of the hour. The chapter deals with the extent of the human trafficking trade within and across the borders of the countries and the role of international laws, international humanitarian law, and human rights law. Human trafficking or the modern-day slavery, as it is known today, has been thriving despite the enforcement of protocols and laws by the United Nations and all other stakeholders who have been a part of the protocol.

The main focus of the chapter has been the role of international laws, UN conventions and protocols, and international organizations such as the ICC, and analysis the effectiveness of the Rome Statute. The distinction between the terms human trafficking and human smuggling, which are used interchangeably, has also been highlighted.

---

[83] Zimmerman, *Health Risks.*

Often these two terms are wrongly used due to which the victims of human trafficking suffer as they are misunderstood as victims of human smuggling and treated in a different manner through stringent laws operational for human smuggling or illegal immigration.

The scope of human trafficking into sexual slavery has been discussed and analysed in detail with the help of data available from UNODC and other international agencies dealing with this organized crime involving women and children as trafficked persons, leading to sexual slavery and forced prostitution.[84] The study further reveals that there is a lack of information and data due to the concealed nature of the trade. The reason for this lack of information further extends to the different methods applied in the collection of data, different legal systems, and enforcement levels between countries, as well as conceptual confusion between trafficking and smuggling and internal and transnational trafficking, which has prevented the collection of accurate information.

The role of organized crime groups have also been discussed and the study has revealed that these groups which are involved in the trade of human trafficking and sexual slavery are well-funded, well-organized, and backed by influential multinational criminal networks that are highly sophisticated and comprise local, national, regional, and international crime syndicates. These crime groups are also backed by corrupt government officials including politicians, law-enforcement officers, immigration officials, and members of the judiciary who extract bribes in the form of money, sexual favours, and political support.

The chapter further dealt with the measures undertaken by international organizations, such as the ICC, in combating human trafficking. The role and effectiveness of the Rome Statute has also been

---

[84] UNODC, *Trafficking in Persons: Global Patterns*, Chapter 2, 57, available at http://www.unodc.org/pdf/traffickinginpersons_report_2006ver2.pdf (accessed on 30 May 2016); UNODC and UN.GIFT, *Responding to Trafficking for Sexual Exploitation in South Asia*, South Asia Regional Conference Compendium, New Delhi, 2007; Asha-Rose Migiro in UNODC.GIFT, *The Global Initiative to Fight Human Trafficking* (Austria: United Nations Publications, 2007), available at https://www.unodc.org/pdf/gift%20brochure.pdf (accessed on 30 May 2016).

discussed, especially the effectiveness of Article 7 of the Rome Statute, in dealing with and preventing trafficking of women and children and forced prostitution. The jurisdiction of the ICC has been studied and its implications have been discussed, in view of its effectiveness in prosecution of cases.

The chapter has also dealt with the nature of recruitment, scams, sale, trade, and exploitation of the victims by the traffickers. Human beings, especially women and children, are trapped into this trade through tricks, deception, false promises, employment opportunities, education opportunities, and matchmaking organizations. Even relatives and members of the family are involved in this trade. The exploitation and torture faced by the victims has also been discussed, as has been the plight of women and the consequences they face if they try to escape.

Trafficking of children into sexual slavery has also been explained in the chapter. It is seen that children are the ones most vulnerable to this trade and they are trapped in sexual servitude very easily.

Further, it has been discussed and analysed as to what are the causes of sex trafficking. The major causes of sex trafficking are mainly socio-economic and political factors. Moreover, the studies have also revealed that globalization has been one of the factors in this trade as it has created a borderless world, improved the infrastructure, increased the mobility of people, and has brought advancement in communication and information. The new forms of media have also made the work of the organized crime groups quicker and easier. Other causes seen behind sex trafficking are natural disasters, armed conflict, breakdown of law and order, and/or political instability.

The chapter has concluded with the discussion on the consequences of sex trafficking. It has been observed that the consequences include various types of dreadful and communicable diseases which are a threat to human health. It has also been studied that sex trafficking sustains organized crime, promotes government corruption, and erosion of government authority; it promotes social breakdown and constitutes severe abuse of human rights. Drug addiction and development of serious psychological and mental problems among the victims is also seen as a serious consequence.

This trade of human trafficking has become a present-day threat to human dignity, human rights, and liberty. It is prevented and eradicated through proper enforcement of laws internationally, by identifying the flaws and deficiencies in the existing laws, taking corrective measures, and proper coordination between the countries. Legal response in dealing with human trafficking and identifying the deficiencies in laws and problems faced in combating the crime is a priority and should be addressed immediately. The next chapter deals with legal prohibition against human trafficking and the legal responses, deficiencies in laws, and problems faced in dealing with human trafficking.

2   The Legal Prohibition

Human trafficking, especially trafficking of women and children, is a dreadful reality in today's modern world. Women and children are trafficked all over the world for forced prostitution, sexual slavery, and forced labour. The mere monetary benefits through this flourishing inhuman trade has encouraged people to accomplish such organized crimes internationally. According to CRS Report for Congress (2010), every year around 800,000 to 900,000 people are trafficked across borders worldwide and around 18,000 to 20,000 are trafficked to the US.[1]

The aim of this chapter is to discuss the state's obligation under international human rights law, international labour law, and international criminal law in order to prevent this hideous act of trafficking in

[1] Congressional Research Service, 'Trafficking in Persons: U.S. Policy and Issues for Congress', available at http://fpc.state.gov/documents/organization/139278.pdf (accessed on 19 September 2014).

persons. Some of the most important and crucial international human rights instruments adopted by the United Nations actually refer to the abolition of slave trade and slave practices along with trafficking in persons. As far as the international labour law is concerned, this chapter discusses the conventions and the legal framework adopted by various labour organizations. Further discussed are the legal responses in dealing with human trafficking, highlighting the various conventions, protocols, and treaties adopted and enforced by the United Nations in curbing and combating human trafficking, with specific focus on the trafficking of women and children.

Many conventions and protocols have been framed by the UNODC under the international law to prohibit and prosecute human trafficking, such as United Nations Convention against Transnational Organized Crime; Supplementary Convention on the Abolition of Slavery, the Slave Trade, and Institutions and Practices Similar to Slavery; United Nations Protocol to Prevent, Suppress, and Punish Trafficking in Persons, Especially Women and Children; and United Nations Protocol against the Smuggling of Migrants by Land, Sea and Air. The UNODC has also instituted the United Nations Global Initiative to Fight Human Trafficking (UN.GIFT) in March 2007 to combat human trafficking in cooperation with the International Labour Organization (ILO), UN Children's Fund (UNICEF), International Organization for Migration (IOM), Organization for Security and Co-operation in Europe (OSCE), and Office of the High Commissioner for Human Rights (OHCHR).[2]

Furthermore, international law has also included the Universal Declaration of Human Rights, 1948; the United Nations Convention for the Suppression of Trafficking in Persons and of the Exploitation of the Prostitution of Others, 1949; the International Covenants on Civil and Political Rights, 1966; and the Convention on the Elimination of all Forms of Discrimination against Women, 1979 towards the initiative of prohibiting and combating trafficking of human beings.

---

[2] J. Fisher, *Human Trafficking: Law Enforcement Resource Guide* (Create Space Independent Publishing Platform, 2009).

Despite the various laws, conventions, and protocols being enforced by the United Nations as well as the countries which have been party to these conventions and protocols, there have been many deficiencies that have aggravated this problem and eventually helped organized crime groups to flourish in this trade of human trafficking. The deficiencies have also given rise to various problems in dealing with cases of human trafficking, especially of women and children who have been the majority among the victims of trafficking and have been exploited repeatedly. This chapter also highlights the gender perspective in human trafficking of women and children and the role of women in the sexual exploitation of other women as well as children. The women involved in human trafficking often take up the role at the top level of this organized crime and facilitate the trafficking of women and children from their country of origin and community.

The Legal Response

Human trafficking has emerged as a flourishing cross-border trade and has become a major area of concern. As per the United Nations, 700,000 to 4 million people are estimated to be trafficked every year all over the world.[3] The majority of the trafficked persons are women and children who are forced into prostitution, slavery, labour, and many other types of exploitation. It is seen that sometimes the trafficked persons are subject to such exploitation voluntarily due to their poor economic condition.

The need for an immediate remedy to this illegal trade, which is a violation of human rights, is of utmost importance in the current scenario. The United Nations has been working on this major issue with the help of its conventions and protocols to prevent, prosecute, punish, and eradicate this problem. But the UN conventions, protocols, and legislations are interpreted differently in different countries and the meaning of the word 'trafficking' also varies from country to country. Since trafficking is a social issue, it also depends on the social and economic conditions as well as traditions and cultures of each country.

---

[3] U.S. Department of State, *Trafficking in Persons Report 2010.*

The legislations of the countries of the world and the UN conventions and protocols need to be streamlined and aligned to deal with human trafficking in a better way.

Human trafficking, as per the UN protocol, is defined as the 'recruitment, transportation, transfer, harbouring or receipt of persons, by means of coercion, of abduction, of fraud, of deception, of abuse of power or of a position, of vulnerability or of the giving or receiving of payments or benefits to achieve the consent of a person having control over another person for the purpose of exploitation.'[4] Exploitation includes exploiting the prostitution of others, sexual exploitation, forced labour, slavery or similar practices, and the removal of organs.[5]

The UN protocol should make sure that the people who are found guilty of trafficking are penalized; the victims should be dealt with sympathy, provided proper protection, and given a temporary or permanent residence in the country of destination.[6] This protocol has been accepted globally but a major question that arises is how far is it effective in preventing or combating human trafficking internationally. This requires a common consensus that is beneficial and efficient for all countries irrespective of the various legislations operative in individual countries.

The legal framework for combating human trafficking was first institutionalized in 1904 as an international agreement to suppress the white slaves by the League of Nations, and later, in 1910, International

---

[4] United Nations Human Rights, 'Protocol to Prevent, Suppress and Punish Trafficking in Persons Especially Women and Children, supplementing the United Nations Convention against Transnational Organized Crime', Article 3, available at http://www.ohchr.org/EN/ProfessionalInterest/Pages/ProtocolTraffickingInPersons.aspx (accessed 30 May 2016).

[5] UNODC, 'Human Trafficking', available at http://www.unodc.org/unodc/en/human-trafficking/what-is-human-trafficking.html (accessed 12 October 2013).

[6] International Criminal Court (ICC), 'Rome Statute of the International Criminal Court', Article 24, available at https://www.icc-cpi.int/nr/rdonlyres/ea9aeff7-5752-4f84-be94-0a655eb30e16/0/rome_statute_english.pdf (accessed on 17 May 2016).

Convention for the Suppression of the White Slave Traffic came into force. In that period, white slaves were referred to as prostitutes and white slavery was referred to as prostitution. In 1921, the convention included children and in 1933, it made provision for female children. This convention was again amended by the Protocol signed at Lake Success, New York, on 4 May 1949.[7]

To combat human trafficking—slavery, servitude, sexual exploitation through forced prostitution, and other forms of exploitation being carried out because of human trafficking—the protocols and treaties enforced by the United Nations must conform to the international law and should be complied to the states/countries at their domestic level. The UNHRC monitors the implementation and compliance of the protocols and conventions in the countries of the parties with the help of its rapporteurs, groups, and non-governmental organizations (NGOs). The parties also prepare an annual report on the activities undertaken and various steps and actions taken towards combating human trafficking in their own countries and submit it to the United Nations for review. The enforcement of legislations at the domestic level, in conformity with the international law and related protocols and conventions enforced by the United Nations is the most effective way of combating human trafficking, especially of women and children. However, in most of the cases, it has been noticed that efficient working of legal mechanisms to combat this crime is not so effective due to the increasing number of cases of trafficking across the world and the sophisticated methods being used by the traffickers in response to these legal prohibitive measures.

With reference to the laws prevalent in South Asia for combating cross-border trafficking of human beings, these laws are majorly domestic legislations since most of the cases are monitored or dealt with locally. This is particularly so because the countries in South Asia

---

[7] United Nations, 'International Convention for the Suppression of the White Slave Traffic', signed at Paris on 4 May 1910, amended by the Protocol signed at Lake Success, New York, 4 May 1949, Treaty Series, vol. 98, , available at https://treaties.un.org/pages/ViewDetails.aspx?src=TREATY&mtdsg_no=VII-9&chapter=7&lang=en (accessed on 21 June 2014).

depend on the criminal justice system prevailing in their own countries for the enforcement of legislations and punishment of the offenders thereby.[8]

Thus, the United Nations has enforced many conventions and protocols to deal with human trafficking and taken various measures to combat this organized crime with the help and support of major countries all over the world. Some of these conventions and protocols which have been enforced towards the prohibition of human trafficking, especially of women and children, and protecting their basic human rights, have been discussed under the following headings.

Universal Declaration of Human Rights

It was on 10 December 1948 that the United Nations adopted the Universal Declaration of Human Rights (UDHR). Its preamble acknowledged that the recognition of inherent dignity and of the equal and inalienable rights of all the members of the human family is the foundation of justice, equality, freedom, and peace in the world. The General Assembly of the United Nations considers the UDHR as a common standard of achievement for all the nations and mankind and expects that every individual and society should promote and respect human rights and freedom by educating people about the declaration.[9]

Article 1 of the UDHR states that everyone is born free with equal dignity and rights and that they should act in a spirit of brotherhood with reason and conscience. From the basic assumption that all human beings are free and equal, it means that the principles of slavery, slave trade, and servitude must be abolished. Further, Article 4 of the UDHR states that no person shall be held in slavery or servitude, and that

---

[8] UNODC, UN Women, and UN.GIFT, 'Responses to Human Trafficking in Bangladesh, India, Nepal and Sri Lanka', review by UNODC—Regional Office for South Asia under the UN.GIFT, New Delhi, 2011.

[9] United Nations, *The Universal Declaration of Human Rights*, available at http://www.un.org/en/documents/udhr/#atop (accessed on 12 August 2014).

slavery and slave trade shall be prohibited in all forms. Furthermore, Article 13 of UDHR states that every person has the right to freedom of movement and residence in any state. Also, Article 23 (1) states that every person has the right to freely choose employment and to obtain favourable conditions of work.[10]

International Covenant on Civil and Political Rights

The International Covenant on Civil and Political Rights (ICCPR) was adopted in 1966 on the guidelines of the UDHR. It recognizes that human beings can enjoy civil and political freedom and can achieve freedom from fear only if the states create an environment in which every individual can enjoy these rights along with the economic, social, and cultural rights. It also lays stress that the states under the Charter of the United Nations should promote universal respect for human rights and freedom and observe the same in every deed. This responsibility should also be spread and instilled among the individuals of the states.

Article 8 clearly states:[11]

1. No one shall be held in slavery; slavery and the slave-trade in all their forms shall be prohibited.
2. No one shall be held in servitude.
3. (a) No one shall be required to perform forced or compulsory labour;

   (b) Paragraph 3(a) shall not be held to preclude, in countries where imprisonment with hard labour may be imposed as a punishment for a crime, the performance of hard labour in pursuance of a sentence to such punishment by a competent court;

   (c) For the purpose of this paragraph the term 'forced or compulsory labour' shall not include:

---

[10] United Nations, *The Universal Declaration of Human Rights*.

[11] United Nations Human Rights, *International Covenant on Civil and Political Rights*, available at http://www2.ohchr.org/english/law/ccpr.htm (accessed on 12 November 2014).

  (i) Any work or service, not referred to in subparagraph (b),
       normally required of a person who is under detention in con-
       sequence of a lawful order of a court, or of a person during
       conditional release from such detention;

 (ii) Any service of a military character and, in countries where
       conscientious objection is recognized, any national service
       required by law of conscientious objectors;

(iii) Any service exacted in cases of emergency or calamity threat-
       ening the life or well-being of the community;

(iv) Any work or service which forms part of normal civil obliga-
       tions.

Notwithstanding any lacunas, ICCPR is determined to its cause—
abolition of slavery and slave trade.

International Covenant on Economic, Social and Cultural Rights

The International Covenant on Economic, Social and Cultural Rights
(ICESCR) was adopted in December 1966.[12] Unfortunately, the
ICESCR does not have any specific provision dealing with slavery or
slave-related trade, although it does state some rights for fair trade and
just conditions of work which apply to people who have been trafficked. For the purpose of labour exploitation, the covenant provides
that the state must recognize the rights of everyone to gain a living by
work and also to join free trade unions to safeguard their stand. Under
this covenant, there was a committee set up that published the *Report
of the UN Committee on Economic, Social and Cultural Rights* of 2006,
which gave recommendations on the issue of trafficking in persons in
Slovenia and Uzbekistan.[13] This committee expressed concern over

---

[12] United Nations, *The International Covenant on Economic, Social and
Cultural Rights*, available at http://www.ohchr.org/EN/ProfessionalInterest/
Pages/CESCR.aspx (accessed on 12 August 2014).

[13] Silvia Scarpa, *Trafficking in Human Beings: Modern Slavery* (New
York: Oxford University Press, 2008), 93–94; UN Committee on Economic,

the trafficking of women and children for sexual exploitation in the Czech Republic and Slovakia. Most recently, this committee has made recommendations on the issue of trafficking in persons to Slovenia and Uzbekistan and in both the cases, the need to assist and protect the victims is a recurring principle. Therefore, it is evident that the focus of this committee has been on the victims of human trafficking.

Convention on the Elimination of All Forms of Discrimination against Women

The Convention on the Elimination of All Forms of Discrimination against Women (CEDAW) was adopted on 18 December 1979 by the UN General Assembly, and entered into force on 3 September 1981 as an international treaty.[14] It was enforced in order to monitor and scrutinize the condition and position of women and to promote their rights. This refers to the work of CEDAW which has been very crucial in throwing light on those areas where women are denied equality with men. Hence, CEDAW's main objective is to work towards upholding the rights of women and protect them from all sorts of discrimination and help them to attain equal rights.

Article 6 of this convention is dedicated to trafficking in women and it provides that state parties shall 'take all appropriate measures, including legislation, to suppress all types of traffic in women and exploitation of prostitution of women'.[15] The proposal of Morocco was

---

Social and Cultural Rights, 'Concluding Observations of the Committee on Economic, Social and Cultural Rights, Slovenia', UN Doc E/C.12/SVN/CO/1 [33], 2006; United Nations, 'Concluding Observations of the Committee on Economic, Social and Cultural Rights, Slovenia', UN Committee on Economic, Social and Cultural Rights, UN Doc E/C.12/UZB/CO/1 [56], 2006.

[14] United Nations, 'Convention on the Elimination of All Forms of Discrimination against Women', available at http://www.un.org/women-watch/daw/cedaw/cedaw.htm (accessed on 12 August 2014).

[15] United Nations, 'Convention on the Elimination of All Forms of Discrimination against Women'.

rejected by the drafting committee of the CEDAW since they did not consider all kinds of prostitutions as exploitation—it recommended to suppress prostitution per se, whether forced or wilful.[16] Such a proposal could have challenged the entire convention and would not have received ratification from many states. Another proposal was made by Denmark, suggesting that it is incorrect to accept the adding of the word illicit before the word trafficking.[17] A committee was set up in 1982 by the United Nations to draft CEDAW. The CEDAW adopted the General Recommendation No. 19 in 1992, stating that trafficking in women and further exploitation by prostitution should be considered as gender-based violence and as a form of discrimination against women.[18]

Since then the committee has been dedicated to the cause and in 2004 the committee concluded its first inquiry regarding the abduction, rape, and murder of women in Mexico. In 2003 more than three hundred women disappeared from this area. The committee recommended that Mexico gravely violated CEDAW.

Convention on the Rights of the Child

The Convention on the Rights of the Child (CRC) was adopted by the United Nations in November 1989 and was entered into force in

---

[16] See also Venla Roth, *Defining Human Trafficking and Identifying its Victim* (Leiden: Martinus Nijhoff Publishers, 2011), 56.

[17] Denmark suggested not to add 'illicit' before 'trafficking' as prostitution is legal in Denmark, which means buying or selling sex is legal while operation of brothels and pimps is illegal. If 'illicit' was added to trafficking, then it would not be accepted in Denmark. See Scarpa, *Trafficking in Human Beings*, 96; 'Prostitution in Denmark', available at https://en.wikipedia.org/wiki/Prostitution_in_Denmark (accessed on 30 May 2016).

[18] United Nations, 'General Recommendation No. 19' in 'Note by the Secretariat, Compilation of General Comments and General Recommendations adopted by Human rights Treaty Bodies', UN Committee on the Elimination of Discrimination against Women, UN Doc HRI/GEN/1/Rev. 8, 302, 8 May 2006.

September 1990.[19] Article 1 of this convention defines a child as a human being below the age of eighteen years. The provisions of this convention are determined to protect the inherent rights of children. The convention considered that since a child is a part of a community and of a fundamental group of the society called a family, s/he should be given the required protection and assistance for the development of personality in a harmonious manner and should grow up in an environment of love, care, affection, happiness, and understanding, be entitled to special care and assistance, and be protected. It also states: 'the child, by reason of his physical and mental immaturity, needs special safeguard and care, including appropriate legal protection, before as well as after birth.'[20]

Article 31 of the CRC obliges the states to take all appropriate national, bilateral, and multilateral measures to prevent the abduction of the children as well as the sale or trafficking of children for any purpose or in any form. The other provisions of the convention must also be taken into consideration:

- Article 19 requires the state parties to protect children from all forms of physical and mental violence, injury or abuse, neglect or neglecting treatment, maltreatment or exploitation including sexual abuse while in the care of parents, legal guardian, or any other individual.
- Article 20 provides for special assistance and protection to be granted by the state to the children who are temporarily or permanently deprived of their family environment.
- Article 21 ensures that the adoption of child shall, in all respect, be in the best interest of the child in case of national or inter-country adoptions.
- Articles 32, 34, and 36 provide for children's protection from economic, sexual, or any other kind of exploitation.
- Article 33 of the convention calls for all the state parties to prevent the use of children for trafficking for the production or use of drugs and psychotropic substance.

[19] UNICEF, 'Convention on the Rights of the Child', available at http://www.unicef.org/crc/ (accessed on 12 August 2014).

[20] UNICEF, 'Convention on the Rights of the Child'.

– Article 39 recognizes the right of the child to physical and psychological recovery and social reintegration in case where they have
been subjected to any kind of abuse.

Protocol to the Convention on the Rights of the Child on the Involvement of Children in Armed Conflict

This protocol is a human rights instrument which supplements the
UN Trafficking Protocol with regard to children, specifically those
trafficked for involvement in armed conflicts. It was adopted in
2000 and is aimed at enhancing the international humanitarian law
on recruitment of children in conflicts.[21] Article 4(2) imposes upon
all the states to take efficient measures to fight against recruitment
and involvement of children in armed conflict and criminalizing the
practice. Article 6(3) provides the states parties to demobilize those
children who have been involved in armed conflict and to assist them
in their physical and psychological needs and bring them back into the
society. Article 70(1) imposes upon them to cooperate to prevent the
involvement of children in armed conflict. This protocol has been ratified by 119 states; however, there are still many states where children
are used during armed conflicts, such as in Iraq, Indonesia, Iran, and
Burma. The committee under this protocol started its work of examin-
ing states in 2005 and is dedicated towards its cause.

Optional Protocol to the Convention on Rights of a Child, on Sale of Children, and Child Prostitution and Child Pornography

This protocol came into force in 2002.[22] Article 2(A) of the protocol
gives the definition of sale of a child as being 'any act or transaction

---

[21] United Nations, 'The Protocol to the Convention on the Rights of a
Child Dealing with Involvement of Children in Armed Conflict', available at
http://www.ohchr.org/EN/ProfessionalInterest/Pages/OPACCRC.aspx
(accessed on 12 August 2014).

[22] United Nations, 'The Protocol to the Convention on Rights of a Child,
on Sale of Children and Child Prostitution and Child Pornography', available

whereby a child is transferred by any person or a group of persons to another for remuneration or any other consideration' and Article 3(1) calls all the state parties to criminalize the following domestic transnational offences committed by individuals or domestic groups: the offering, delivering, or accepting a child for the purpose of sexual exploitation, removal of organs for profit, and forced labour; acting as an intermediary for inter-country/interstate illegal adoption; offering, obtaining, procuring, and providing a child for child prostitution; and producing, distributing, disseminating, importing, exporting, offering, selling, or possessing child pornography. Finally, Articles 8, 9, and 10 provide for the responsibility of the state to provide assistance to the victims.

International Convention on Elimination of All Forms of Racial Discrimination against Women

This international convention was adopted in 1965 by the UN General Assembly.[23] It does not contain any measure directly dealing with trafficking in person or the forms of slavery even though its monitoring body, the Committee on the Elimination of Racial Discrimination against Women, was created to monitor the implementation of the convention by the state parties, who were required to submit a report after one year from the accession. Notwithstanding the lack of measures specifically dedicated to human trafficking, the committee recognizes that Azerbaijan, for example, protects and assists trafficking victims, well implementing the convention for fighting this crime of human trafficking.

---

at http://www.ohchr.org/EN/ProfessionalInterest/Pages/OPSCCRC.aspx (accessed on 12 August 2014).

[23] United Nations, 'International Convention on Elimination of All Forms of Racial Discrimination against Women', available at http://www.ohchr.org/EN/ProfessionalInterest/Pages/CERD.aspx (accessed on 12 August 2012).

International Convention against Torture and Other Cruel, Inhuman or Degrading Treatment or Punishment

The international convention (CAT or Torture Convention) was adopted by the UN General Assembly in 1984 and it entered into force three years later, in 1987. Although it does not contain any measure specifically dealing with trafficking of women and children or any kind of slave trade, it does include the various kinds of treatments against human beings which come under the purview of torture as acts 'by which severe pain or suffering, whether physical or mental' is imposed on humans.[24]

Since human trafficking involves torture of human beings for the purpose of slavery, servitude, prostitution, sexual slavery, labour, and other forms of exploitation by force or coercion, this convention has its share of responsibility in protecting human trafficking.

International Convention on the Protection of the Rights of All Migrant Workers and Members of their Families

It was in the year 1990 that the UN General Assembly adopted this convention; it finally came into force on 1 July 2003. The convention provides for elimination of the exploitation of migrant workers throughout the entire process of migration and for the protection of the human rights of both documented and undocumented migrants. This treaty also contributes to the fight on transnational trafficking in human beings. As per Article 2 of this convention, a migrant worker is a person 'who is to be engaged, is engaged or has been engaged in a remunerated activity in a State of which he or she is not a national'.[25]

---

[24] United Nations, 'The International Convention against Torture and Other Cruel, Inhuman and Degrading Treatment or Punishment', available at http://www2.ohchr.org/english/law/cat.htm (accessed on 12 August 2012).

[25] United Nations, 'The International Convention on the Protection of Rights of All Migrant Workers and Members of their Families', available at http://www2.ohchr.org/english/law/cmw.htm (accessed on 12 August 2014).

Till date, only 37 states have ratified this convention and the most unfortunate thing is that the countries which are the destination hubs of trafficking are not signatories to this convention. It took thirteen years for this convention to come into force due to very low ratification as ratification by a minimum of twenty states was required for the convention to come into force. Unfortunately, there are other issues, such as fight against illegal migrants, which are generally on the top of the agenda of these states.

The Committee on the Protection of the Rights of all Migrant Workers and Members of their Families is a monitoring and supervisory body under this convention. It monitors the proper implementation of this convention in the member states. All the state parties to this convention are required to submit their reports to this committee within one year of their ratification and are also obliged to send their periodic reports after every five years, regarding the implementation of the convention in their states and conformation to the convention. Their reports also contain the present scenarios in the individual countries and the activities being undertaken to protect the rights of all migrant workers. After receiving the reports, the committee examines and gives its recommendations and also expresses its concerns to the state parties in the form of 'concluding observations'. The committee holds two sessions in a year and meets in Geneva every year.[26]

Convention and Protocol Relating to the Status of Refugees

The 1951 Convention and the 1967 Protocol relating to the status of refugees are the most important international steps taken for the protection of the refugees. Article 1 of the Refugee Convention defines a refugee as an individual who is outside the country of his or her nationality or a habitual resident who has a well-founded fear of persecution for reasons of race, religion, membership of a particular social group, nationality, or a political opinion and is unable or unwilling to avail himself of the protection of that country or return to it.

---

[26] United Nations, 'Committee on Migrant Workers', available at http://www2.ohchr.org/english/bodies/cmw/ (accessed on 12 August 2014).

In 2002, the UNHRC adopted guidelines dealing with the issue of gender persecution and recognized that it did not mention gender among the list of the five persecutions. Further, the UNHRC recognized that even if being a victim of trafficking is not sufficient to claim the recognition of the refugee status, there are some cases in which the well-founded fear of persecution and the inability or unwillingness of the state to act and justify the claim exist.[27]

Although the guideline is restricted to women and children trafficked for the purpose of forced prostitution or other forms of sexual exploitation, it is recommended that the state parties to the convention extend their purpose to all the victims—women and children—who are trafficked for the purpose of exploitation (sexual, labour, or other forms).

Deficiencies Embedded in the Laws Dealing with Human Trafficking

Though the United Nations has enforced protocols, conventions, and treaties in conformity with international law and international humanitarian law to safeguard human rights and to combat human trafficking, slavery, organized crimes, as well as to prevent such crimes, some drawbacks/flaws are still in existence due to which this trade is still flourishing and the players of this trade are still untouched and out of reach from the hands of law protectors. The major reason behind this is the huge difference in the economic and cultural conditions prevailing between the developing and the developed nations, and the lack of compliance of the legislations or enforcement of stringent laws in every country, including those who are a party to the UN protocols and conventions with regard to human trafficking.

During the drafting of the UN protocol for combating human trafficking, especially trafficking of women and children, all stakeholders of the Protocol have taken into account human trafficking for

[27] United Nations, 'Convention and Protocol Relating to the Status of Refugees', available at http://www.unhcr.org/3b66c2aa10.html (accessed on 30 August 2014).

prostitution (whether forced or voluntary) and sexual slavery, since it has been a major concern worldwide. Countries all over the world which have tried to deal with it through various legislations at the domestic level but ultimately a legislation/protocol was sought internationally to stop cross-border trafficking and also within the borders of the country. The trafficking of human beings is also a violation of human rights as it involves forced prostitution and slavery and damage to human dignity. The difference in the economic conditions prevailing in the nations has been a major cause for this crime. The UNHRC has taken several steps in controlling this violation, considering it as a major issue, and ultimately with a target of abolishing this exploitation.[28]

Many activists and members of various organizations who are dealing with issues such as human trafficking, human rights, and gender advocacy have mentioned in their reports that the protocol itself has contradictory definitions and is interpreted differently in different countries. According to many such members of organizations and lobbies working for the protection of human rights, all forms of prostitution—whether voluntary or forced—must be considered as a violation of human rights and sex workers and migrants are to be considered the victims of human trafficking. The study reveals that the word 'exploitation', which is mentioned in the protocol, is understood or interpreted differently by different countries. Some organizations and countries consider and interpret all acts of migration involving sexual exploitation of people as trafficking, and the persons being migrated as victims of trafficking, and do not include other forms of exploitative trafficking such as trafficking for labour, domestic work, and forced bondage.[29] On the other hand, in some countries, the term has included all types of exploitation, including forced prostitution,

[28] UNHCR, 'Principles and Guidelines on Human Rights and Human Trafficking', E/2002/68/Add.1, 2002, available at http://www1.umn.edu/humanrts/instree/traffickingGuidelinesHCHR.html (accessed on 16 August 2014).

[29] UNODC, 'The Concept of "Exploitation" in the Trafficking in Persons Protocol', available at https://ec.europa.eu/anti-trafficking/sites/antitrafficking/files/unodc_ip_exploitation_2015.pdf (accessed on 30 May 2016).

and these countries have taken various steps towards abolishing it. Such misinterpretations by various countries, organizations, and people have raised a question—how far is this protocol going to address the issues of human trafficking in any form, especially those involving women and children. It has become a matter of major concern. It has also been observed that the lack of proper explanation and misinterpretations of terms such as 'trafficking' and 'exploitation' by different countries have helped traffickers to move around and commit such crimes without any legal complications. Such ambiguous and contradictory definitions and laws have given opportunities to traffickers to flourish further and have given rise to disagreements among the member countries and law makers.[30]

Another question that arises here is how far are the victims of such crimes of trafficking and exploitation being protected and given their basic and fundamental human rights. It has been noticed that the most important person—the victim—in this heinous act is being ignored. This has revealed a flaw in the UN protocols for the prevention of this crime. It has also been noticed that the enforcement of various international laws for preventing trafficking of women, gender bias, and for ensuring women's rights of equality, non-discrimination, and economic stability are dependent on the UN protocols, which have been framed based on the predominant concepts of male-dominated governments of various countries. This very dependency permeates the UN system for enforcement of laws, protocols, and conventions to protect the organized crime against women.[31]

Furthermore, it has been noticed that a lack of coordination between the nations all over the world, which has provided a platform for the persons involved in such trans-border organized crimes. There is also a lack in imposing stringent punishment on traffickers and

[30] ILO, 'Human Trafficking and Forced Labour', Guidelines for Legislation and Law Enforcement, Special Action Programme to Combat Forced Labour, 2005.

[31] Phyllis Coontz and Catherine Griebel, 'International Approaches to Human Trafficking: The Call for a Gender-Sensitive Perspective in International Law', Women's Health Journal 4 (2004).

proper enforcement of laws in these countries. Another flaw noticed in combating human trafficking is the lack of protection of the victims of such crimes, due to which the victims are never willing to come forth to fight for their rights and punish the traffickers.

Studies of laws enforced in prohibiting human trafficking have revealed that there is a dearth of integrated laws in combating human trafficking among many countries, despite the fact that most of the countries have enforced laws against trafficking.[32] It has also been noticed that various countries interpret laws against human trafficking differently. In some parts of Europe, laws against trafficking were used to prosecute victims of both trafficking and smuggling whereas in some countries, trafficking in persons refers to victims of trafficking for prostitution only. It is a big flaw in the laws that consider trafficking equivalent to prostitution and this has created an adverse impact on the persons who are being trafficked or being subjected to other forms of exploitation, and thereby on the prosecution of these victims.

Problems Experienced While Dealing with Human Trafficking

It is well-known that human trafficking is a thriving business and ranks third in the world among the organized crimes, just after arms and ammunition and drug trafficking in the global market.[33] Among the trafficked victims all over the world, around 80 per cent are women and 50 per cent are children.[34] Enforcement of law at the international

[32] UNODC and UN.GIFT, *Global Report on Trafficking in Persons*, 2009; UN.GIFT, *Human Trafficking: An Overview* (New York: United Nations, 2008).

[33] B. Jamal, *Women Victims of Human Trafficking in Globalized world of Entertainment and Sex Industry: and Humiliation of Human Dignity and Existence* (New York: Columbia University, 2007).

[34] Rochelle L. Dalla, Lynda M. Baker, John DeFrain, and Celia Williamson, *Global Perspectives on Prostitution and Sex Trafficking: Africa, Asia, Middle East, and Oceania* (Plymouth, UK: Lexington Books, 2011), 69; 'Statistics: Estimation of the Impact of Human Trafficking', available at http://www.trafficking.org/learn/statistics.aspx (accessed on 30 May 2016).

level as well as at the state level is not stringent enough to rescue the victims and protect them from the traffickers. The victims of organized crime are forced into slavery and prostitution and are left in a pathetic condition by the traffickers.[35]

It has been noticed that they are mostly helpless and are deprived of their basic human rights. To protect their rights, the United Nations High Commissioner for Refugees (UNHCR) has undertaken various initiatives to ensure the basic human rights to be provided to the victims of this trade and also helps them to obtain refugee status in the destination country.

Despite the initiatives taken by UNHCR, the victims of human trafficking face various problems in the destination country during their slavery and exploitation and also in their countries of origin they are after they escape from the traffickers and return to the country of origin, or when they are deported by the immigration officials of the destination countries. During their stay in the destination country, the trafficking victims are left totally at the mercy of the traffickers, and they are often found to be living in inhuman conditions, and facing ill treatment and exploited continuously. Their passports are seized and they are left with no hope of liberty, but to be exploited forcefully. Even if they escape from the hands of the traffickers or are rescued from the traffickers, their plight does not seem to end. They still face problems such as lack of protection, danger of being caught and exploited again, difficulty of getting a refugee status, difficulty in immigration, difficulty in getting a valid visa, deportation, and many others. In many cases, it is found that after they are deported to their countries of origin, they are re-trafficked, outcast from the society, and faced with retaliation from the traffickers. Research and study has identified significant reasons of retaliation by the traffickers and the members of their families and friends in the country of origin.[36]

---

[35] UNODC, UN Women, and UN.GIFT, 'Responses to Human Trafficking'.

[36] Aronowitz, *Human Trafficking, Human Misery : The Global Trade in Human Beings* (Connecticut: Greenwood Publishing Group, 2009); J. Winterdyk et al., *Human Trafficking: Exploring the International Nature, Concerns and Complexities* (CRC Press, 1st edition, 2011).

Studies have even revealed that police protection provided for the witnesses and victims of trafficking was inappropriate as they were not informed about the suitable measures taken for their protection.[37] In some cases, the confidentiality and safety measures taken to protect the victims in the countries of destination were seen effective but despite that, the traffickers troubled members of the family in the country of origin. Retaliation faced by the victims assisting in the investigation and taking legal action against the traffickers, which often also impacts relatives of these victims, include threats, bribes, coercion, violence, and terrorization by the traffickers and even the officials involved in trafficking. The local law enforcers are even found to be unprepared to deal with such cases of victim protection and are found corrupt most of the time.[38]

There is an incongruity noticed between laws for the migrants, especially those without any documentation, and the laws which provide protection to the trafficked persons and permit them to reside in the country of destination. It has been noticed that the persons who are found to be trafficked and are not recognized by the law enforcers are immediately deported to the country of origin and these persons also face detention at the immigration department. These persons who are the victims of trafficking, or the illegal migrants, are mostly unaware about their rights. They face discrimination even after being sexually exploited. There are many cases where they are accused, criminal actions are taken against them, and they are arrested and punished for being forced into prostitution and sexual exploitation.

The UNHCR and other human rights organizations have been working towards rescuing and providing justice to the victims and in eradicating this serious crime across as well as within the borders. But it has been noticed that members of the organizations working towards this objective also face threats of death and other serious consequences from the society as well as the governments of various countries, especially in Southeast Asia. This is due to the corruption in the criminal justice system, the deficiency in proper enforcement

[37] Winterdyk et al., *Human Trafficking*; Aronowitz, *Human Trafficking, Human Misery*.

[38] Winterdyk et al., *Human Trafficking*.

of anti-trafficking laws, misinterpretation of UN protocols by the government and other officials, and a lack of knowledge about these laws and protocols among the citizens. Another reason is that the victims, their family members, and the society do not cooperate with law-enforcement organizations in this noble cause as they fear facing serious retaliation from the traffickers. The organizations working towards the objective of eradicating this crime globally face threats from the traffickers as well.[39]

Another problem faced in dealing with human trafficking cases is the lack of coordination between the stakeholders of law-enforcement organizations and government officials, as they have their own conflicting agendas while dealing with the victims of trafficking and such illegal migrants.[40] There also exists a lack of trust, lack of cooperation, and sometimes also difficulty in communicating as there are language barriers in many cases. There are also problems in getting government sponsorship for services towards the protection and safety of the victims.

The delay in prosecution of human trafficking cases and investigations is yet another problem faced while dealing with the victims and their cases. The victims are, therefore, held in the destination country, not given a refugee status, and face the risk of being exploited again. These victims are not even provided residence permits despite such provisions being included in the laws for protecting the victims of trafficking. These victims are not apprised of their rights and hence face difficulty in getting justice for the crime being done against them.[41]

Lack of clarity, lack of proper understanding of anti-trafficking laws by the law-enforcement officials, and lack of availability of resources also add up to the impediment in prosecuting human trafficking victims.

[39] William Pretorius, 'Law Enforcement Responses to Trafficking in Persons in South East Asia', 2006, available at http://www.aaptip.org/2006/artip-project/documents/Paper_LE-Responses%20to%20TIP_22Oct08_fnl.pdf (accessed on 30 May 2016).

[40] H.J. Clawson, N. Dutch, M. Cummings, *Law Enforcement Response to Human Trafficking and the Implications for Victims: Current Practices and Lessons Learned* (US Department of Justice, 2006).

[41] ILO, *The Cost of Coercion*, Report of the Director General, 2009.

Human Trafficking and Gender

Human trafficking is probably the only area of transnational organized crime in which women are significantly represented—be it as victims, perpetrators, or activists seeking to combat this crime. According to the ILO, women are disproportionately the victims of human trafficking, particularly in cases of trafficking for sexual exploitation, domestic servitude, and marriage.[42] But it is also seen that women have often been facilitators and perpetrators of human trafficking. On the other hand, they are increasingly mobilizing themselves at the regional and national levels to combat human trafficking. While women and girls are victimized all over the world, it is more frequent in countries where they are denied the right to education, the right to live with dignity, or economic and political rights—they have no social status at all.[43]

A research suggests that women and children have been the greatest sufferers in the process of globalization.[44] The 2008 global crisis led to women and girls being pulled out of schools, given less to eat, and forced to work at a young age to support their families. At the same time, women have also been seen as the facilitators of this illicit trade of human trafficking: women exploit other women for servitude. They support the trafficking activities of their lovers and husbands; of course, a woman can act independently too. In many countries, they run brothels. It must be mentioned here that their role in human trafficking is, thus, significantly different than in drug trafficking, where women rarely have any position of authority.

---

[42] ILO, *A Global Alliance against Forced Labor*, Global Report on the Follow-Up to the ILO Declaration on Fundamental Principles and Rights at Work (Geneva: ILO, 2005), available at http://www.ilo.org/wcmsp5/ groups/public/@ed_norm/@declaration/documents/publication/wcms_ 081882.pdf (accessed on 30 May 2016).

[43] R. Masika, *Gender, Trafficking and Slavery* (Oxfam Publishing, 2002).

[44] 'Women and the Economy Globalization', available at www.unpac. ca/economy/g_migration.html (accessed on 12 December 2013); Debra Bergoffen, Paula Ruth Gilbert, Tamara Harvey, and Connie L. McNeely (eds), *Confronting Global Gender Justice: Women's Lives, Human Rights* (New York: Routledge, 2011), 36.

Studies have shown that gender plays a very important role in human trafficking and exploitation of women.[45] Women themselves are mostly, and often primarily, involved in facilitating human trafficking and sexual exploitation of other women and girl children, even across borders. Although, in many countries, men also play the role of a recruiter and hire women through fake employments and false marriages, facilitating trafficking of women, cases which are reported in the Arab countries, Russia, Turkey, and Africa, for example, have women in the roles mentioned earlier. These women involved in human trafficking and facilitating movement of women across the borders for sexual exploitation and forced prostitution are generally between twenty and fifty years of age. Since these women are the biggest facilitators of trafficking of women, they are placed at the top level of their organized crime groups.[46]

Research has further revealed that the women who are involved in trafficking of women are among those who have earlier been victims of trafficking themselves and have been sexually exploited. After being into the trafficking business for a considerable time and being sexually exploited in their life as prostitutes these women turn into pimps and brothel owners in the latter part of their life and act as predators. These women are set free and allowed to go back to their country of origin on the condition that they will continue with the trafficking business and recruit and facilitate other women and girls for human trafficking. But they are kept under control by the traffickers who constantly monitor their movements and activities.[47]

It is evident from various findings in different countries that these women continue to be involved in the human trafficking crime due to various reasons such as debts, pressure from traffickers, fear of punishment from police, fear from the members of the family and friends, fear from society, receiving incentives and gaining profits from traffickers, getting a higher position in the business, and even a sense or feeling of revenge for the sufferings from exploitation.[48]

---

[45] J. D'Cunha, 'Trafficking in Persons: A Gender and Rights Perspective', Expert Group Meeting on Trafficking in Women and Girls, New York, 2002.

[46] D'Cunha, 'Trafficking in Persons'.

[47] D'Cunha, 'Trafficking in Persons'.

[48] D'Cunha, 'Trafficking in Persons'.

Apart from women becoming perpetrators and facilitating the crime of trafficking, women getting trapped and becoming vulnerable to human trafficking more than men are based on some of the situations which they face in society. These reasons and factors can be enumerated as follows:[49]

- inequality in the status of the women in the family as well as in the society
- unequal opportunity to education
- lack of proper employment
- lack of proper information and awareness regarding employment
- culture and tradition of society and community
- tolerance of violence against women in the society
- lack of access to legal redressal
- poor economic and living condition of the families

The fact that women are enemies of fellow women is evident in several cases of human trafficking, sexual exploitation, and voluntary or forced prostitution. These women take advantage of the aforementioned factors and exploit other women, thereby facilitating human trafficking across the borders. Such incidents take place majorly in Southeast Asia, Africa, Russia, Turkey, Arab countries, and some European nations. This is also evident from the first global report of the UNODC which states: 'Indeed, female offenders have a more prominent role in trafficking in persons than in any other crime. In Eastern Europe and Central Asia, females account for more than 60 percent of convictions for trafficking in persons.'[50]

Responses to Law Enforcement against Human Trafficking: A Regional Outlook

The increasing rate of human trafficking for labour, sexual servitude, slavery, and prostitution all over the world has led to the enforcement

---

[49] D'Cunha, 'Trafficking in Persons'.
[50] UNODC, 'Global Report on Trafficking in Persons', Vienna, 2014.

of various laws worldwide to combat this crime. The response to law enforcement in human trafficking is different in different countries. Various international laws, conventions, and protocols have been adopted and enforced by the United Nations and its allied organizations such as UNODC, UNTOC, and UN.GIFT. In addition to this, many more legislations have been enforced by countries all over the world to combat human trafficking.

Major activities related to human trafficking take place in developing nations, such as the South Asian region including the Indian subcontinent, Central Asia, the Middle Eastern region, the African region, and some parts of Eastern Europe. These regions have strived to combat human trafficking by enforcing various laws at the domestic level in conformation with the international laws and protocols of the United Nations. The legal systems in these regions are diverse and the responses to the law enforcement against trafficking are also varied. The region-wise outlook of the responses to the laws enforced in these regions is illustrated in the following sections.

South Asia

In the South Asian region, cross-border trafficking of women and children is a major area of concern. The trafficking activities take place in the countries of this region which act as countries of origin, destination, as well as transit. Human trafficking is a very severe form of organized crime in this region. But it is very difficult to find out the exact number of victims of trafficking because of the subversive nature of the crime and the insufficient response and lack of proper effective measures to tackle this heinous crime. The exploitation of women and young girls in this region is continuously on the rise despite the enforcement of various domestic laws in the countries of this region.[51]

Most of the women and girls trafficked in the South Asian region hail from the Indian subcontinent, such as Bangladesh, Nepal, and

[51] A. Derks, 'Combating Trafficking in South East Asia: A Review of Policy and Programme Responses', 2/2000, IOM Migration Research Series, 2000.

India, and even from Sri Lanka and Pakistan. These women and girls are mostly sent to brothels operating in India and also trafficked to the Middle East region for exploitation, sexual servitude, and prostitution. The trafficking of women and children takes place in this region mainly because of the poor economic condition, lack of employment, lack of education, and poor societal status of women living in this region. Due to these reasons, the response to the law enforcement in this region is not much effective since these factors give rise to corruption and thus the region becomes traffickers' haven. The rules and regulations, protocols and conventions are not followed but are seriously violated while anti-trafficking legislations are also not implemented properly in these regions. Hence, the plight of the victims of trafficking is worse here. The victims of trafficking are not properly taken care of as per the standards laid down by the UN protocols and conventions. They do not receive any protection during prosecution and also after being released. They always have a fear of being trafficked again.[52]

The South Asian region has a different legal system. It has a domestic legislation to combat human trafficking that takes place in this region. This is primarily based on the criminal justice system predominant in the region and comprises the police, the prosecutors, and the judiciary.

As per the National Human Rights Council and National Crime Records Bureau (NCRB) reports of 2005, the reported crimes under the Immoral Trafficking Prevention Act were 5,908. Further, as per the study of UNIFEM of 2006, in a survey of over 4,000 persons, the rate of reporting of trafficking cases was only 40 per cent as compared to the huge number of estimated illegal trafficking acts. The number recorded or reported with regard to the survivors of commercial sexual exploitation and trafficking is still very low due to the high rate of corruption and the fear of being re-victimized.[53] According to an NHRC report, the registered number of cases and conviction rate of the

[52] UNODC and UN.GIFT, 'Responding to Trafficking for Sexual Exploitation in South Asia', South Asia Regional Conference Compendium, New Delhi, 2007.

[53] T. Krishna Prasad, *Trafficking in Persons: Tip of the Iceberg* (United Nations Development Fund for Women, 2006), 65; National Crime Records

victims are low due to the insufficient law enforcement in the region. The studies also state that the rate of corruption among the police, judiciary, bureaucrats, and prosecuting officers is ever-increasing. The victims are re-victimized and even re-trafficked, involving these personnel with the help of the organized crime groups.[54]

The government initiatives and various measures undertaken as part of responses to law enforcement has greatly helped in prosecuting the traffickers, rescuing the victims, and reducing the number of trafficked humans in the South Asian region. Training of police personnel and law-enforcement officers as well as the involvement of NGOs have greatly encouraged in bringing down the rate of human trafficking rate in this region, though this region still holds the highest rank among the various other countries of origin. The government as well as the NGOs provide shelter, protection, and support to the victims of trafficking. Awareness programmes are also conducted to spread information about human trafficking, especially of women and children, and this most vulnerable community is apprised of the severity of the crime as well as the laws enforced to curb this crime, so that they do not fall prey to the traffickers.

The Middle East and Central Asia

The Middle Eastern countries are primarily considered as countries of transit and destination for the victims of trafficking. The trafficked persons generally hail from South Asia, such as from India, Bangladesh, Nepal, Pakistan, Sri Lanka, Thailand, Indonesia, and China. The trafficked persons are also found hailing from Africa, mainly the East African countries. Women and children are trafficked as migrants for forced labour, domestic services, and other employment purposes. But when the trafficked persons reach the country of destination, they are forced into the condition of exploitation. The exploitation begins with seizing of their passport and other legal documents, they

---

Bureau, *Crime in India: 2005* (New Delhi: Ministry of Home Affairs, 2006); UNODC and UN.GIFT, 'Responding to Trafficking'.

[54] UNODC and UN.GIFT, 'Responding to Trafficking'.

are kept captive in places depriving them the basic human needs, and then subjected to severe ill treatment, sexual exploitation, abuse, forced labour, and debt bondage, later forcefully indulged into prostitution. The employment agencies working in the South Asian countries as well as in the United Arab Emirates, Oman, Iran, Iraq, Syria as well as other countries of this region lure the vulnerable persons by providing fake employment opportunities.[55]

The countries of the Central Asian region are mostly and exclusively categorized as the countries of origin. These countries include Kazakhstan, Turkey, Turkmenistan, Tajikistan, Ukraine, and Russia. The victims hailing from this region are trafficked to the neighbouring countries of Asia and also to parts of Europe such as Western and Central Europe. The victims are mostly adult women who are trafficked for sexual exploitation and forced labour and servitude.[56]

The governments of the countries in this region, like all other countries dealing with this organized crime, are also working towards combating the trafficking of the labour force which comprises mostly women, but the measures and initiatives undertaken by the governments are just not enough in eradicating this crime from the region.[57] However, effective and important initiatives are being undertaken by way of proper enforcement of laws as per the international standards laid down by the United Nations.[58] The governments in this region are also prosecuting the offenders, arresting them, punishing them through imprisonment by means of the enforced laws but are still unable to completely combat this crime in the region. Better laws are still required to be put into effect in this region. Though the governments are helping and supporting the victims of trafficking by

---

[55] UN.GIFT, 'Human Trafficking: An Overview', United Nations, New York, 2008.

[56] UN.GIFT, 'Human Trafficking'.

[57] For a study of the measures taken, see UNODC, *Global Report on Trafficking in Persons*, 2009.

[58] UNODC, *International Framework for Action to Implement the Trafficking in Persons Protocol* (New York: United Nations Publications, 2009).

providing them with shelters and protection and also assisting them in leading a normal life without any bondage or threat, there is a lack of proper infrastructure for the victim. The governments are required to look after the legal provisions, enforce effective legal measures, frame better policies with regard to the migrants, punish the traffickers, and take adequate measures in terms of immigration, identification of the traffickers as well as the victims of forced labour and prostitution.

The governments in the region are still trying to establish an effective anti-trafficking law to be enforced to completely eliminate the crime of trafficking of human beings from this region. They are bringing changes in the prevalent laws as per the international guidelines and standards so as to effectively tackle the problem of forced labour, forced prostitution, migration, and sexual exploitation of women and children specifically through the act of human trafficking. The citizens are also apprised of this growing crime rate and are made aware of the possible traffickers; the immigrant officials and law-enforcement officers are also given adequate training to identify the violators of immigration and the offenders of the anti-trafficking laws. The education system is being developed in the region, better economic policies are being framed and, socio-cultural condition of the people is being developed through various awareness programmes through governmental agencies as well as NGOs.

The African Region

The African continent, specifically the eastern part of the continent, is the most vulnerable region in terms of human trafficking of women and children.[59] This region mainly consists of the countries of origin for the victims of trafficking. Due to the fact that these countries are among the underserved, underprivileged communities and have severely poor economic, social, and political conditions, besides the other crimes related to drug trafficking and arms trafficking, the orga-

---

[59] UNODC, 'The Problem of Drug and Organized Crime in West and Central Africa', available at http://www.unodc.org/westandcentralafrica/en/regional-programme-framework.html (accessed on 21 August 2014).

nized crime of human trafficking has spread its roots in this region. Women and children are trafficked on the pretence of better employment opportunities and better living conditions in other developed nations. Children are trafficked through adoption process and are thereafter forced into labour, domestic servitude, and sexual exploitation. The young girls are forced into sexual servitude and forced prostitution. These victims are mostly trafficked to the Middle Eastern countries, the US, European countries, and other developed nations. They are even trafficked to other parts of the African continent such as western, central, and southern Africa.[60]

Since these people are not aware of their basic human rights and the laws enforced to protect them and prevent human trafficking and labour exploitation, they are easily lured by the traffickers to the countries of destination—mostly the developed nations—where they are exploited. The government, in recent times, is striving to enforce effective legal measures to prevent and eliminate the crime of human trafficking and slavery or the debt bondage of the people.[61] Many NGOs have also come forward to assist and help the government to effectively manage this act of preventing human trafficking. They offer education to the people, make them aware about their rights, tell them about the laws enforced to protect them, and thus help in preventing trafficking in the region. They also provide shelters for the rescued victims of trafficking, provide them education, and help them lead a normal life again. The government is also trying to improve the economic conditions of the region by facilitating various policies for protecting the rights of its citizens, providing education to the children and women, and curbing this menace of human trafficking.

The European Region

The countries of the European region are among the destination countries for the victims of trafficking. However, there has also been some evidence of this region being that of origin, whereby, victims from the

---

[60] UN.GIFT, 'Human Trafficking'.
[61] UNODC and UN.GIFT, *Global Report on Trafficking in Persons*.

eastern part of Europe are trafficked to the western and the central parts of the region. So, while several people from the Asian region are trafficked here, the victims from this region are mostly adult women trafficked for sexual exploitation, sexual servitude, prostitution, domestic services, abuse, and forced labour.[62]

Law enforcement in this region is as per international standards; it strives to comply with the various protocols and conventions of the United Nations by providing fundamental human rights, victim protection, refugee status to the victims of trafficking in the country of destination, proper deportation and framing of immigration laws to combat human trafficking, and enforcement of various anti-trafficking laws to combat trafficking for labour, slavery, and sexual servitude.[63] Thus, the government, with the help of the United Nations and various NGOs, is trying to bring down the rate of human trafficking in this part of the world.

The officials, law-enforcement officers, and bureaucrats are given proper training and information about the prevalent laws—international as well as domestic—so as to help them identify the traffickers and their activities, their nature of working in the region, and the possible victims of trafficking, and thus take effective measures and actions to combat and prevent organized crime.

Latin America and the Caribbean

The Latin American and the Caribbean regions are identified as the intra-regional and interregional trafficking zones. The victims are trafficked to European, North American, Asia, and Middle Eastern countries. The countries of origin in the case of intra-regional trafficking have been found to be mostly the Dominican Republic, Ecuador, Bolivia, and Paraguay; countries such as Chile and Guatemala, and the East Caribbean countries are those of destination.[64]

[62] UN.GIFT, *Human Trafficking*.

[63] UNODC and UN.GIFT, *Global Report on Trafficking in Persons*.

[64] Office for Victims of Crime Training and Technical Assistance Centre, 'Human Trafficking', available at http://www.ncdsv.org/images/OVCTTAC_HumanTraffickingResourcePaper_2012.pdf (accessed on 21 September 2014).

The victims of human trafficking in this region are mostly found to be adult women, in addition to men and boys. They are trafficked for forced labour, forced begging, and domestic servitude. The children are also used for sex tourism in the countries of this region, such as in Brazil, Costa Rica, Mexico, Jamaica, the Dominican Republic, Colombia, Nicaragua, and Guatemala.[65]

The major reason of human trafficking and sexual servitude here is due to poor economic conditions. The poor families themselves facilitate trafficking by sending their children and young girls for prostitution and sexual servitude in exchange of money, gifts, and other monetary favours.

The government has enforced various anti-trafficking laws to combat trafficking in this region and has also put in place conventions and protocols of the United Nations for the purpose.[66] Development in various sectors of the economy of this region has been very important in combating this organized crime. Various NGOs and government agencies have been working towards helping and coordinating with immigration officials, judiciary, and law-enforcement officers to save the victims, prosecute the traffickers, and thus help in reducing the crime in the region. They have also been providing shelters and protection for the rescued victims and the refugees of human trafficking. Further, the government has enforced various immigration policies to keep a check on illegal migration to and from the nations.

Statistics of Human Trafficking as per ILO, UNODC, IOM, and UN.GIFT: Qualitative Reports

The nature of the organized crime involving trafficking of humans is very subversive and hidden, and hence, to get an exact and actual figure of the number of men, women, and children being trafficked for forced labour and sexual servitude is a very difficult task. Even to get the actual profits earned by the actors of this organized crime group is not possible. Nevertheless, international organizations such as the

---

[65] Office for Victims of Crime Training, 'Human Trafficking'.

[66] UNODC and UN.GIFT, *Global Report on Trafficking in Persons*.

ILO, UNODC, International Organization for Migration (IOM), and UN.GIFT have provided statistical data about the number of persons being trafficked, the profits earned by the traffickers, and costs incurred in the transportation of the trafficked persons, which is quite alarming. The data provided by these international organizations has helped us get the knowledge and information about the severity of this crime which takes place across as well as within the borders. These figures and statistics help various countries, governments, and other organizations working towards the eradication of human trafficking in framing and implementing relevant laws at the domestic and regional levels.[67]

From this data, it has come to light that the highest percentage of the victims are trafficked solely for sexual exploitation and servitude. As per the ILO, the number of victims trafficked were more than 2.45 million during the period 1999 to 2004.[68] As per UNODC, the type of exploitation of the trafficked persons has been the highest in commercial sex, which is 87 per cent, and in economic or forced labour, it has been 28 per cent. In the gender- and age-related data on human trafficking, the majority of the victims have been found to be women and children. The UNODC reported that the victims comprised 77 per cent female, 9 per cent male, and 3 per cent children. The ILO reported the statistics as 80 per cent female and 40 per cent minors. IOM reported that 83 per cent were female, 15 per cent were male, 13 per cent were minors, and 2 per cent remained unidentified.[69]

It is already known that the business of human trafficking is a high-profit business with a low risk of getting caught and ample growth opportunities; it holds the third rank in the world trade among the organized crimes. The profits earned and costs incurred due to the human trafficking business can be summarized in Tables 2.1 and 2.2, as per the ILO *Global Alliance* report and database.[70]

---

[67]   ILO, 'Action against Trafficking in Human Beings', 2008.

[68]   GAO, 'Human Trafficking: Better Data, Strategy, and Reporting Needed to Enhance U.S. Antitrafficking Efforts Abroad', Report to the Chairman, Committee on the Judiciary and the Chairman, Committee on International Relations, House of Representatives, July 2006, victim profiles.

[69]   GAO, 'Human Trafficking', victim profiles.

[70]   ILO, *Global Alliance*, 55–56; ILO, *The Cost of Coercion*, 32.

Table 2.1   Annual Profits from All Trafficked Forced Labourers (in USD)[71]

Region/Type of Economy/ Country	Profits per Forced Labourer (Exploitation– Commercial Sex)	Profits per Forced Labourer (Exploitation– Other Economic Exploitation)	Total Profit
Industrialized economies	67,200	30,154	15,513
Transition economies	23,500	2,353	3,422
Latin America & the Caribbean	18,200	3,570	1,348
Asia and the Pacific	10,000	412	9,704
Sub-Saharan Africa	10,100	360	159
Middle East and North Africa	45,000	2,340	1,508
Global Profits	–	–	31,654

The ILO, in its recent global report, has given an estimation of the financial cost of coercion on the victims of human trafficking by way of forced labour and other means of exploitation.[72] The report has also estimated the total amount as 20 billion USD[73] but this data which has been made available does not include the data of trafficked victims for forced commercial sexual exploitation. This estimated cost given in the report includes loss of income due to non-payment and underpayment of wages, recruiting fees, travel cost, fees paid to the agents, and other related costs. Table 2.2 depicts the estimation of the cost of coercion.

Identification of the Victims of Human Trafficking

The victims of human trafficking have been identified as mostly adult women in the age group of eighteen to twenty-four years as per the

---

[71] ILO, *Global Alliance*, 55–56.
[72] ILO, The Cost of Coercion, 32.
[73] ILO, The Cost of Coercion.

Table 2.2 Estimate of the Total Cost of Coercion (in USD)[74]

	Number of Victims: Forced Labour	Number of Victims Trafficked	Total Underpaid Wages	Total Recruiting Fees	Total Cost of Coercion
Industrialized economies	113,000	74,133	2,508,368,218	400,270,777	2,908,638,995
Transition economies	61,500	59,096	648,682,323	42,675,823	691,358,145
Asia and the Pacific	6,181,000	408,969	8,897,581,909	142,855,489	9,040,437,398
Latin America & the Caribbean	995,500	217,470	3,390,199,770	212,396,124	3,602,595,894
Sub-Saharan Africa	537,500	112,444	1,494,276,640	16,994,438	1,511,271,079
Middle East & North Africa	229,000	203,029	2,658,911,483	551,719,286	3,210,630,769
Total	8,117,500	1,075,141	19,598,020,343	1,366,911,936	20,964,932,279

74 ILO, The Cost of Coercion, 32.

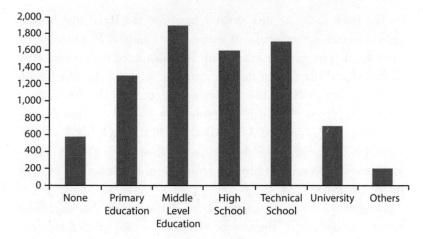

Figure 2.1 Education Level of the Victims of Human Trafficking[75]
Note: Others implies vocational/any other courses.

IOM database. These trafficking victims have, on an average, acquired middle-level education. They are identified during their movement across the border, during transit, and when they are rescued after exploitation in the country of destination. Figure 2.1 depicts the education level of the victims of human trafficking where it is clearly evident that the victims are mostly of middle-school level, high-school level, and technical-school level. Besides, there are also a number of victims who have acquired primary school education.

***

The trafficking of women and children is increasing day by day, and is becoming a booming trade all over the world, across borders. This crime has undermined the legal framework of all the countries across the world. Considering it is the biggest threat to humanity and human dignity, governments, law enforcers, peacemakers, and human rights organizations have come together from across the world to work towards the common goal to eradicate this transnational crime.

[75] UN.GIFT, Human Trafficking, 17.

The main focus of this chapter has been the legal prohibitions against trafficking, especially of women and children. In its introduction, the chapter gave an insight on the statistics of the people being trafficked and the UN protocols, conventions, and laws which have been enforced to check the trafficking nuisance. It also highlighted the various protocols and laws enforced by United Nations organizations such as UNODC, UN.GIFT, UNICEF, ILO, IOM, OSCE, and OHCHR towards the eradication of this crime. It gave an insight into various laws enforced by the United Nations under the aegis of international law.

Further, various' legal responses in dealing with this organized crime were discussed. The United Nations has adopted and enforced a considerable number of conventions, protocols, and treaties to combat human trafficking and deal with this organized crime in an efficient manner. These conventions, protocols, and treaties have been highlighted and discussed in the chapter. The chapter also described how people are victimized in this crime, human rights are violated, and human dignity shattered. The reasons discussed have majorly been poor economic conditions, fake and attractive employment opportunities, lack of education, lack of information and awareness, and unequal status of women in the society. The crime and those who commit this crime are still far away from legalities and legal prohibitions. The UN protocols and conventions in combating trafficking of women and children have been highlighted in the chapter, and also described ways in which the United Nations works in every country all over the world in helping and coordinating with the nations in dealing with this organized crime was also described. The chapter also discussed the various steps taken towards combating this crime in different nations.

A focus on the flaws and loopholes in legislations, protocols, and conventions of the United Nations and misinterpretations of some terms by different states has been described, explaining how due to these reasons the crime has not yet been eradicated completely from the world; moreover, the traffickers have become the biggest gainers in this business, taking advantage of such loopholes in the legal prohibitions. Such deficiencies observed in the legal prohibitions have been one of the reasons behind this flourishing trade.

The plight of the victims has raised questions about proper justice, proper prosecution and punishment to traffickers, as well as protection and provision of human dignity and the basic rights to the victims—these have been highlighted mainly while describing the deficiencies and problems faced while dealing with human trafficking. Various studies and reports revealed that the people who are victimized in this crime are often left in a miserable condition and even after they are rescued from the hands of the traffickers and brothels, their problems never seem to end. They face problems in living in the destination country, face problems in getting the refugee status, have the risk of being victimized in another crime, and if deported to the country of origin, they face immigration problems and the risk of being re-trafficked. Even the people and organizations working with the objective of combating human trafficking and assisting the victims face threats from the traffickers. Besides this, the legalities to combat human trafficking face problems due to lack of coordination between the government and other officials, including the ones involved in immigration. Problems are too many and coordination between states, officials, and governments is still lacking.

The chapter has also highlighted the gender perspective in human trafficking and the role of women in sexual exploitation. As discussed, women who have themselves been victims of human trafficking and sexual exploitation have been observed to be getting into the trade of human trafficking, thus facilitating trafficking of other women in the country of origin of these victims and their communities. This chapter has thus highlighted the various reasons and factors due to which women get involved in this organized crime.

Further, the chapter has discussed and highlighted the responses of law enforcement against human trafficking at various regions across the world, taking a region-wise look at the extent of human trafficking and the laws enforced to combat it. With reference to the reports published by UNODC and UN.GIFT, the major regions identified and discussed are South Asia, the Middle East and Central Asia, the African region, Europe, Latin America, and the Caribbean. In the discussion and highlights on these regions, it has been found that most of the countries of the South Asian, African, Latin American,

Caribbean, and Central Asian regions are identified as the countries of origin whereas the countries of the European region, the Middle Eastern region, and some parts of the European and African regions have been identified as the countries of destination.

This chapter has highlighted the statistical data which has been made available from the reports of the ILO, UNODC, IOM, and UN.GIFT. The reports of these international organizations have revealed that most of the trafficked victims are women and young girls who are trafficked only for the reason of sexual exploitation and forced prostitution. These reports have also been seen to have highlighted the severity of this crime carried out efficiently and successfully across the borders all over the world. The data has also stated that the age of the women who are trafficked for sexual exploitation is between eighteen and twenty-four years, and the majority of the victims of trafficking are of middle-school level though many of these victims have also acquired education at the high school and technical school level and a few of them are at the university level.

This discussion now poses a need of a proper and effective legal response in dealing with human trafficking, especially of women and children. The following chapter deals with the importance of a strong legal response, evaluates how effective are the international legal responses towards human trafficking, gives an overview of the international law and human trafficking with a brief description of various approaches towards prevention of human trafficking and also gives an overview of the human rights aspect and the crime, providing a description on the enforcement action of the state and the success of ICC in prosecuting human trafficking cases, thereby giving an effective legal response to deal with this heinous form of organized crime and combat trafficking of women and children.

3 *Establishing an Effective Legal Response*

The severity of human trafficking has already been discussed in the previous two chapters. Human trafficking is cancerously spreading all over the world. Thus, the need for combating this heinous crime was strongly felt by the United Nations, various NGOs, and many government organizations; but before these law-enforcement agencies could take a step, a great deal of exploitation was already done by the traffickers.

It will be wrong for anyone to believe that trafficking of women and children will be entirely eliminated with the help of the protocols and conventions which have been enforced as measures to combat this crime since there is too much money and profit involved in this business—traffickers make billions of dollars annually. It is like trying to eliminate smuggling of narcotic drugs when there is such a huge market available for it.

To combat human trafficking, the United Nations has framed an international legal framework with the cooperation of the states all over the world. It has enforced the UNTOC and established the UNODC, which later enforced the Protocol to Prevent, Suppress and Punish Trafficking in Persons, also known as the Trafficking in Persons Protocol or the Palermo protocol. However, trafficking has increased at an alarming pace in recent times despite the various legal frameworks and stringent laws being enforced at the international as well as domestic levels, as is evident from the alarming data collected from various studies and research.[1] The UNODC, ILO, and IOM have provided us with shocking figures of human trafficking across the borders.[2] Hence, a more effective law to combat this heinous crime is needed to save humanity and human dignity.

A Comparison of the United Nations Trafficking Protocol and the CoE Trafficking Convention

The two most important legal instruments enforced at the international level are the United Nations Trafficking in Persons Protocol and the Council of Europe Convention on Action against trafficking in human beings, which is also known as the CoE Trafficking Convention. Although both work towards preventing and combating human trafficking, they work in different ways. The UN Trafficking Protocol seeks to ensure the prosecution of those who commit the crime of human trafficking by enhancing law as well as cross-border cooperation, whereas the CoE Convention seeks to promote the protection of trafficked persons' human rights. Table 3.1 illustrates the major similarities and differences between these two laws by identifying the main features from the human rights perspective.

---

[1] Social development 'Notes: Conflict, Crime and Violence, Human Trafficking: A Brief Overview', No. 122 (2009)

[2] P. Belser, *Forced Labour and Human Trafficking: Estimating the Profits*, Declaration of Fundamental Principles and Rights at Work, International Labour Office, Geneva, 2005.

Table 3.1 Comparison of the UN Trafficking Protocol and the CoE Trafficking Convention[3]

Basis	UN Trafficking Protocol	CoE Trafficking Convention	Observations
Defining 'trafficking'	Article 3	Article 4	The definitions vary since the CoE Convention defines trafficking victims as well
Scope of the law	Transnational trafficking connected with organized crime.	All forms of trafficking— transnational or national— connected with organized crime.	The CoE Convention has a wider scope.
Article identifying victims of trafficking	No provision available.	Article 10	The CoE Convention prohibits removal of a person from the territory of a state party if there are reasonable grounds to support trafficking.
Protection of privacy and identity	Article 6: in appropriate cases and to the extent possible under domestic law.	Article 11: obligatory.	The CoE Convention additionally obliges to ensure that the identity of the child victims are not made public through media or any other means, except under exceptions, as per the provisions of Article 11 of the convention.

(Cont'd)

[3] INTERPOL, 'Trafficking in Human Beings', available at http://www.interpol.int/Crime-areas/Trafficking-in-human-beings/Trafficking-in-human-beings (accessed on 20 October 2013).

Table 3.1 (*Cont'd*)

Basis	UN Trafficking Protocol	CoE Trafficking Convention	Observations
Assistance to victims of trafficking	Article 6.3: discretional—state parties to consider in appropriate cases.	Article 12.1: Some rights are given to all victims of trafficking. It is obligatory to ensure that assistance is not made conditional on his or her willingness to act as witness.	Rights guaranteed by CoE Convention include accommodation, psychological and material assistance, emergency medical aid, counselling, education for children, access to labour markets, rights to criminal proceedings, among others.
Protection of victims of trafficking	Article 6.5: Obligatory, while trafficked person remains within the territory of the state party.	Article 12.2: Obligatory to take into account the safety needs and provide protection to the victims of trafficking and to their families from potential retaliation or intimidation. In particular, during and after investigation and prosecution of perpetrators. Article 30 obliges to ensure	Ambit is wider in case of the CoE Convention. Article 33 of the CoE Convention talks about missing and endangered persons and their protection.

(*Cont'd*)

Table 3.1   (*Cont'd*)

Basis	UN Trafficking Protocol	CoE Trafficking Convention	Observations
		in the course of judicial proceedings the protection of the private life of the victims of trafficking and, where appropriate, their identity.	
Protection of witness	No specific article in the UN protocol, Parent Convention Article 24 obligatory to provide effective protection from potential retaliation or intimidation of witnesses and, when appropriate, for their relatives and other persons close to them.	Article 28: Obligatory to provide effective and appropriate protection of witnesses and, when necessary, members of their families from potential retaliation or intimidation. Obligatory to ensure and offer various kinds of protections such as physical protection, relocation, identity change, and assistance in obtaining jobs. Child victims are to be afforded	The CoE Convention has a wider ambit since it includes the provisions for protection of witnesses as well apart from victim protection.

(*Cont'd*)

Table 3.1   *(Cont'd)*

Basis	UN Trafficking Protocol	CoE Trafficking Convention	Observations
		special measures so that the best interest of the child is protected.	
Provisions on non-punishment of victims	No provision in this regard	Article 26: Obligatory to provide for the possibility of not imposing penalties on victims of trafficking stemming from their involvement in unlawful activities to the extent they have been compelled to do so.	The CoE Convention aims to protect the victims.

The Importance of a Strong Legal Response

Trafficking of human beings is increasing at an alarming rate throughout the world. These organized crimes are taking place across as well as within the borders of states. Organized crime syndicates work in such a way that the states find it increasingly difficult to track them down and combat the trafficking business. It is already evident from the previous discussions that human trafficking is ranked among the world's third largest trade among the organized crime businesses. With the help of this fast-growing trade, the traffickers are minting money. Trafficking of human beings takes place with the help of powerful and influential criminals who operate internationally through a network, and comprises local, regional, national, and international crime syndicates. They use global routes to transport victims and are linked to international mafias who are supported by financers, brothel owners, and other operators in the destination country. These crime groups are also backed by corrupt government officials, including politicians, law-enforcement officers, immigration officials, and members of the judiciary who accept bribes in the form of money, sexual favours, and political support. They also include the relatives and members of the family by offering them huge monetary benefit. The magnitude of the crime can be measured through the bitter reality that has been uncovered through research and studies by international organizations that are continuously working towards eradicating this crime. Thus, there is a need for a strong legal response towards combating human trafficking and proper enforcement of stringent laws is essential, considering the present scenario all over the world.[4]

Trafficking is a violation of the laws enforced in most of the states across the world. The states that have been party to the protocols and conventions of the United Nations have enforced various laws to act as a basis or standard to combat trafficking at the domestic level in their own countries. But not all countries have effective anti-trafficking laws adopted, enacted, and/or enforced at the domestic level, based on the international laws and protocols. As it is, the adoption and ratification of the laws and policies takes considerable time to become operational and effective at the state level. Such delays have always helped the actors of the trafficking crime groups to take advantage, run their business, and become successful in their activities. Many countries are devoid of any kind of anti-trafficking laws in action and this deficit in the legal framework has facilitated such countries to be the hub of human trafficking business. Such countries even include those that have been party to various protocols and conventions of the United Nations to prevent trafficking and slavery. This has occurred despite the clause

---

[4] A. Gallagher and P. Holmes, 'Developing and Effective Criminal Justice Response to Human Trafficking', *International Criminal Justice Review* 18, no. 3 (2008).

of obligation of the state parties to secure rights and freedom and to prohibit acts amounting to torture and inhuman treatment and take strict measures to prevent such acts under their jurisdiction. Besides, it has also been observed that some countries have never been a party to the protocols and conventions of the United Nations to curb this menace of human trafficking, but they still have anti-trafficking laws operational and effective in their countries. These countries have ensured the protection of human rights, thereby preventing trafficking of human beings by enacting and enforcing strict and stringent anti-trafficking legislations.

The deficiency in the laid-down legislations in the countries and the lack of proper and effective laws against the crime of human trafficking is a matter of serious concern. It is an impediment towards preventing and uprooting the crime which violates humanity, human dignity, and integrity. Without an effective legislation and a proper legal framework, it is a huge task to fight this crime and punish the traffickers.[5] The UN protocols and conventions which have been enforced to prevent human trafficking and slavery and punish the traffickers have been differently interpreted in different countries. Some countries base their anti-trafficking legislations of anti-trafficking only on women and children and their sexual exploitation and ignore the fact of trafficking of men and their exploitation for forced labour. Such cases of labour exploitation are not dealt with effectively despite the fact that they are also a part of human trafficking crime which also constitutes the exploitation of human rights. Thus, it is very important to have a clear understanding of the anti-trafficking legislations and implementation of more effective legislations to combat trafficking and related issues.

International legislations such as the various protocols, treaties, and conventions of the United Nations—UNHRC, UNODC, UNTOC—and various other organizations under the aegis of the United Nations have taken up this matter of human trafficking and exploitation very seriously through various initiatives which are carried

---

[5] The Action Group, 'Recommendations for Fighting Human Trafficking in the United States and Abroad', 2008, available at http://www.freetheslaves.net/Document.Doc?id=96 (accessed on 20 October 2013).

out by them in combating the same.[6] Despite the fact that majority of the UN member states have ratified the Protocol to Prevent, Suppress and Punish Trafficking in Persons, especially Women and Children (Trafficking in Persons Protocol), supplementing the United Nations Convention against Transnational Organized Crime[7] and various other instruments in order to stop human trafficking, findings have revealed that the rate of the crime has increased manifold and many countries of the world are facing problems in combating this crime. The studies and findings have also revealed that the victims of human trafficking are often confused with the victims of smuggling and thus there is no proper implementation of appropriate laws and the victims face lack of protection in the country of destination and are prevented from receiving their fundamental rights. Thus, a need for a proper initiative to protect humanity, to stop human trafficking, and to ensure punishment of the traffickers was strongly felt and various organizations of the United Nations came forward and implemented the UN.GIFT.

The UN.GIFT has been one of the most important steps taken towards identifying the causes, problems, and conditions with respect to human trafficking and has been helping to combat the crime through its various initiatives and activities across many countries. It has been an initiative and a combined effort to combat human trafficking, which has been undertaken by UNODC in association with the ILO, UNICEF, IOM, OSCE, and UNHCHR in March 2007.[8]

Thus, as the United Nations has taken up various initiatives, enforced various laws, and implemented protocols, conventions, and treaties towards preventing the crime at the international level, it is also noticed that similar but specific laws are required to be enacted

[6] United Nations, *Toolkit to Combat Trafficking in Persons: Global Programme against Trafficking in Human Beings*, 2008.

[7] UNODC, 'United Nations Convention against Transnational Organized Crime and the Protocols Thereto', available at https://www.unodc.org/unodc/treaties/CTOC/ (accessed on 30 May 2016).

[8] UN.GIFT, *Human Trafficking: An Overview* (New York: United Nations, 2008).

and enforced in each country at the domestic level so as to prevent this organized crime. It has been noticed that many terms of the protocol and international laws towards preventing human trafficking are being misinterpreted or differently interpreted by many countries at the domestic level. If the laws are specific and strong enough at the domestic level in each country then the rate of human trafficking will automatically reduce worldwide. A serious need has been felt for the rescue and protection of the victims of trafficking and proper identification and differentiation of the trafficked persons/victims from the smuggled migrants to ensure that the victims are able to receive protection in the country of destination as well as the country of origin, and are addressed with sympathy. Thus, more stringent and unambiguous laws are required to be enacted and enforced internationally in each country to fight human trafficking in an efficient and effective manner.[9]

The definitions and terms mentioned in the protocols and conventions should have some clarity so that they are not misunderstood and misinterpreted while dealing with the crime and also while framing laws of anti-trafficking at the national or domestic level by the states. The definitions and legal terms should commensurate with the international laws and protocols and should follow international standards. This is very important for having an effective legal prohibition to assist in protecting the victims of human trafficking and prevent the crime and related exploitation. There is a dire need for the states to amend and implement effective laws in accordance with the international laws and international standards; these laws should include all types of exploitation involved in human trafficking, be it with women, children, or men. The legislations should have proper and clear definitions of the act of crime and the punishment of the traffickers. The laws should also be assisted with related laws to control and monitor the businesses which work or facilitate human trafficking through hidden agendas. Such businesses could be employment

---

[9] Office for Victims of Crime Training and Technical Assistance Centre, 'Human Trafficking', available at http://www.ncdsv.org/images/OVCTTAC_HumanTraffickingResourcePaper_2012.pdf (accessed on 21 September 2014).

agencies, travel agencies, marriage bureaus, beauty salons, wellness clinics, hotels, and others. Thus, an effective and strong legislation to combat this organized crime should also look into various businesses which could be a facilitator and a part of this crime. Another aspect to be looked into is the adoption system and policies in the countries. This is because there are various such adoption agencies which carry out the business of human trafficking under the guise of adoption. All this should also be taken into consideration while framing effective laws on anti-trafficking.

Effectiveness of International Legal Response and Human Trafficking

Human trafficking, which has emerged as a transnational organized crime, has shown its severity with its ever-increasing network across the borders all over the world. This has urged the international community to come forward and frame a legislation to combat it. In this, international law has played an important role by providing a basis for the United Nations to frame the legislation to define, prevent, and prosecute the trafficking of human beings. The states which are party to the convention are required to sign and ratify international law, and thereby, enforce legislations at the domestic as well as local level so as to have a stronger legal framework in their countries.

This present-day scenario and the severity of the crime reveals the flaws and weaknesses in the effective implementation of international laws and various international legal frameworks and the responses towards eradicating this crime. This section describes the questions it poses about the effectiveness of these legal frameworks towards fighting trafficking and the extent to which the laws are efficient to provide protection to the victims of trafficking.

The trafficking protocol has included provisions wherein the state parties are required to prevent trafficking in their own countries and also protect the victims of human trafficking and prosecute and punish the traffickers. They are also required to provide residence or a refugee status to the victims of human trafficking if that particular country is a country of destination.

The protocol also describes and points out the differences between smuggling and trafficking with the help of the provisions which state that the people do not have any right to choose to be trafficked or their children to be trafficked. In case of smuggling, if the smuggled person is later exploited again or forced into slavery and sexual servitude, then it comes under the provision of the trafficking protocol. The same provision includes persons who do not have any other option but to abide by the instructions of the traffickers. The norms and standards laid down for the treatment of trafficking victims have been stated in various conventions and treaties which are also based on international law. These protocols, treaties, directives, and guidelines are framed to ensure a sympathetic and humane approach towards victims of trafficking, and also to ensure that they are not treated as criminals. Many NGOs and special rapporteurs of the United Nations work towards providing these victims proper justice against exploitation and abusive treatment from traffickers. Reports from rapporteurs and NGOs assist the United Nations to keep a check and monitor the compliance of the state parties with the trafficking protocols and international law.

But, it has been observed that in most of the occasions, the victims of human trafficking are further victimized as smuggled migrants and face humiliation in the country of destination as well as in the country of origin even after they are rescued from traffickers. The reason behind this has been the overlapping and conflicting laws, misinterpretation of laws and protocols in various countries, lack of knowledge of a proper legal framework, lack of cooperation amidst all the countries, and lack of efficient policies in combating this crime. Thus, an effective legal response towards addressing problems of the victims and of people and countries working towards fighting this shameful crime is immediately required.

At the domestic level, the enforcement of legislations in accordance with international law is very important and plays a vital role in the effective implementation of the laws and efficiently dealing with human trafficking and its prevention from the region. These legislations enforced at the domestic and regional levels have been designed in a manner to prevent and combat trafficking with the help of the provisions laid down by the international guidelines of the United Nations, but are enforced and enacted in a manner that they address the issues aimed at the region, which means they should be region specific or country specific. Some of these domestic legislations which have been enacted in various countries are the Council of Europe Convention on Action against Trafficking in Human Beings, 2008, the European Convention for the Protection of Human Rights and Fundamental Freedoms, 1950, the United States Victims of Trafficking and Violence Protection Act, 2000, Trafficking Victims Protection Act (TVPA), 2000 (US), the Immoral Traffic (Prevention) Act, 1956 (amended in 1986, India), Anti-Trafficking in Persons Programme (Indonesia), Inter-Agency Council against Trafficking (Philippines), Trafficking in Persons and Transportation (Control) Act, 2007 (Nepal), and Sexual Offences Act, 2003 (UK).

Although these legislations have been enacted and enforced to combat trafficking at the domestic level, there are many problems that these countries face in dealing with this crime and prosecuting the traffickers. Since it is a transnational crime, curbing trafficking requires active cooperation and coordination among the governments, law-enforcement officers, and immigration offices of the countries involved. It also requires various resources such as time and money, and requires the willingness of the victims/witnesses to cooperate with the law-enforcement officers for identification of the traffickers and thereafter punishing them. In many cases, it has been noticed that the victims are reluctant to reveal any kind of information about the traffickers in fear of retaliation towards them and the members of the family, friends, and relatives.

It is a challenging and awkward issue that many countries which are member states of the United Nations have not yet ratified the protocol for combating human trafficking, due to which proper and effective implementation of these international legislations have been hampered. There are also countries that lack in implementing the anti-trafficking protocol, which is due to the lack of knowledge, expertise, and proper legislation to fight trafficking. The lack of efficient implementation of a legal framework to fight human trafficking has posed a need to work towards an internationally acceptable legal framework across all nations.

Studies have highlighted numerous problems in dealing with human trafficking cases including labour exploitation, and in prosecuting the offenders. These problems are due to the fact that there is a serious lack of coordination and cooperation among the countries dealing with human trafficking, their police personnel, judiciary system, and prosecutors. This lack of cooperation between the countries impacts the prosecution of cases and protection of witnesses and victims. Hence, it is very important that the legislations of anti-trafficking and protection of victims at the domestic level and cooperation with other countries in effectively dealing with this transnational crime be at par with the international standards and should comply with the UN protocols and conventions enforced in eliminating human trafficking. There is seen to be a lack of cooperation and mutual distrust among countries fearing evidences collected by them getting misplaced or lost if shared with other nations. Such ground realities make it difficult to fight human trafficking at the domestic level and hinder the investigations to prosecute the traffickers.

The United Nations Convention on Transnational Organized Crime (UNTOC) was enacted and enforced to overcome these issues and problems of non-cooperation among the countries to deal effectively with human trafficking cases. The United Nations has also established a number of agencies and various programmes to deal with such human trafficking cases effectively for enhance cooperation between the parties. Examples of such agencies are Europol, Eurojust, Europe Programme against Corruption and Organised Crime in South Eastern Europe, Southeast European Prosecutors Advisory Group, European Judicial Institute, and CIS Co-ordination Council of General Prosecutors.

The victims of human trafficking for sexual and labour exploitation who have been potential witnesses for prosecuting such cases are still facing difficulties in getting proper justice for the exploitation and protection from the traffickers in the country of their origin and destination. There have been many reports where the law enforcers have themselves handed back the victims to the traffickers instead of protecting them, deported them with the assistance of the immigration officials without proper investigation and often, rescued victims have been deprived of investigation and justice because of dearth of documentary evidence and lack of identity proof.

In case of victims of labour exploitation, the labour organizations in various countries are required to look after the compensation systems for the victims. They should be compensated financially for the damages caused to them by way of abuses, injuries, loss of wages, or breach of contract, with the assistance of the funding agencies of the states. These victims should be redressed and be given justice through a civil justice system instead of the criminal justice systems prevailing in many countries. There are countries where such redressal systems have been implemented to protect the victims but it is still evidenced that the victims of trafficking for labour exploitation face difficulties in getting their grievances heard by the labour agencies and governments, and do not receive the financial compensation for the loss and abuses they have faced.

There are various reasons of such a failure to provide justice to the victims of trafficking and labour exploitation. In some cases, the victims are deported without getting any opportunity of being heard by the legal authorities or the justice system prevalent in the country of destination. Their cases are not heard because of their illegal entry and lack of identity documents, which is again unjust towards the victims because they have been deceived by their fake employers. Some victims are financially very poor and they cannot afford to pay the expenses incurred for the civil justice system, compensation cases, or even to sustain themselves to live in the country to follow up with these cases. Many victims are neither aware of their rights and the legalities of labour laws, nor do they have access to legal assistance to hear their case and fight for compensation and justice. In some countries, the compensation system to such victims does not exist, due to which the victims face difficulties in the fight for their rights and get justice.

There are some immigration policies and regulations in some countries due to which many persons are exposed to human trafficking and labour exploitation. This is because the weak immigration policies and regulations in such countries have facilitated the traffickers who run their businesses through recruitment agencies, fake employers who charge fees in exchange of their services of providing employment in other countries and providing valid working visas and work permit in those countries. Even the types of visas add up to the advantage of the traffickers. Countries where working visas are associated with only a single employer, the persons employed are deprived of the option of changing their employer. Such cases are reported in a number of countries, especially for the labour employed as domestic servants, who are then treated as bonded labour. When such victims escape from the employer's captivity, they are reported to the immigration personnel, who then treat them as illegal immigrants. Often, such immigration policies of such type do not go into the detailed investigation of whether the victims are exploited, forced into slavery, or trafficked for such purpose. They just consider them as illegal immigrants and deport them, depriving them of protection. Due to lack of proper legislations and regulations in migration of labour force required for specific purpose and skills in some countries, migration is often carried out without proper documentation and this enhances the human trafficking and thereby exploitation of persons.

Hence, to curb this practice and such exploitation of human beings, specific and effective measures need to be undertaken, but this again purely depends on the legal system of the country in which they have to be actually operational. To make the policies and regulations effective, it also depends on the administrative practices of the government, the infrastructural resources, and the justice system.

Approaches towards Prevention of Human Trafficking

To combat human trafficking, there is a need to have effective measures and approaches towards minimizing the severity of the crime. The major approaches identified by the United Nations are the three-P and three-R strategies. The three-P strategy includes prevention, protection, and prosecution.[10] The most important is prevention of trafficking. Prevention requires the states parties to establish comprehensive policies to prevent trafficking and adopt or strengthen the

---

[10] U.S. Department of State, *Trafficking in Persons Report 2010.*

measures to exploitation and demand for sexual services. Preventive measures also include effective attempts in regulating and monitoring the recruitment of labour force and contributing various other practices through public awareness campaigns, training programmes, and advocacy measures. Protection and prosecution are some other effective approaches for combating trafficking.

Beside these already laid down approaches towards minimizing and combating human trafficking, there could also be some alternative measures which could be implemented to prevent, minimize, and effectively combat human trafficking.

Legalizing Prostitution

Legalizing prostitution has been a debatable issue in almost all the countries. It is a matter of chance—it may work for good, thereby minimizing the rate of trafficking of women and young girls, or it may aggravate the rate of human trafficking. The consequence mainly depends on the legal framework of that particular country. There might also be cases where legalizing prostitution improves the working and safety conditions for women in this profession and allow sex businesses to recruit from among the domestic women who would choose prostitution as their free choice of occupation.[11]

Thus, although many people consider prostitution as immoral, they also believe that it should be legalized with strict enforcement of laws to monitor and control it. This will help in reducing the trafficking of women and young girls for the purpose of sex trade and other related crimes of exploitation. Legalizing prostitution will hopefully reduce the abuse of women and young girls, who are sold and resold, used and reused forcefully into prostitution. The legalization of prostitution would also help in securing the health requirements of the prostitutes and would considerably reduce the spread of STDs. The prostitutes

---

[11] Seo-Young Cho, Axel Dreher, and Eric Neumayer, 'Does Legalized Prostitution Increase Human Trafficking?', paper presented at the Workshop on Human Trafficking, International Crime and National Security: A Human Rights Perspective at the University of Göttingen, Germany (2012)

will have access to healthcare and medical facilities which will ensure proper medication for various health-related problems, whether mental, emotional, psychological, or physical.

Legalizing prostitution will minimize the rate of illicit sex trafficking of women and young girls and in turn will reduce the exploitation and abuses of these victims at the hands of traffickers, pimps, and customers. Legalizing it will convert it into an industry regulated by government rules and regulations and will ensure strict compliance to health and safety measures. It will also be regulated by the taxation policies of the governments. The illegal ways of earning money and thriving in the business of trafficking through prostitution will be minimized and eliminated, and money laundering and other financial crimes will also reduce. Since it will be a taxable profession after legalization, the government will monitor the income generated by prostitution, and this tax will also add up to the government economy.

Further, legalizing and regulating prostitution will eliminate the illegality of related activities, such as reduction in forceful inclusion of girls and women into prostitution. It is often found that most of the prostitutes belong to the vulnerable sections of society—illegal immigrants, minors, and drug addicts, for example. Legalizing it will put a limitation on the age and health condition of the prostitutes; further, it will be a monitoring and control measure on the pimps and brothel owners and also reduce abuses and violence.

It will help the government to regulate the activities of prostitutes and brothel owners, ensuring the rights of willingness of the prostitutes in view of their legal age and health, safety, and other precautionary measures.

Though, legalization of prostitution has some advantages, there are also some concerns which might misfire at the government and the citizens. Legalizing prostitution can increase the rate of human trafficking and expand the trafficking market—it will fuel the demand for women and girls in the sex industry and thus increase human trafficking. The legalization of prostitution does not imply lenient enforcement of anti-trafficking laws. On the contrary, the current fact of prostitution being illegal does not mean stricter enforcement of anti-trafficking laws; human trafficking will always be illegal even after legalizing prostitution.

Though, legalizing prostitution is an attempt to solve the problem of human trafficking, it will not make situations better. The traffickers abduct women and girls and sell them for money to sex traders not just for prostitution but also as slaves. Legalizing prostitution will not be able to stop the traffickers from holding a woman in captivity. The problems of legalized prostitution are evident from the realities existing in the countries where it has been legalized. One such country is Sweden. Though legalizing prostitution has helped in reducing trafficking of women and girls, it has not been able to control the abuses and exploitation of the prostitutes by the pimps and customers; they are actually treated as sex slaves. There are also many brothels that have close association with criminal organizations.[12] The Swedish government has thus enforced measures such as punishing the persons who buy sex by imposing fines, and publishing their names in the newspapers, thereby humiliating them for the offence they have committed.[13]

Thus, along with legalizing prostitution, the government would need to note the other side of the picture and enforce stricter laws to control, monitor, and reduce the other types of exploitation and abuses, such as rape and sexual slavery.

Effective Employment Laws, Unemployment Benefit

Human trafficking has a major reason fuelling it—unemployment in the countries of origin. Poor employment opportunities and social and economic disadvantages, particularly of women and children,

[12] 'Can Legalizing Prostitution Help Prevent Human Trafficking for Sexual Exploitation?', available at http://www.traffickingproject. org/2009/04/can-legalizing-prostitution-help.html (accessed on 25 December 2013).
[13] 'Can Legalizing Prostitution Help Prevent Human Trafficking for Sexual Exploitation?'

urbanization, and migration for employment are push factors of human trafficking. Most of the victims of human trafficking are unemployed, in search of jobs, seeking better opportunities in foreign lands; in this manner, they fall into the trap of the traffickers. Victims are often attracted with false promises of high-paying jobs, manipulated by people they trust, and when they fall prey to them, they are forced or coerced into prostitution, domestic servitude, farm or factory labour, or other types of forced labour. The traffickers hire employment agencies for luring unemployed youth with attractive opportunities, take away their passports and other identity documents, and finally traffic them into different places for accomplishing the aim of the trafficking business, where they are fully exploited.[14]

Hence, effective laws are required to be enforced by the governments of these nations to combat the trafficking methods of fake employment by monitoring the activities of employment agencies and also to enforce regulations and policies for employment of persons in any kind of an organization. These need to be checked for adherence to the prescribed regulations and legislations pertaining to employment and recruitment of persons. Better infrastructure, in terms of opportunities for the unemployed persons to develop themselves, and financial stability so that they do not get trapped by the traffickers while looking for better employment opportunities, is required. The countries should strive for economic growth so as to generate and provide employment opportunities to the unemployed citizens.[15]

Unemployment benefits, also known as unemployment insurance or unemployment compensation, depending on the jurisdiction of the individual states, are payments made by the state or other authorized bodies to its people or citizens who are unemployed. Depending on the jurisdiction of the state and the status of the person, this sum

[14] Sallet Elizabeth P., 'Human Trafficking and Modern Day Slavery', Human Rights and International Affairs, November 2006, available at http://www.socialworkers.org/diversity/affirmative_action/humantraffic1206.pdf (accessed on 20 October 2013).

[15] Elizabeth, 'Human Trafficking and Modern Day Slavery'.

may be small, covering only basic needs, or may compensate the lost time proportional to the previously earned salary. The unemployment benefits could be based on a compulsory para-governmental insurance system. They are often a part of a social security scheme.[16] These unemployment benefits are generally given only to those registering as unemployed, and fulfilling the conditions which ensure that they seek jobs and are not employed anywhere. In some of the countries, a significant proportion of unemployment benefits are distributed by trade and labour unions. This arrangement is known as the Ghent system. Unemployment benefit was included by the ILO in its Employment Promotion and Protection against Unemployment Convention, adopted in 1988 for promotion of employment against unemployment and as an initiative towards social security, including unemployment benefit.[17]

Such measures and initiatives will serve the purpose of securing people from being trapped for employment opportunities by fake employment agencies run by traffickers. This initiative should be taken up in all the countries so as to save citizens from the hands of organized crime groups; it will, thereby, protect the human rights of its citizens, in turn maintaining the demography and human capital of the country.

Strengthening Immigration/Emigration and Border Control

Human trafficking, being a transnational organized crime, tends to violate the laws of immigration and security of the countries. Thus, strong immigration and border-control measures are required so as to prevent the traffickers from carrying out their activities across and within the borders. The countries all over the world need to frame stringent policies to control the migration of people to their countries and from other countries.

---

[16] 'Unemployment Benefit', available at http://en.wikipedia.org/wiki/Unemployment_benefits (accessed on 25 December 2013).

[17] 'Unemployment Benefit'.

Traffickers misuse the weak immigration policies of various countries, effectively move around across international borders, and efficiently run their business of trafficking of persons for forced labour, prostitution, and sexual slavery. After analysing the extent and gravity of human trafficking, the United Nations, with the help of UNODC, framed some effective immigration policies and border control measures among the states. There are a number of measures included in the trafficking in persons protocol that states can refer to in order to make it more difficult for traffickers to move people across borders. These measures are also included in the Migrants Protocol.

Fabrication and forgery of all kinds of legal documents has been taking place all over the world. Development of new technologies is helping criminal organizations and traffickers to produce false documents by making it easier, and thus the traffickers are now able to provide the victims of trafficking false passports and other travel documents such as visas. There are also instances of corruption among the immigration officers who form a part of the trafficking network and assist the traffickers in migration of persons without properly verifying the documents. Such corrupt immigration officials also help in providing visas from embassies for the victims of trafficking.[18]

Therefore, stricter measures are required to make the documents impossible to forge, fake, or alter. Administrative and security elements are also required to protect the process of production and issuance against corruption, theft, or other means of diverting documents. There are many new technologies and processes which are being developed to create new types of documents which could identify individuals in a unique manner since they would completely rely on information stored in the database, which would be out of the reach of these offenders.[19]

Over the recent years, border control has greatly reduced due to various factors. The permeability of borders helps criminal organizations in trafficking persons, regionally as well as internationally. The

[18] United Nations, *Toolkit to Combat Trafficking in Persons*.
[19] United Nations, *Toolkit to Combat Trafficking*.

technical capacity of border control agencies to detect and prevent trafficking is often found to be inadequate. For example, at border crossings of many states, there are no telecommunication facilities, and there is an absence of persons who cross the borders for commercial purposes. Moreover, it is also seen that the border-control agencies and border police forces lack adequate staff, infrastructure, and funding from the governments. Criminal organizations take advantage of such situations and transport people across borders.[20]

Thus, there is an urgent need to strengthen the basic border controls, thereby making it more difficult for traffickers to use conventional means of transport to enter countries. Strengthening the border-control measures should include making border controls more effective and prevent the misuse of passports and other travel or identification documents. Moreover, cross-border cooperation among the countries is very much required to prevent the movement of the traffickers across borders.[21]

New International Treaties

With the aim of combating the most heinous crime of human trafficking, considerable number of bodies established by the United Nations, various other international and non-governmental organizations, and academic and business groups including responsible and committed citizens of the countries, work in their own ways and with their own initiatives to addresses the problem. The people and groups which act alone and operate within the national or local borders have only a limited impact on human trafficking. Hence, combining the efforts and resources of all these stakeholders and channelizing their efforts and initiatives into a lucid and effective strategy can form a strong and focused initiative in combating the crime.

Since it is an international problem, affecting all the countries of the world which are facing similar consequences, various conventions,

---

[20]　UNODC and UN.GIFT, *Human Trafficking*.
[21]　UNODC and UN.GIFT, *Human Trafficking*.

protocols, and treaties have been enforced internationally to combat and deal with this crime. Many important protocols and conventions have been adopted and enforced by the United Nations, such as the Palermo protocol, often known as the Trafficking in Persons Protocol, the UNTOC convention, and various anti-trafficking laws towards fighting the crime. Beside these protocols and conventions, organizations such as UNODC and UN.GIFT have also been established by the United Nations in order to combat human trafficking with the ratification of all its member states.[22]

Despite so many important trafficking protocols and conventions and various other organizations working towards combating the crime, it is seen that trafficking is still increasing day by day with more sophistication in its operation; its rate has aggravated and it is rising at an alarming pace. It is among the topmost transnational crimes in the world. There are still several member states that have not yet ratified the Trafficking Protocol and hence working towards a globally applicable legal framework remains to become a priority issue to combat trafficking. Therefore, there is a dire need to enforce more new, strong, and effective anti-trafficking legislations and treaties at the international level. This can actually bring down the trafficking rate considerably, thereby preventing and finally eliminating the crime.

Regional Treaties

Although there are various regional legislations and protocols to prevent, fight, and combat human trafficking and to protect the victims of trafficking, there is still a need to have more efficient regional treaties to fight this crime against humanity more effectively. The Trafficking in Persons Protocol has been the first internationally agreed legislation of human trafficking that obliges all the countries to criminalize human trafficking; therefore many countries that have ratified the protocol have adopted the legislation by translating the protocol's obligations

---

[22] UNODC and UN.GIFT, 'UNODC Human Trafficking Case Law Database', available at http://www.ungift.org/knowledgehub/en/about/unodc.html (accessed on 15 July 2014).

into their national and domestic laws to combat the crime. In addition to this, many regional organizations have also followed up with regional instruments, action plans, and initiatives towards fighting human trafficking. However, there are still a considerable number of countries where effective legislation is still not in place to fight human trafficking, or where only certain elements of the protocol have been adopted while framing anti-trafficking laws.[23]

Although it appears that human trafficking places itself high on the agenda of the member states, it is evident that even with anti-trafficking legislation in place, many governments still do not have the necessary knowledge, expertise, or national capacity to fight trafficking in persons in its multidimensional aspects. This is because the crime is transnational in nature. Only a limited number of governments have been able to adopt national action plans, create inter-agency coordination mechanisms, and identify the role of all different departments concerned in order to counter human trafficking in a coordinated and multidisciplinary manner. In addition to this, it is also seen that only a few countries have the necessary knowledge, skills, and expertise and have received training for efficient investigation and prosecution of human trafficking cases. Thus, it is essential that these professional skills are used to enforce effective regional legislations and treaties, and also channelize them effectively to prosecute the traffickers at the regional level.[24]

Human Trafficking and Human Rights

Human trafficking is a form of modern-day slavery. Persons who have been victims of human trafficking have been deprived of their basic fundamental rights, their human rights. Trafficking has led to severe violation of human rights and human dignity. The trafficked persons are considered as a commodity and are used and reused, purchased and sold, a number of times. The trafficked persons are ill-treated and often abused by traffickers. They are kept in very unhygienic conditions

---

[23] UNODC and UN.GIFT, *Human Trafficking*.
[24] UNODC and UN.GIFT, *Human Trafficking*.

and are subjected to severe violation of human rights. The victims are sexually abused and pushed into forced sex and prostitution, forced labour, slavery, warfare activities, or are forced to work in mines and other dangerous workplaces.[25]

Human rights is a major concern in such cases when victims' movements are restricted and they are detained in shelters, under inhuman conditions, whether it is in the country of origin, country of destination, or in transit. There are even some instances where the victims face dire consequences due to societal status and racism existing in their country, which again entails violation of human rights.[26]

In response to such ill treatment and severe violation of human rights by the traffickers and the increasing degradation of humanity by these offenders, international organizations such as the United Nations have enacted legislations to protect the human rights. Thus, the international human rights law was enacted and enforced. Besides this, there are a considerable number of legal instruments and at the regional as well as international level. The trafficking protocol has included a human rights aspect in it while being drafted. The following clauses of the protocol define the human rights aspect of the protocol.

Protection and Assistance

The Trafficking in Persons Protocol states: 'Trafficked persons shall not be detained, charged or prosecuted for the illegality of their entry into or residence in countries of transit and destination, or for their involvement in unlawful activities to the extent that such involvement is a direct consequence of their situation as trafficked persons.'[27] This means that the states should ensure that the trafficked persons should not be prosecuted for their illegal entry into the country of destination

[25] United Nations, *Recommended Principles and Practices on Human Rights and Human Trafficking: Commentary* (United Nations Publications, 2010).

[26] UNODC and UN.GIFT, *Human Trafficking*.

[27] UNODC, Inter-Parliamentary Union, and UN.GIFT, *Combating Trafficking in Persons: A Handbook for Parliamentarians*, available at https://www.unodc.org/documents/human-trafficking/UN_Handbook_engl_core_low.pdf (accessed on 30 May 2016).

or any kind of illicit activities which are the consequences of their situation as trafficked persons. It also mentions that 'states shall ensure that trafficked persons are protected from further exploitation and harm and have access to adequate physical and psychological care. Such protection and care shall not be made conditional upon the capacity or willingness of the trafficked person to cooperate in legal proceedings.' This means that it is the duty of the states to ensure that the trafficked persons are protected from further exploitation and they should be given adequate physical and psychological care, which should not be based on any kind of conditions as to the capacity or willingness of the trafficked persons to cooperate in the legal proceedings of prosecution of the traffickers.[28]

Again, the Trafficking in Persons Protocol states in Article 6 the need for assistance to and protection of victims of trafficking, and the need to ensure some of the critical rights to the victims of trafficking as per the international standards for the protection of human rights.[29] Following are examples of these rights identified:

- right to safety
- right to privacy
- right to information
- right to legal representation
- right to be heard in court
- right to compensation for damages
- right to assistance
- right to seek residence
- right to return

The victims are entitled to these rights irrespective of their immigration status or their willingness to testify in court. These are briefly explained here.

---

[28] UNODC, Inter-Parliamentary Union, and UN.GIFT, *Combating Trafficking in Persons.*

[29] UNODC, Inter-Parliamentary Union, and UN.GIFT, *Combating Trafficking in Persons.*

Right to Safety

'Each State Party shall endeavour to provide for the physical safety of victims of trafficking in persons while they are within its territory.'[30] This means that the countries where the victims have been held should ensure the safety of the victims and they should be protected while they testify against the traffickers during the prosecution. They should also be given proper and safe residence in their countries.

Right to Privacy

The Trafficking in Persons Protocol entails that state parties shall protect the privacy and identity of victims of trafficking in persons legal proceedings relating to such trafficking confidential.[31] This means that the states should ensure to protect the confidentiality of the victims and the legal proceedings and should also shield the identity of the victims. The courts could further keep the proceedings and trial confidential by excluding the media and the public.

Right to Information

The Trafficking in Persons Protocol provides that states parties should make available to victims of trafficking 'information on relevant court and administrative proceedings' and 'information, in particular as regards their legal rights, in a language that the victims of trafficking in persons can understand.'[32] This means that the states should ensure that relevant information is provided to the victims about the court and administrative proceedings during the prosecution of the traffickers and such information should be provided to the victims in a language which they will understand.

---

[30] UNODC, Inter-Parliamentary Union, and UN.GIFT, *Combating Trafficking in Persons*, Article 8.

[31] UNODC, Inter-Parliamentary Union, and UN.GIFT, *Combating Trafficking in Persons*, Article 8.

[32] UNODC, Inter-Parliamentary Union, and UN.GIFT, *Combating Trafficking in Persons*, Article 8.

Right to Legal Representation

The OHCHR recommendations and the Trafficking in Persons Protocol mention that states shall ensure 'providing trafficked persons with legal and other assistance in relation to any criminal, civil or other actions against traffickers/exploiters'.[33] This means that the victims should be provided with legal assistance, counseling, and other information regarding their legal rights but in a language that is understandable by the victims.

Right to Be Heard in Court

The Trafficking in Persons Protocol provides that the state parties should provide victims of trafficking in persons with 'assistance to enable their views and concerns to be presented and considered at appropriate stages of criminal proceedings against offenders'.[34] This means that the states should ensure that the trafficked persons or the victims are provided with assistance to express their views and concerns and should be considered during the court proceedings for the prosecution of the traffickers.

Right to Compensation for Damages

The Trafficking in Persons Protocol provides that 'each state party shall ensure that its domestic legal system contains measures that offer victims of trafficking in persons the possibility of obtaining compensation for damage suffered'.[35] This refers to the right of the victims to be provided with compensation for the damages caused to them during exploitation and for the trauma they have experienced and suffered due to trafficking.

---

[33] Center for Study of Democracy, 'Antimafia: The Italian Experience in Fighting Organized Crime', Policy Brief No. 31, October 2011.

[34] Center for Study of Democracy, 'Antimafia'.

[35] Center for Study of Democracy, 'Antimafia'.

Right to Assistance

The protocol states that 'each state party shall consider implementing measures to provide for the physical, psychological and social recovery of victims of trafficking in persons'. It explains that victims have the right to:

a) appropriate housing;
b) counselling and information, in particular as regards their legal rights, in a language that the victims of trafficking in persons can understand;
c) medical, psychological, and material assistance; and
d) employment, educational, and training opportunities.[36]

This refers that the state parties should ensure that the victims of trafficking are provided with assistance in terms of medical/physical, psychological, and social recovery and should also be provided with appropriate residence or housing and assistance regarding their legal rights, access to education, employment, and training.

Right to Seek Residence

According to Article 7 of Trafficking in Persons Protocol, 'each state party shall consider adopting legislative or other appropriate measures that permit victims of trafficking in persons to remain in its territory, temporarily or permanently, in appropriate cases' and 'give appropriate consideration to humanitarian and compassionate factors'.[37] This means that the parties should adopt certain legislations or some measures to permit the victims of trafficking to reside in that country, either temporarily or permanently, and in certain cases should also consider the humanitarian and compassionate factor. In some cases, it has been noticed that the victims, upon arrival in their country of origin, were again made vulnerable to retaliation from the traffickers. Even immediate deportation of the victims makes it difficult for the

---

[36] Center for Study of Democracy, 'Antimafia'.
[37] Center for Study of Democracy, 'Antimafia'.

legal personnel and the government to retrieve information about the traffickers from the victims. Thus, this right was considered in the protocol.

Right to Return

Article 8 of the protocol provides that state parties of which victims of trafficking are nationals or residents should 'facilitate and accept, with due regard for the safety of that person, the return of that person without undue or unreasonable delay'.[38] Repatriation of victims 'shall preferably be voluntary'. This right was included so as to ensure that the victims of trafficking have the right to return to their country of origin with dignity. The state parties should ensure that the victims have their consent to return and that they are provided with proper protection.

The OHCHR also works towards protecting the human rights of the trafficked victims. The anti-trafficking activities of the OHCHR are at the country level and serve as modes of better coordination and cooperation among the governments, NGOs, and the victims at the ground level. The United Nations and OHCHR teams in each country work very well in cooperation and assist in guiding, implementing, and protecting the rights of the victims of trafficking, along with the government. The government also benefits from their support, establishes and implements better legislations, and monitors the trafficking activities, preventing them, while also protecting the victims and their rights. Such activities and good coordination among the United Nations, OHCHR, other human rights groups, and NGOs eliminates violation of human rights and thereby helps in combating the transnational organized crime of human trafficking.[39]

The advantages could be better understanding of the problems faced by the victims of trafficking as well as the victims of smuggling. These problems and abuses faced by the victims of both categories can change the perspective and make the state consider them as victims

---

[38] Center for Study of Democracy, 'Antimafia'.
[39] United Nations, *Recommended Principles*.

of human rights violation instead of criminals for their illegal entry to the country of destination. This will be a victim-centred approach in dealing with the human trafficking crime. Such an approach can help the victims reinstate their dignity, self-respect, and self-image and also assist them in getting out of the traumatic psychological condition and undignified situation in which they were and because of which they were isolated from their family, friends, relatives, and the society. Such a human rights framework and approach to the protocol also helps us to understand the various issues related to the protection and promotion of human rights, the reasons behind trafficking, and the consequences faced by the trafficked persons or the victims.

Enforcement Action of the State: Deterrence of the Existing Mechanism

The United Nations has enforced various protocols to fight human trafficking, especially trafficking of women and children. The UNODC and UNTOC implemented the Protocol to Prevent, Suppress and Punish Trafficking in Persons (Trafficking in Persons Protocol or the Palermo protocol)[40] and the United Nations Convention against Transnational Organized Crime[41] to fight the crime against humanity. The Palermo protocol was signed by 117 countries in 2003 while 132 countries ratified the protocol in 2009.[42]

Further, the UNODC launched the United Nations Global Initiative to Fight Trafficking (UN.GIFT) in March 2007 to fight this transnational organized crime which has grasped most of the nations of the world.[43] But not all member states have ratified this global initiative to fight human trafficking.

[40] UNODC, 'United Nations Convention against Transnational Organized Crime', available at http://www.unodc.org/pdf/crime/a_res_55/res5525e.pdf (accessed on 28 September 2014).

[41] UNODC, 'United Nations Convention against Transnational Organized Crime'.

[42] UNODC and UN.GIFT, *Human Trafficking*.

[43] UNODC and UN.GIFT, 'UNODC Human Trafficking Case Law Database'.

The aforementioned UN protocol, commonly known as the Palermo protocol, has identified three types of interventions—prevention, protection, and prosecution. This is known as the three-P strategy.[44] This strategy is followed by subsequent three-R strategy—rescue, rehabilitation, and reintegration.

Three-P Strategy

Figure 3.1 is a diagrammatic representation of the three-P strategy.

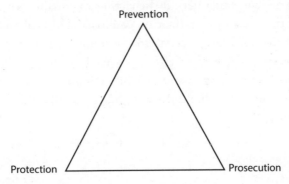

Figure 3.1   Three-P Strategy[45]

Prevention

The prevention of trafficking includes measures to establish information and media campaigns in order to raise awareness of the issue, for economic empowerment, to provide education, to alleviate the

---

[44] United Nations Human Rights, 'Protocol to Prevent, Suppress and Punish Trafficking in Persons Especially Women and Children, supplementing the United Nations Convention against Transnational Organized Crime', Article 3, available at http://www.ohchr.org/EN/ProfessionalInterest/Pages/ProtocolTraffickingInPersons.aspx (accessed on 30 May 2016).

[45] Figure source: Venla Roth, *Defining Human Trafficking and Identifying its Victims: A Study on the Impact and Future Challenges of International, European and Finnish Legal Responses to Prostitution-Related Trafficking in Human Beings* (Leiden: Martinus Nijhoff Publishers, 2011), 10.

vulnerability of potential victims of human trafficking, to discourage the demands for sexual services and exploitable labour, to provide training to relevant actors on the phenomenon and its counter measures.[46]

Protection

The second element—the protection of victims—consists of measures such as providing assistance and physical safety to the trafficking victims and witnesses as well as the members of their family, adopting measures that permit the victims to remain within the territory of the transit or destination countries, and facilitating a safe return of the trafficking victims to the country of origin, including the prevention of revictimization, provision of proper shelter, and provision of counselling sessions to the victims of trafficking to come out of the trauma and build their confidence so that they feel a part of the society.[47]

Prosecution

The measure to ensure the prosecution of perpetrators comprise criminalization of trafficking in human beings globally, implementation of the anti-trafficking laws, ensuring the functionality and adequacy of criminal and procedural legislation, and other measures as regards pre-trial investigation and criminal proceedings against the offenders.[48]

Three-R Strategy

The three-P approach has subsequently been complimented with the three-R approach to emphasize that anti-trafficking strategies and activities needed to internalize the victim-centred approach.

---

[46] U.S. Department of State, *Trafficking in Persons Report 2010*.

[47] U.S. Department of State, *Trafficking in Persons Report 2010*.

[48] U.S. Department of State, *Trafficking in Persons Report 2010*.

The three-Rs stand for rescue, rehabilitation, and reintegration of trafficking victims. This is a victim-centred approach of the Trafficking in Persons Protocol.

Rescue

This element refers to the victim's freedom and liberation from the captivity and detention.

Rehabilitation

This entails providing shelter to the rescued victims of trafficking, providing the general needs of the trafficking victims, access to medical facilities, access to counselling, and training after being rescued.

Reintegration

It refers to the support, and assistance from the authorities, cooperation between the authorities of the countries, and coordination among the country of origin and destination, which is very important for the victims after their return.

The Success of the International Criminal Court in Countering Instances of Human Trafficking

The ICC statute or the Rome Statute of the International Criminal Court came into force on 1 July 2002, and thus was established the first international criminal court which had jurisdiction over crimes of genocide, war crimes, crimes against humanity, and crimes of aggression.[49] The ICC statute includes enslavement among the 11 acts constituting the crimes against humanity, and consequently its Article 7(1) states the following.

---

[49] International Criminal Court (ICC), 'Rome Statute of the International Criminal Court', Article 5(2), available at https://www.icc-cpi.int/nr/rdonlyres/ea9aeff7-5752-4f84-be94-0a655eb30e16/0/rome_statute_english.pdf (accessed on 17 May 2016).

For the purpose of this statute, 'crime against humanity' means any of the following acts when committed as part of a widespread or systematic attack directed against any civilian population, with knowledge of the attack:[50,51]

- murder;
- extermination;
- enslavement;
- deportation or forcible transfer of population;
- imprisonment or other severe deprivation of physical liberty in violation of fundamental rules of international law;
- torture;
- rape, sexual slavery, enforced prostitution, forced pregnancy, enforced sterilization, or any other form of sexual violence of comparable gravity;
- persecution against any identifiable group or collectivity on political, racial, national, ethnic, cultural, religious, gender, or other grounds that are universally recognized as impermissible under international law;
- enforced disappearance of persons;
- the crime of apartheid;
- other inhumane acts of a similar character intentionally causing great suffering, or serious injury to the body or mental or physical health.

This is surely the most detailed definition of crimes against humanity. Enslavement was already included among the crimes against humanity in Article 6(c) of the Nuremberg Charter of the International Military Tribunal at Nuremberg, and by Article 5(c) of the charter of

---

[50] ICC, 'Rome Statute', Article 7.

[51] ICC, 'Rome Statute of the International Criminal Court', available at http://legal.un.org/icc/statute/99_corr/cstatute.htm (accessed on 30 May 2016); Coalition for the International Criminal Court, *Core Crimes Defined in the Rome Statute of the International Criminal Court*, available at http://www.iccnow.org/documents/FS-CICC-CoreCrimesinRS.pdf (accessed on 30 May 2016).

the International Military Tribunal for the Far East. Also, the charter of the statutes of the ICTY and ICTR include enslavement as a crime against humanity. However, none of these four tribunals define the practice, while, for the purpose of The Rome Statute, enslavement means the exercise of any or all the powers attaching to the right of ownership over a person and includes the exercise of such power in the course of trafficking in persons, in particular women and children.[52]

According to Article 7(1), enslavement is to be considered as a crime against humanity when the act has been committed either as a widespread or asystematic attack against civilian population. Article 7(2)(a) of the Rome Statute also defines the expression 'attack directed against any civilian population' as including any attack carried out both by state and non-state actors even outside of an armed conflict and directed against any civilian population. Another necessary element for the attack to be considered as a crime against humanity is that it has to be committed with full knowledge of it.[53]

As the definition states, even though a criminal act must be 'widespread' or 'systematic' to be considered as a crime against humanity, even if a single act committed is of an organized nature or has been committed against a number of persons or victims, then this will constitute a crime against humanity. The ICTY has established this rule and follows it to prosecute various cases of crimes against humanity, including cases of trafficking. Thus, according to this explanation stated, the ICC can prosecute cases of trafficking in persons, sexual slavery, and forced prostitution.[54]

Further, as per the definition of 'enslavement', the ICC can prosecute cases which include the trafficking of persons for labour. The persons who are trafficked as labour are subjected to servitude, physical restraint, restricted movement, and forced or compulsory labour. The crime against humanity includes any 'systematic' or 'widespread' acts,

---

[52] ICC, 'Rome Statute', Article 7(c).

[53] D. Robinson, 'The Elements of Crime against Humanity', in R.S. Lee (ed), *The International Criminal Court, Elements of Crimes and Rules of Procedure and Evidence* (New York: Transnational Publishers, 2001).

[54] ICC, 'Rome Statute', Article 7.

and such labour trafficking, forceful servitude, and exploitation constitute such act under the crime against humanity of the ICC statute.[55]
The ICC statute also includes 'trafficking in persons' without limiting
the intention of the trafficking act to sexual exploitation only and thus
includes trafficking for human organs or trafficking for slavery, servitude, and forced labour, which constitutes a crime against humanity
under the 'enslavement' provision. Thus, the ICC statute has been very
instrumental and important in identifying the crime of human trafficking, identifying the victims and the extent of exploitation, and the
provisions for prosecution of the traffickers.[56]

***

Trafficking was a matter of international human rights law and
international law long before it became an issue of migration or
transnational organized crime. However, trafficking and the forms of
exploitation which are associated with it have traditionally not been
served well by the international human rights system. In other words,
it was the chronic inability of the human rights law and the human
rights mechanisms to deal effectively with contemporary forms of
exploitation, including trafficking, which provided a number of states
with the incentive to move outside that system for a more effective
response.

The historical factors and the political preferences were more influential than law in maintaining the marginalization of trafficking as an
international human rights issue. The United Nations adopted various conventions and protocols to address these issues of human rights
violation and formed these legislations on the basis of international
law. The member states of the United Nations facing these issues of
human rights violation in the form of trafficking and exploitation came
together to bring a strong legal response against the transnational
organized crime in the form of UNTOC; further with the help of
UNODC, it further enforced the Trafficking in Persons Protocol. The

---

[55] Center for Study of Democracy, 'Antimafia'.
[56] Center for Study of Democracy, 'Antimafia'.

chapter highlighted the severity of the crime and the various conventions and protocols enforced in combating it.

The chapter has provided the similarities and the differences of the two most important instruments to combat human trafficking—the United Nations Trafficking Protocol and the CoE Trafficking Convention. Both these instruments have been enforced with the aim of preventing and combating human trafficking and strive to uphold human dignity and human integrity. Both these instruments have the human rights aspect, but differ in their method of working towards the aim. These similarities and differences have been portrayed in the chapter, giving us a clear view of each of these instruments with a human rights perspective.

The need for stringent laws to combat human trafficking had been felt strongly all over the world. This is due to the bitter fact that the crime has surfaced and penetrated its roots in almost all the countries of the world and has also spread its network globally, violating human rights, state legislations, and international legislations. Thus, stricter action and stringent legal response against human trafficking is of utmost importance. The traffickers carry out their activities through a network of international mafias supported by financers and brothel owners in the destination country. They have a global route for transporting the victims with the help of the network of the organized crime syndicate present at the local, national, and international levels. The corrupt government officials including politicians, law enforcement officers, immigration officials, and members of the judiciary also support such activities and accept bribes in the form of money, sexual favours, and political support. The traffickers are also assisted by the relatives and family members of the trafficked victims by offering them huge monetary benefits. The chapter thus highlighted the importance of a strong legal response to fight human trafficking. It highlighted the various legislations and legal framework enacted and enforced across the world at the domestic, regional, and national levels, in accordance with the international legal framework prepared by the UN conventions and protocols enforced in order to combat trafficking of humans and exploitation of human beings. It has also thrown light on some realities regarding the countries which do not have any legislation against human trafficking and have become a hub of this transnational organized crime. The shocking part is that these countries have been a party to the Trafficking Protocols and various conventions in combating this crime. It has also mentioned a few countries that are not party to these anti-trafficking protocols and conventions but have enforced very effective anti-trafficking laws to deal with this crime very efficiently. The chapter has discussed the importance of strong legislations enforced at the domestic level by the countries as an effective measure to deal with trafficking and further exploitation of the victims in the form of forced labour, slavery, sexual servitude, and forced prostitution. The misinterpretation of the term 'trafficking' in different countries and the confusion created thereby has affected a proper implementation of anti-trafficking laws impacting the trafficking victims who are often considered illegal migrants. Many countries have also enforced legislations to combat trafficking, keeping in mind only the women and children; thus the male labour force which is also trafficked and exploited by forced labour and slavery is neglected.

Further, the need and importance of effective implementation of the anti-trafficking laws have been seen in the chapter, discussing ways to have a proper and efficient legal framework at the domestic level so as to curb this menace. It has highlighted the human rights aspect of the human trafficking crime and stated the need for full compliance by all the nations with the international legislations while implementing laws to prevent human trafficking and protect the victims. Also discussed is the need for an amendment and effective implementation of laws which not only take into account the exploitation of women and children but also the exploitation of men through forced labour, forced slavery, and other ways. The importance of clear definitions and terms have been explained in the chapter and so have been the advantages of this clarity, to help in proper prosecution of the traffickers and stricter punishment of the criminals for such acts. The chapter has highlighted the importance of receiving support and assistance of related laws for controlling and monitoring the hidden crime which is carried out with the help of various fake employment agencies, marriage bureaus, beauty salons, and others.

The effectiveness of the legal responses at the international level has not been very pleasing. Although measures to curb trafficking require immediate and stringent actions to eradicate it from its roots, it has been very difficult since the crime has spread its network all over the world and is deeply rooted. This chapter has highlighted the effectiveness of the international legal responses. The United Nations, through its various initiatives to fight and combat this crime, is still striving to achieve a balance between the international legislations and the domestic- and region-level legislations. The legislations against human trafficking have been found to be not as effective as they should be or as they had been thought to be. The chapter has discussed the weaknesses and flaws in these legislations, both at the international level and at the domestic, regional, and national levels, and also highlighted the reasons behind such weaknesses and non-compliance or less compliance. The confusion created in identifying the victims of trafficking with illegal immigrants or victims of smuggling is a drawback in the effectiveness of the anti-trafficking legislations. There are also some conflicting and overlapping laws in the countries which again compliance with the international legislations. The chapter has also highlighted the lack of cooperation between the nations in effective implementation of anti-trafficking laws and proper coordination in dealing with the prosecution of the traffickers and protecting the victims, which is due to distrust and fear of losing documents or evidences. There are also problems in dealing with the trafficking cases and protecting the victims because of the lack of knowledge, training, and awareness about the anti-trafficking laws and the measures to be taken in dealing with such cases among the law-enforcement officers and immigration officials. The effectiveness of the legal response is also impacted by the lack of coordination and cooperation among the countries, its police personnel, the judiciary system, and the prosecutors. The chapter has thus drawn attention towards the processes to enhance cooperation among the countries in various programmes working towards this objective. It further explains the appropriate methods and steps to be taken to protect the victims of trafficking after their return to their country of origin or getting refugee status and residing in the country of destination. Also emphasized is the protection of the victims who are potential witnesses in the prosecution cases, whereby many such victims have often been denied justice and have faced difficulties to get protection. Highlighted is the compensation system applicable and available for the victims of trafficking of labour. The chapter has explained the redressal mechanism for the victims of trafficked labour and the justice system required, and explained the justice system prevalent in various countries. The types and nature of visas are also reasons for trafficking and exploitation, which can be rectified with the help of better and improved immigration policies.

Ways in which regulatory frameworks have been formed to prevent trafficking has also been analysed in the chapter. Ranging from the UN conventions and protocols to the enforcement of anti-trafficking laws at the regional level, the chapter looked at the various approaches to combat human trafficking.

Then has been emphasized the significance of human rights law and has highlighted instances where the trafficked persons have been deprived of their basic human rights. Human trafficking is in itself a violation of human rights and degradation of human dignity. The chapter has described the aspects of human rights in the international machineries and legal instruments in preventing and combating human trafficking and exploitation. The status of the victims, their exploitation by way of forced labour, sexual abuse, prostitution, ill treatment, restriction on movements unhygienic living conditions, victimization and commodification are illustrations of violation of human rights. Rescuing the trafficked victims and protecting them from retaliation by the traffickers is a very important aspect to assist the government to take action against the traffickers and prosecute them. The trafficking protocol has included various clauses and sections to provide fundamental rights to the trafficked victims, assistance for their physical and psychological well-being, and help to overcome the traumatic experiences of exploitation and sexual abuse. The chapter explained how various rights of the trafficked victims have been stated in Article 6 of the Trafficking in Persons protocol.

The enforcement actions of the state have been discussed, which include the Palermo protocol, and the UNODC and UN.GIFT and their initiatives. The victim-centred approach which is usually known as the three-P strategy of the Palermo protocol has been described, followed by a brief explanation of the three-R approach. Apart from this, the ICC statute on crimes against humanity has also been a very successful instrument towards preventing, protecting, and prosecuting the trafficking cases. It has been a step forward in addition to the Trafficking Protocol in combating the organized crime of trafficking. The success of the ICC statute, which is also commonly known as the Rome Statute, has been very instrumental in prosecuting traffickers. Article 7 of the Rome Statute, and the Crime against humanity has clearly explained the clauses of exploitation of human beings through human trafficking with the help of clear and specific definitions of each possible criteria. Thus, this chapter ends with the role of the ICC statute in combating trafficking with the help of its provisions in identifying the crime of human trafficking, identifying the victims and the extent of exploitation, and the provisions for the prosecution of the traffickers.

This chapter thus explains and describes the importance of various international legal responses and its effectiveness in combating human trafficking crime, the role and relation of the International Law in framing the conventions and protocols of the United Nations towards fighting this crime, and also highlights the problems experienced by the victims, and the reasons for the low rate of effectiveness of the anti-trafficking laws at the domestic level. Lastly, it describes the ICC statute and its role in preventing human trafficking and prosecuting the traffickers.

The following chapter mainly deals with Article 7 of the Rome Statute and trafficking as crime against humanity. It also deals with the characterization of crime against humanity and various statutes and laws for crimes against humanity. The chapter further describes various international problems, makes a hypothetical study of the arms, drugs, and human trafficking, and describes trafficking as a severe deprivation of physical liberty which constitutes Article 7(1)(a)–(h) of the Rome Statute–The Elements of Crime, and also describes the *mens rea* element of the Elements of Crime.

4 International Institutions vis-à-vis Crimes against Humanity

In recent times, trafficking of human beings has increased so much that it has taken up the form of a global trade. Human beings are used as commodities and reusable products; they are purchased and sold in global markets, used and exploited, and degraded to such an extent that they lose their dignity.

The United Nations defines human trafficking as a crime against humanity and includes in its definition of human trafficking the act of recruiting, transferring, transporting, harbouring, and receiving of person by coercion, force, or any other means for exploitation.[1] The world has been facing this crime since ages and has been continuously trying

---

[1] UNODC, 'Human Trafficking', available at http://www.unodc.org/unodc/en/human-trafficking/what-is-human-trafficking.html (accessed on 12 October 2013).

to combat it through various legislations and protocols. The countries across the world act as either a country of origin, transit, or destination. Millions of people are trafficked every year, be it men, women, or children. They are exploited through forced labour, servitude, sexual abuse, and many other forms of exploitation, even in warfare. The United Nations, with the assistance of UNODC and UN.GIFT, enforced the United Nations Convention against Transnational Organized Crime (UNTOC) and Protocol to Prevent, Suppress and Punish Trafficking in Persons (Trafficking in Persons Protocol) to fight this crime against humanity.

Further success has been achieved with the establishment of the ICC, and with the enforcement of the ICC statute or the Rome Statute. The shocking data about the trade and the extent of victimization has aroused concern and awareness in the legal arena, leading to the establishment of the ICC, besides various other laws and conventions to combat the trade and the heinous crime.

The Rome Statute of the ICC came into force in 2002 for combating human trafficking. It was enacted with reference to 'trafficking in persons', considered as a crime against humanity under the enslavement provision of the statute. Since the enforcement of the ICC, 124 countries of the world have given their consent to the Rome Statute to deal with crimes against humanity including enslavement, sexual slavery, enforced prostitution, and any other form of sexual violence of comparable gravity.[2]

Article 7(1) of the Rome Statute enumerates that acts 'when committed as part of a widespread or systematic attack directed against any civilian population, with knowledge of the attack' constitute a 'crime against humanity'.[3] Article 7(1)(c), the 'enslavement' provision, is further elaborately defined under Article 7(2)(c) as the 'exercise

---

[2] Center for Study of Democracy, 'Antimafia: The Italian Experience in Fighting Organized Crime', Policy Brief No. 31, October 2011.

[3] International Criminal Court (ICC), 'Rome Statute of the International Criminal Court', Article 7(1), available at https://www.icc-cpi.int/nr/rdonlyres/ea9aeff7-5752-4f84-be94-0a655eb30e16/0/rome_statute_english.pdf (accessed on 17 May 2016).

of any or all the powers attaching to the right of ownership over a person and includes the exercise of such power in the course of trafficking in persons, in particular women and children'.[4] The Elements of Crimes of the Rome Statute elucidate that exercising 'any or all powers attaching to the right of ownership over one or more persons' includes, but is not limited to, 'purchasing, selling, lending or bartering such a person or persons, or by imposing on them a similar deprivation of liberty'. [5]

Article 7(1)(c) of the Rome Statute has also included 'trafficking in persons, in particular women and children'. It is also defined in the Elements of Crimes but the definition of trafficking is not accurate and appropriately expressed in the statute except the portion defined as 'attaching to the right of ownership over one or more persons' and/or 'by imposing on them a similar deprivations of liberty'.[6]

Characterization of Crimes against Humanity

Crimes against humanity are crimes committed against a civilian population, violating human rights and depriving people of their fundamental rights. These crimes differ from the others such as genocide in the way they are committed. The major difference is that these crimes are aimed at civilian population or groups of persons whereas crimes like genocide are committed with the main aim or intention of destroying an entire group or population.

The idea of the inclusion of crimes against humanity in a legal framework that dates back to more than 100 years. It has its origin in the Hague Convention concerning the Laws and Customs of War on Land of 1907. The Preamble of the Convention, which is stated

---

[4] ICC, 'Rome Statute', Article 7(2)(c).

[5] ICC, 'Rome Statute', Article 9.

[6] W. Duncan, 'The Hague Conference on Private International Law and its Current Programme of Work Concerning the International Protection of Children and Other Aspects of Family Law', *Yearbook of Private International Law* II (2000): 48.

in the Martens Clause, is referred to as the 'laws of humanity'.[7] This formed the basis of the inclusion of crimes against humanity in various other charters, statutes, and conventions. Later, crimes against humanity were included as a separate category in the Nuremberg Charter. Article 6(c) of the charter describes crimes against humanity.[8] Furthermore, this crime was included in Tokyo Charter in its Article 5(c). Both the Nuremberg Charter and the Tokyo Charter have drawn connection of crimes against humanity with war crimes. Thereafter, the ICTY and ICTR statutes reaffirmed crimes against humanity.[9]

Besides these charters and statues, namely Nuremberg Charter, Tokyo Charter, ICTY, and ICTR, the most significant one has been the Rome Statute and its Article 7, which has helped to a great extent to define clearly the crimes against humanity with its Elements of Crime.[10] Following are some of the important statutes and charters framed against crimes against humanity. These definitions help in bringing clarity in the views and different aspects of crimes which are defined as the crimes against humanity.

The London Charter of the International Military Tribunal (Nuremberg Charter), Article 6(c)

The Nuremberg Charter or the Charter of the International Military Tribunal is an annexe to the agreement for the prosecution and punishment of the major war criminals of the European Axis. It is also known as the London Charter. It was a decree issued on 8 August 1945, which laid down the laws and procedures. These laws and

---

[7] B.V. Schaack, *The Definition of Crimes against Humanity: Resolving the Incoherence* (Santa Clara Law Digital Commons, 1998), available at http://digitalcommons.law.scu.edu/facpubs, (accessed on 20 December 2013).

[8] J.N. Aston, 'Genesis of International Criminal Law', *Social Science Research Network* August (2011), available at http://papers.ssrn.com/sol3/papers.cfm?abstract_id=1928908 (accessed on 26 September 2014).

[9] ICC, 'Rome Statute', Article 29.

[10] R. Chaikin, *Trafficking and the Global Sex Industry 2009* (MD Lexington Books).

procedures formed the basis of the Nuremberg trials. This charter also stipulated that crimes of the European Axis Powers could also be tried and further defined the following three categories of crimes—war crimes, crimes against peace, and crimes against humanity.[11]

Article 6(c) of the London Charter or the Nuremberg Charter defines crimes against humanity as 'murder, extermination, enslavement, deportation, and other inhuman acts committed against civilian populations, before or during the war; or persecutions on political, racial or religious grounds in execution of or in connection with any crime within the jurisdiction of the Tribunal, whether or not in violation of the domestic law of the country where perpetrated'.[12] This definition was also used in the Charter of the International Military Tribunal for the Far East.

The Rome Statute, Article 7(1)

The Rome Statute was constituted by the ICC in 2002 to have a universal jurisdiction on crimes which comprise genocide, crimes of aggression, war crimes, and crimes against humanity. It was done well before the Palermo protocol was brought into effect, which defined the crime of trafficking and included threats, deception, and abuse of authority, power, or a dominant position while the drafting of the Palermo protocol.

Article 7 of the Rome Statute[13] constituted the crimes against humanity to include sexual slavery, enforced prostitution, enslavement, and any other form of sexual violence of comparable gravity. Article 7(1) of the Rome Statute defines crimes against humanity as

---

[11] R. Cryer, 'Prosecuting International Crimes: Selectivity and the International Criminal Law Regime', *Cambridge Studies in International and Comparative Law* (2005).

[12] United Nations General Assembly, *The Charter and the Judgment of the Nuremburg Trial*, 4, available at http://www.cininas.lt/wp-content/uploads/2015/06/1949_UN_ILC_N_statuto_koment.pdf (accessed on 30 May 2016).

[13] ICC, 'Rome Statute', Article 7.

'any of the acts when committed as part of a widespread or systematic attack directed against any civilian population, with knowledge of the attack'.

The Statute of the International Criminal Tribunal for the Former Yugoslavia (ICTY), Article 5

This statute, commonly known as ICTY, was established by the Security Council acting under Chapter VII of the Charter of the United Nations, the international tribunal for the prosecution of persons responsible for serious violations of international humanitarian law committed in the territory of the former Yugoslavia since 1991, and was adopted on 25 May 1993 by the Resolution 827. The ICTY was constituted to function in accordance with the provisions of the present statute. It has its jurisdiction over four types of crimes committed on the territory of the former Yugoslavia since 1991. These crimes include grave breaches of the Geneva Conventions, violations of the laws or customs of war, genocide, and crimes against humanity.

Article 5 of the statute of the ICTY defines crimes against humanity.[14] It states that 'the International Tribunal shall have the power to prosecute persons responsible for the following crimes when committed in armed conflict, whether international or internal in character, and directed against any civilian population:

(a) murder;
(b) extermination;
(c) enslavement;
(d) deportation;
(e) imprisonment;
(f) torture;
(g) rape;

---

[14] ICTY, 'United Nations International Criminal Tribunal for the former Yugoslavia', available at http://www.icty.org/sid/135 (accessed on 11 December 2012).

(h) persecutions on political, racial, and religious grounds;

(i) other inhumane acts.'

The Statute of the International Criminal Tribunal for Rwanda, Article 3

The statute of the International Criminal Tribunal for Rwanda (ICTR) was established in November 1994 by the United Nations Security Council by Resolution 955. It is an international tribunal established with the purpose of prosecuting the persons who were responsible for the genocide in Rwanda and various other serious violations of international humanitarian law committed in the territory of Rwanda, or by the Rwandan citizens in nearby states, between 1 January and 31 December 1994. The tribunal has its jurisdiction over genocide, crimes against humanity, and war crimes. These are defined as violations of Common Article 3 and Additional Protocol II of the Geneva Conventions (dealing with war crimes committed during internal conflicts).[15]

Article 3 of the ICTR states crimes against humanity[16] thus: 'The International Tribunal for Rwanda shall have the power to prosecute persons responsible for the following crimes when committed as part of a widespread or systematic attack against any civilian population on national, political, ethnic, racial or religious grounds:

(a) murder;

(b) extermination;

---

[15] International Committee of the Red Cross, 'Special Protection of Women and Children', *International Review of the Red Cross*, available at https://www.icrc.org/eng/resources/documents/misc/57jmj2.htm (accessed on 30 May 2016); International Committee of the Red Cross, 'Geneva Conventions and Commentaries', available at https://www.icrc.org/en/war-and-law/treaties-customary-law/geneva-conventions (accessed on 30 May 2016).

[16] International Criminal Tribunal for Rwanda, 'Statute of the International Tribunal for Rwanda', available at http://www.icls.de/dokumente/ictr_statute.pdf (accessed on 11 December 2013).

(c) enslavement;
(d) deportation;
(e) imprisonment;
(f) torture;
(g) rape;
(h) persecutions on political, racial, and religious grounds;
(i) other inhumane acts.

The Statute of the Special Court for Sierra Leone, Article 2

The Special Court for Sierra Leone, also known as the 'Special Court' or the SCSL, is a judicial body jointly set up by the government of Sierra Leone and the United Nations. It was set up to 'prosecute persons who bear the greatest responsibility for serious violations of international humanitarian law and Sierra Leonean law' committed in Sierra Leone since 30 November 1996 and during the Sierra Leone Civil War.[17]

Article 2 of the statute of the SCSL states the crimes against humanity[18] and defines them as follows: 'The Special Court shall have the power to prosecute persons who committed the following crimes as part of a widespread or systematic attack against any civilian population:

(a) murder;
(b) extermination;
(c) enslavement;
(d) deportation;
(e) imprisonment;
(f) torture;

---

[17] Special Court for Sierra Leone, 'The Statute of the Special Court for Sierra Leone', available at http://www.sc-sl.org/ (accessed on 11 December 2013).

[18] SCSL, available at http://www.sc-sl.org/LinkClick.aspx?fileticket=u Clnd1MJeEw%3d&tabid=70. [Accessed on 11th December 2013]

(g) rape, sexual slavery, enforced prostitution, forced pregnancy, and any other form of sexual violence;

(h) persecution on political, racial, ethnic, or religious grounds;

(i) other inhumane acts.'

The Law on the Establishment of the Extraordinary Chambers in the Courts of Cambodia (ECCC), Article 5

The reason for the enactment and the rationale for this law is to bring to trial all senior leaders of Democratic Kampuchea and those who were the most responsible persons for the crimes committed and serious violations of Cambodian Penal Law, International Humanitarian Law and Custom, and International Conventions recognized by Cambodia. These crimes were committed between 17 April 1975 and 6 January 1979.[19]

Article 5 of the ECCC[20] includes in its provisions crimes against humanity and states: 'The Extraordinary Chambers shall have the power to bring to trial all suspects who committed crimes against humanity between 17th April 1975 and 6th January 1979. Crimes against humanity, which have no statute of limitations,[21] are any acts that are committed as part of a widespread or systematic attack directed against any civilian population, on national, political, ethnical, racial, or religious grounds, such as

(a) murder;

(b) extermination;

(c) enslavement;

---

[19] Extraordinary Chambers in the Courts of Cambodia (ECCC), available at http://www.eccc.gov.kh/sites/default/files/legal-documents/ KR_Law_as_amended_27_Oct_2004_Eng.pdf (accessed on 11 December 2013).

[20] ECCC, available at http://www.eccc.gov.kh/sites/default/files/legal-documents/KR_Law_as_amended_27_Oct_2004_Eng.pdf (accessed on 11 December 2013).

[21] ICC, 'Rome Statute', Article 29.

(d) deportation;
(e) imprisonment;
(f) torture;
(g) rape;
(h) persecutions on political, racial, and religious grounds;
(i) other inhumane acts.'

The International Law Commission's Draft Code of Crimes against the Peace and Security of Mankind, Article 18

The text for the draft code was adopted by the International Law Commission in its 48th session in 1996, and was submitted to the General Assembly as part of the commission's report. Article 1 of the draft code states the application of it as:

1. The present code applies to the crimes against the peace and security of mankind set out in part two.
2. Crimes against the peace and security of mankind are crimes under international law and punishable as such, whether or not they are punishable under national law.[22]

Article 18 of the ILC's Draft Code of Crimes against Peace and Security of Mankind (1996)[23] defines crimes against humanity as follows.

'A crime against humanity means any of the following acts, when committed in a systematic manner or on a large scale and instigated or directed by a government or by any organization or group:

[22] 'The International Law Commission's Draft Code of Crimes against the Peace and Security of Mankind', 1996, available at http://untreaty.un.org/ ilc/texts/instruments/english/draft%20articles/7_4_1996.pdf (accessed on 11 December 2013).

[23] 'International Law Commission's Draft Code', available at http:// untreaty.un.org/ilc/texts/instruments/english/draft%20articles/7_4_1996. pdf (accessed on 11 December 2013).

(a) murder;

(b) extermination;

(c) torture;

(d) enslavement;

(e) persecution on political, racial, religious or ethnic grounds;

(f) institutionalized discrimination on racial, ethnic or religious grounds involving the violation of fundamental human rights and freedoms and resulting in seriously disadvantaging a part of the population;

(g) arbitrary deportation or forcible transfer of population;

(h) arbitrary imprisonment;

(i) forced disappearance of persons;

(j) rape, enforced prostitution and other forms of sexual abuse;

(k) other inhumane acts which severely damage physical or mental integrity, health or human dignity, such as mutilation and severe bodily harm.'[24]

Aforementioned are some of the important statutes and legislations which have been entered into force by the United Nations in association with particular countries as a consequence of severe crimes committed, such as genocide and war crimes, which were considered to be a serious violation of the international humanitarian law and thus were brought under the ambit of crimes against humanity. These crimes or attacks were committed against a civilian population and were widespread and systematic in nature and included murder, enslavement, extermination, persecution on political, racial, religious or ethnic grounds, enforced prostitution, and other inhumane acts.

Among these statutes and legislations, the most important one is Article 7 of the Rome Statute, besides the ICTY and ICTR. Article 7 defines the crimes against humanity as attack directed against a civilian population.[25] The 'attack' is described as a conduct

---

[24] 'International Law Commission's Draft Code', available at http://untreaty.un.org/ilc/texts/instruments/english/draft%20articles/7_4_1996.pdf (accessed on 11 December 2013).

[25] ICC, 'Rome Statute', Article 9.

which involves the violent acts committed and such conducts must include 'multiple commissions'. The 'widespread' nature of such attacks further describes the number of persons victimized or the extension of the crime in a geographic area and 'systematic' defines the organized nature of the crimes committed against a civilian population.

Thus, the crimes against humanity, as defined in all these aforementioned important and significant statutes which are operating globally, have described and included such acts of violence committed against a human population in a systematic and widespread manner which comprised severe violation of human rights and the international humanitarian law.

International Problems in Dealing with Human Trafficking

Human trafficking has posed a big threat to humanity and human dignity. It has been the reason behind a lot of problems across the borders. It has given rise to smuggling of human beings and increased the rate of trafficking through fraud, deception, force, coercion, and abuse of power. This increased rate of trafficking takes place through fake employment offers, matchmaking services, and in other ways, which has helped the traders of trafficking to flourish and make profits in this illegal business. The victims of trafficking have been found to be mostly those who are financially weak and are deprived of social status and education; importantly, most of these vulnerable victims have been found to be women and children in a majority of the cases.

The countries all over the world are facing this problem of trafficking and smuggling of human beings which has given rise to a higher and increased rate of exploitation of human beings, mostly of women and children. The exploitations are mostly in the form of forced labour, slavery and servitude, sexual abuses, forced prostitution, and sometimes extermination.

Various international laws have been enforced to combat trafficking of human beings for forced labour and sexual exploitation, but these laws have not yet been much useful to the extent to which they were considered or expected to be.[26] In fact, it has been observed that the crime is spreading its network all over the world at an alarming rate, as is evident from various reports and numbers made available by the United Nations through its network and establishments such as the UNODC, UN.GIFT, ILO, IOM, and others.

The rapidly increasing human trafficking has caused various problems globally and has posed a serious threat to the legal framework of nations, human dignity, and humanity, overall. Human trafficking is a multidimensional problem and has close connections to other organized crimes of drug trafficking and arms trafficking.

One of the issues faced due to human trafficking is the health problem and the spread of various communicable and dangerous diseases such as HIV/AIDS, tuberculosis, and hepatitis. Trafficking of human beings poses a serious threat to the health of the victims. The victims of trafficking are often found to be going through severe mental, emotional, physical, and psychological trauma due to brutal and violent forms of exploitation experienced by them. Trafficking has forced many victims to become drug addicts and they have also developed serious psychological and mental problems.[27] Serious health problems including physical, emotional, and psychological problems are on the rise among the victims due to the severity of exploitation experienced by them at the hands of the traffickers as well as the customers. They are often found to be left in unhygienic conditions, deprived of their basic needs and fundamental rights. They are totally left at the mercy of the traffickers who just use them as a reusable commodity and not as human beings. These victims also face abuse, forced abortion, and other related complications and diseases. There are cases in which women victims of trafficking are forced into brothels for prostitution

---

[26] Office for Victims of Crime Training and Technical Assistance Centre, 'Human Trafficking', available at http://www.ncdsv.org/images/OVCTTAC_HumanTraffickingResourcePaper_2012.pdf (accessed on 21 September 2014).

[27] L.J. Lauderer. 'End Human Trafficking: A Contemporary Slavery', Election Symposium, USA, 2012, available at http://www.thepublicdiscourse.com/2011/09/3706/ (accessed on 15 December 2013).

soon after their forceful abortions. Trafficking is thus a crime threatening the world, and a threat of the spread of dangerous and communicable diseases.[28]

Further, it poses a threat to national security and a country's citizens and their fundamental rights and freedom. Owing to its transnational nature, it disapproves and violates the legal framework of nations. Since it works across the borders, it encourages and also assists terrorists to carry on their activities to penetrate a country's security system and attack.

Almost all the nations have enforced various laws against human trafficking but very often these laws prove to be inadequate in preventing the crime and ensuring prosecution of the traffickers. Further, most of the time, the laws are also insufficient to provide protection to the victims of trafficking in the country of their origin as well as in the country of their destination. The law-enforcement officers and other officers of the judiciary, immigration officers, and even the prosecutors face difficulties due to the dearth of appropriate and effective laws. Mostly, a victim-centred approach of the laws is required, which would provide with shelters and assist them to come forward and become mainstream citizens.

Human trafficking, just like drug trafficking business, involves a triangle of activities including supply, demand, and distribution. But it differs from drug trafficking in that there is less focus on the demand side—victims are just forced into the trafficking business whether or not they have a demand. The traffickers only focus on the supply and distribution of the trafficked persons.[29]

Human trafficking is a more organized form of business, better than any administration system of any country. The criminals of the organized groups of human trafficking carry out their activities across the borders and also within the borders of the countries in such a manner

---

[28]   L.J. Lauderer. 'End Human Trafficking'.

[29]   A.M. Banks, *Sexual Violence and International Criminal Law: An Analysis of the Ad Hoc Tribunal's Jurisprudence & The International Criminal Court's Elements of Crimes* (The Hague, Netherlands: Women's Initiatives for Gender Justice, September 2005).

that it becomes very difficult to trace and catch hold of them. Their way of working has become more sophisticated, with these organizations hiring professionals and taking their organizational structure at par with any business enterprise. It is a decentralized one and thus it has become more difficult to get into the roots of trafficking. These crime groups are more organized, and they work actively irrespective of the linguistic, cultural, and ethnic differences that come up owing to their respective national and geographic boundaries. They are up-to-date with the new and advanced technologies for carrying out sex trade—for example, they transmit sexually exploitive images, create sex-oriented chat rooms and global sex clubs, and have apt techniques for online stalking. They use encryption and encoding techniques to hide their identity and location base. These organizations have formed a network of professionals who work towards new strategies in facilitating the human trafficking business effectively and have recruited persons to identify and traffic the most vulnerable victims, especially women and children. They work through agencies such as recruitment agencies, brothels, massage parlours, strip clubs, beauty salons, and spas.[30]

Human trafficking is a global problem of the twenty-first century. It has created problems for the legal machinery and health sector because of the heinous and brutal nature of crime and violation of human rights. It is a multi-billion dollar trade which comprises a victim base of shocking millions who have been trapped as slaves, prostitutes, and bonded labourers.

Another big and serious problem faced globally is the lack of cooperation between the nations in dealing with human trafficking cases, their victims, and prosecuting the traffickers. The non-cooperation and low level of coordination between the officials of the nations affected by this transnational organized crime has aggravated the problem and helped the organized crime syndicates to carry out their cross-border trafficking business effectively and efficiently. The reasons behind such non-cooperation is the distrust on each other in dealing with

[30] Banks, *Sexual Violence and International Criminal Law.*

trafficking victims, distrust with their protection, lack of knowledge and awareness about the laws and its methods and provisions, and a fear of losing the documents or evidence against traffickers.

The rapid growth of the trafficking business is also another international problem and it has been noticed that this business of human trafficking is often facilitated by the members of the family, friends, relatives of the victims, and corrupt government officials and agents. Sometimes, it is also due to the fact that the facilitators of trafficking receive huge monetary benefits from the traffickers. They are actively involved in this crime, in assisting the criminals, and in earning millions. The organized criminal groups are operational at different levels. Trafficking has sustained the organized crime groups and given rise to higher rates of corruption by government authorities. It has also encouraged social breakdown and has resulted in severe abuse of human rights.

The victims are being trafficked by way of abduction, recruitment, use and abuse of power in the country of origin, transfer across borders, and exploitation in the destination country. Trafficking also takes place within the borders of the country of origin. The governments of these countries have tried to put an end to this crime but have not yet been successful, despite the enforcement of domestic laws, international laws, and establishment of the ICC and the Rome Statute, especially Article 7 of the Rome Statute, which deals with crimes against humanity.

Among various problems of human trafficking, one of the major problems is the victim's protection after being rescued from the hands of the traffickers. The victims face threat to their existence and also a threat of being sold and resold. The problems faced by the victims are also concerned with their deportation to their country of origin and their protection and safety and acceptance in their own country and society. Such problems arise due to the ineffective and insufficient immigration policies and lack of knowledge and awareness of the policies among the immigration officials of the government of that country. The victims of human trafficking are often misunderstood as illegal migrants and are deported to the country of origin without even investigating the case of that victim and the situation and reason behind the non-availability of identification documents. There are also some countries that have enforced appropriate and effective immigration policy to identify victims of trafficking and also to prevent the crime, but the problem still exists due to the lack of awareness and lack of knowledge about the policies among the immigration officers.[31]

The prosecution of the victims and traffickers have been a major problem at the international level; but before that, another major problem is to catch hold of the criminals. Often, it is seen that traffickers put forward consent of the victims and the court has to go for validation of the consent and evidences of consent. Whenever the consent is broken at any given stage through coercion, deception, force, or abuse of authority and exploitation, it is considered to be trafficking and the consent is nullified. Finding out the actual evidences and validity of the consent of the victim in this crime of forced labour, sexual exploitation, and prostitution in any country or a country of destination by the court is a time-consuming activity and the victim has to face all the difficulties and threats from the organized criminal groups.[32]

The nature of this crime is transnational and its causes are very complex. The victims are mostly unaware or are aware only to a certain extent. The problem also lies in factors such as poor living conditions, poor socio-economic conditions, poor social status, unemployment problem, and poor security measures at the international borders, among others. Even unseen natural disasters, wars, and political instability lead to the propagation of this organized crime across the borders and severe violation of human rights.

Often, women, children, and even men fall victims to such exploitation in terms of forced labour, forced prostitution, slavery, and servitude. Men and children are mostly smuggled and trafficked as migrants to countries across the world for forced labour, slavery, and domestic servitude whereas women are mostly trafficked for sexual slavery and forced prostitution. These victims are generally kept in very dreadful

---

[31] 'Combat Trafficking', available at http://www.humantrafficking.org/combat_trafficking/protection (accessed on 19 November 2013).

[32] UN.GIFT, *Human Trafficking: An Overview* (New York: United Nations, 2008).

conditions; it has also been found that major costs are borne by the victims in terms of their health and physical as well as psychological conditions in the destination country, so as to be alive. They owe debt to the traffickers since they do not have any funds or money of their own and they depend on the traffickers for their expenses. They often do not have any access to health and medical facilities.

Trafficking also poses a serious threat to the integrity and security of a nation as well as to the freedom and human rights of the victims or the people who are vulnerable to the organized crime syndicate. Trafficking even poses a serious concern in the demographic pattern of a country or a region of destination as well as the country of origin. It affects the demographic statistics of the country, increases the number of illegal migrant workers, and causes an imbalance in the human capital of that country or region. It also gives rise to increased corruption and propagation of this crime.[33]

Arms, Drugs, and Human Trafficking—A Paradigm

It is a grave reality that this fast-growing crime includes smuggling of arms, trafficking of drugs, and trafficking of human beings. Human trafficking is done for the sole purpose of forced labour, slavery, servitude, and forced prostitution. These are the three most dreadful organized crimes which are spread across the world—across and also within the borders. These three dimensions of the organized crime are at present a major international issue, the most important among these being the crime of human trafficking.

Transnational organized crime is present in various forms such as trafficking of drugs, firearms, and human beings. Organized crime syndicates take advantage of human mobility to smuggle humans as migrant workers and thus weaken the financial systems of the countries by way of money laundering. An enormous amount of money is involved in these organized crimes, which affects the economic

---

[33] G. Connor, *Human Trafficking—A Global Issue*, January 2004, available at http://gbgm-umc.org/umcor/ngo/issues/trafficking.cfm (accessed on 8 October 2013).

conditions of the countries involved and thereby encourages corruption. These organized crimes bring huge profits to the perpetrators and pose a threat to the lives and freedom of thousands and millions of people who fall prey to these criminal groups.[34] As UNODC states: 'Every year, countless individuals lose their lives at the hands of criminals involved in organized crime, succumbing to drug-related health problems or injuries inflicted by firearms, or losing their lives as a result of the unscrupulous methods and motives of human traffickers and smugglers of migrants.'

Many conventions and protocols have been framed by the UNODC under international law to prohibit and prosecute human trafficking, such as UNTOC, Supplementary Convention on the Abolition of Slavery, the Slave Trade, and Institutions and Practices Similar to Slavery, United Nations Protocol to Prevent, Suppress, and Punish Trafficking in Persons (also called the Trafficking in Persons Protocol or the Palermo protocol), especially Women and Children and the United Nations Protocol against the Smuggling of Migrants by Land, Sea and Air. But the crime thrives despite such measures, legal frameworks, and strict law enforcements, along with the arms and ammunitions trade and trafficking of drugs being efficiently carried out across the national and international borders.

As described by the UNODC, the organized crime group has spread its network globally and reached macro-economic proportions. The illicit goods which are bought from one state/country are trafficked across the borders of another country and are marketed in the third country or state. This is how the trafficking business thrives across the borders and continues its activities. Transnational organized crime pervades the 'government agencies and institutions, fuelling corruption, infiltrating business and politics, and hindering economic and social development'.[35] These three organized crimes—arms, drugs, and human trafficking—destabilize the governance and democracy of

---

[34] UNODC, 'Organized Crime' available at http://www.unodc.org/unodc/en/organized-crime/index.html (accessed on 12 October 2013).
[35] UNODC, 'Organized Crime'.

a country and make the criminals powerful and help them to thrive in this business, thereby exploiting human lives.

These criminals build links across the borders, overcoming the cultural and language barriers with the help of local persons and partners in the crime, thus stretching their networks. The relationship between criminal networks of the organized crime is flexible and sophisticated, and becomes stronger with each and every big achievement in their world of crime. They recruit people in the countries of origin, who act as professional executives. Their main activity is to find the weak spots in a country and identify vulnerable persons who could be prospects for human trafficking and victimization. Their nature of the crime and the way in which it is operated is already hidden and now it has become so sophisticated with the advancement of technology that it is very difficult to know the whereabouts of the criminals of such organized crime groups. The drug mafia and firearms mafia work in collaboration and also facilitate the trafficking of human beings. These three organized crime groups are very much interconnected and benefit from each other in committing the grave offences and making huge profits.[36]

Mapping the extent and the serious impact of the illicit trafficking of drugs and arms across the globe, which in turn promotes human trafficking and migrant smuggling, the United Nations Convention against Illicit Traffic in Narcotic Drugs and Psychotropic Substances was enforced in 1988. The parties to the convention realized the need to bring about a strong and effective legal measure internationally, with the cooperation of all states across the globe, to combat illicit trafficking. The convention was adopted by the United Nations Conference for the adoption of a Convention against Illicit Trafficking in

---

[36] General Assembly of the United Nations, 'Thematic Debate of the 66th Session of the United Nations General Assembly on Drugs and Crime as a Threat to Development On the Occasion of the UN International Day against Drug Abuse and Illicit Trafficking', 26 June 2012, New York, available at http://www.un.org/en/ga/president/66/Issues/drugs/drugs-crime.shtml (accessed on 20 December 2013).

Narcotic Drugs and Psychotropic Substances, held at Vienna between 25 November and 20 December 1988.[37]

The leaders of the world realized and reaffirmed the danger and threat posed to the civilians by drug trafficking and its links to, inter alia, transnational crime, money laundering, and arms trade, and also encouraged governments to deal with the threat effectively and to cooperate to prevent the channeling of funds to and between those engaged in such activities.[38] In Section IV of its Resolution 50/148, the General Assembly further proposed an international conference to combat the illicit production, sale, demand, trafficking, and distribution of narcotic drugs and psychotropic substances and related activities, and also laid stress on the fact that the Commission on Narcotic Drugs needs to consider that the focus of the proposed conference should actually aim at a balanced and integral approach on the assessment of existing strategies, consider new strategies, methods and practical measures, and take concrete actions so as to strengthen international cooperation for addressing the problem of illicit drugs trafficking and illicit arms trade related to drug trafficking.[39]

Drug trafficking is one of the largest organized crimes and this illicit trafficking of drugs has, in turn, facilitated terrorist groups to carry out their activities in cross-border terrorism in many nations. Thus, it has given a strong base for another organized crime, giving rise to the illicit trafficking of arms across the borders.[40] Further, trafficking of drugs has given a strong financial support to arms trafficking. Together, they have been closely linked and related to the most dreadful transnational organized crime—human trafficking. Thus, a very close and viable link exists among all the three organized crimes, which has become

---

[37] United Nations, 'United Nations Convention against Illicit Traffic in Narcotic Drugs and Psychotropic Substances', Vienna, 20 December 1988.

[38] General Assembly resolution 50/148 of 21 December 1995.

[39] General Assembly resolution 50/148 of 21 December 1995.

[40] Antonio García Revilla, 'Interrelationship between Small Arms Trafficking, Drug Trafficking and Terrorism', Curbing Illicit Trafficking in Small Arms and Sensitive Technologies, available from http://unidir.org/pdf/articles/pdf-art922.pdf (accessed on 15 December 2013).

a bane to the world and humanity. These crimes have exploited the economic, social, cultural, and demographic DNA of many countries. Arms trafficking and human trafficking are also closely related since the groups work together for carrying out their illicit trade. The use of human beings in arms trafficking also helps in human trafficking for the purpose of forced labour and other forms of exploitation such as sexual slavery and forced prostitution.

Drug trafficking thus affects the human capital and the society. It reduces the quality of life of the people and compels skilled labour to leave the country, leading to their exploitation, humiliation, and victimization. It hinders the development of the society through its nature of crime and thus limits people's access to education and employment. Hence, at the end, it changes the demography of a country or a region drastically.[41]

These three organized crimes further affect the economy by depicting a poor picture of the country as a socially, democratically, and economically unstable one. As a result of this, potential business opportunities and investors do not enter that country to establish their businesses. These organized crimes further weaken the development processes and build distrust among its citizens, the government, the legal framework, and the judiciary. Transnational organized crimes target these countries in particular as they seem vulnerable to trafficking. These countries are mostly affected by war, internal conflicts, weak democracy, and inefficient legal framework, and are thus corrupted incredibly to the core. Due to this reason, organized crime syndicates flourish in these regions.[42]

The economic development of the countries across the globe is threatened by these transnational organized crimes of drugs, arms, and human trafficking. The countries need to come together with various effective and quality approaches and responses to counter these illicit crimes. The approaches should include the economic and social development strategies.[43] The nations need to take up efforts to address the

---

41 ICC, 'Rome Statute', Article 7(1)(g)–6.
42 ICC, 'Rome Statute', Article 7(1)(g)–6.
43 ICC, 'Rome Statute', Article 7(1)(g)–6.

issues which are a result of the organized crimes and illicit trafficking business, such as increased rate of corruption and money laundering, among others. The development strategies to counter these organized crimes should comprise awareness programmes, employment opportunities, access to educational facilities, and various other measures, to help the nations to develop and elevate the status of the people who are most vulnerable to the crimes.

Trafficking as Severe Deprivation of Physical Liberty

Trafficking of human beings entails men, women, and children being forced into crimes such as exploitative labour, slavery, and prostitution or sex trade. This deprives them of physical liberty since the victims are not allowed to have any kind of access to the outside world or medical and health facilities, and are solely at the mercy of the crime syndicates.

This grave reality has been felt, identified, and understood by law enforcers such as the United Nations, whereby they have adopted and enforced Trafficking in Persons Protocol and further enforced the Rome Statute of the ICC, besides the other statutes, to address the issues and cases of crimes against humanity.

Article 7(1)(e) of the Rome Statute is described in the Elements of Crime of the ICC as the crime against humanity of imprisonment or severe deprivation of physical liberty. According to the elements stated in this article, if one or more persons trafficked are imprisoned and are severely deprived of their physical liberty, the act is said to be a crime against humanity. This is followed by finding out about the gravity of the conduct, violating fundamental rules of international law, and conducting the crime as a part of a widespread or systematic attack directed against a civilian population about which the traffickers are aware.

As millions of men, women, and children fall prey to this organized crime, women, especially, are often subjected to inhuman and unhygienic living conditions, while being driven forcefully into slavery, servitude, and sexual exploitation, and ultimately into forced prostitution. Men and children are mostly driven into forced labour, servitude, domestic slavery, and even begging; they are beaten up like animals, forcefully given drugs, and are often left at the mercy of the traffickers or their owners.[44] The victims' identification documents are taken away and they are threatened about the possible violence that would be inflicted on them and to members of their family, if they do not follow the orders. The victims also face the problem of communication since they are not aware of the language spoken in that country and they do not know anyone in that country. In addition to this, the victims are also afraid of going out or contacting any person for assistance due to their illegal status and lack of identification documents.

Trafficking is a very serious and heinous crime which is against humanity. It is a violation of human rights by putting control over the basic rights of the people to live, freedom of movement, and expression. Trafficking is now gaining control over the earning capacity of the people who fall victims to this organized crime, mostly who belong to the weaker section of the society. This grave offence has also been violating the integrity of the victims and degrading human dignity.

Trafficking as Torture

Human trafficking has always been associated with torture faced by victims—physically, mentally, and emotionally. Article 7(1)(f) of the Rome Statute defines this as a crime against humanity involving torture, under the Elements of Crime of the ICC. The elements further describe this crime as one in which the perpetrator inflicts severe physical or mental pain or suffering upon one or more persons, and such persons are in the custody or control of the traffickers or the owners of the trafficked persons. This crime also validates that such pain or suffering did not arise only from, and was not inherent in or incidental to, lawful sanctions and such a conduct was committed as part of a widespread or systematic attack directed against a civilian population, constituting a crime against humanity.

---

[44] Global Alliance Against Traffic in Women (GAATW), *Collateral Damage: The Impact of Anti-Trafficking Measures on Human Rights around the World* (Bangkok, 2007).

Article 7(2)(e) of the Rome Statute further defines 'torture' as 'the intentional infliction of severe pain or suffering, whether physical or mental upon a person in the custody or under the control of the accused; except that torture shall not include pain or suffering arising only from, inherent in or incidental to, lawful sanctions'.[45] It is said to be a crime against humanity when the torturer is doing the act which is a widespread or systematic attack against a civilian population. This meaning of 'torture' is broader in its definition when considered at the international level.

Torture generally includes severe pain and suffering done for a specific purpose such as to find out 'information or a confession, or at punishing, intimidating or coercing the victim or a third person, or at discriminating, on any ground, against the victim or a third person'. The ICC does not include this element but there is a specific mention in the Elements of Crimes of the ICC for torture as a crime against humanity; it states: 'It is understood that no specific purpose need be proved for this crime.'[46]

The elements for torture as a crime against humanity defined before the ad hoc tribunals are mentioned as follows:

1. The infliction, by act or omission, of severe pain or suffering, whether physical or mental.
2. The act or omission must be intentional.
3. The act or omission must aim at obtaining information or a confession, or at punishing, intimidating or coercing the victim or a third person, or at discriminating, on any ground, against the victim or a third person.

The acts of torture include all kinds of serious abuses which are of sexual nature and have been inflicted on the integrity of a person, both physically and morally, by means of coercion, threat of force, or intimidation in a manner which is degrading and humiliating to the dignity of the person. The victims are subjected to severe physical torture for

---

[45] ICC, 'Rome Statute', Article 7(2)(e).
[46] ICC, 'Rome Statute', Article 7(1)(f).

disobeying orders and are forced to do everything for which they have been trafficked. The trafficked persons are treated horribly, worse than even animals, and are often beaten up brutally. The victims, especially the women and children, are put into sexual slavery and servitude and they are generally a debt bondage. If they resist from doing any act which they have been asked to do, the traffickers scare them, blackmail them, by informing them about their status in the country of destination where they are illegal immigrants and are likely to face problems as per the laws of that country. The traffickers also ask the victims to repay all the expenses incurred in bringing them to the country of destination, and only after which they might be released. The victims are also often subjected to starvation, imprisonment, physical abuse (beatings and rape), and verbal abuse, which causes physical as well as mental agony. Many of them eventually become affected mentally and psychologically and later on attempt or commit suicide to escape the regular abuse and torture.

Trafficking as Rape

Trafficking as rape is described as a crime against humanity in Article 7(1)(g) of the Rome Statute, Article 5(g) of ICTY Statute, and Article 3(g) of ICTR Statute. It is described in the Elements of Crime as a crime against humanity of rape of the ICC as: 'The perpetrator invaded the body of a person by conduct resulting in penetration, however slight, of any part of the body of the victim or of the perpetrator with a sexual organ, or of the anal or genital opening of the victim with any object or any other part of the body. The invasion was committed by force, or by threat of force or coercion, such as that caused by fear of violence, duress, detention, psychological oppression or abuse of power, against such person or another person, or by taking advantage of a coercive environment, or the invasion was committed against a person incapable of giving genuine consent.' Further, this crime is validated as a crime against humanity of rape as per the Elements of Crime of the ICC when the conduct is committed as part of a widespread or systematic attack directed against a civilian population and the person responsible for conducting the crime is aware of this. Rape and other acts of sexual violence are considered as torture at the ad hoc tribunals. Rape constitutes torture when the elements of torture are met. [47]

Rape, as stated by the Kvočka Trial Chamber, is a 'violation of sexual autonomy' whereas the *Foca* defines rape as focused on sexual autonomy and various ways in which it can be violated.[48] The sexual activity to be defined as rape must fall within one of the two categories:

1. The sexual activity must be accompanied by force or threat of force to the victim or a third party.
2. The sexual activity must be accompanied by force or a variety of other specified circumstances which made the victim particularly vulnerable or negated her ability to make an informed refusal; or the sexual activity must occur without the consent of the victim.

The Convention against Torture and Other Cruel, Inhuman and Degrading Treatment or Punishment can be related to the crime as rape which comes under inhuman and degrading treatment. Just like torture, rape is used for purposes such as intimidation, humiliation, degradation, discrimination, punishment, control, or destruction of a person. It is a violation of personal dignity and can be considered as torture when inflicted by or at the instigation of or with the consent of a public official or other person in an official capacity.[49]

The trafficked persons, especially the women and children, are often forced into sexual slavery and sexual abuse. The victims are subjected to sexual activity constituting rape which occurs without the consent

---

[47]   ICC, 'Rome Statute', Article 7(1)(g)–1.

[48]   United Nations, 'International Tribunal for the Prosecution of Persons Responsible for Serious Violations of International Humanitarian Law Committed in the Territory of the Former Yugoslavia since 1991', available at http://www.icty.org/x/cases/kvocka/acjug/en/kvo-aj050228e.pdf (accessed on 30 May 2016).

[49]   Preparatory Commission for the International Criminal Court, 'Commentary submitted by Switzerland on Article 7 of the Statute of the International Criminal Court', available at http://www.iccnow.org/document s/3rdSesProposalArticle7.pdf (accessed on 30 May 2016)

of the victim, by force, threat of force, or coercion, by taking advantage of a coercive environment, or against a person incapable of giving genuine consent.[50] The traffickers often work with the help of persons employed for the purpose of identifying prospective victims. They kidnap the young girls, keep them in captivity, and continuously rape them. Later on, these girls are sent to various places across the borders and supplied to brothels and strip clubs.

Thus, rape is a heinous and severe crime which constitutes crimes against humanity. Trafficking as rape is committed against a civilian population, such as women and girls of a particular region and age, spread across nations, which justifies the crime against humanity as 'widespread and systematic' attack 'directed against a civilian population'. The perpetrator is aware of the nature of the act and that it is aimed against a civilian population. Rape and other acts of sexual violence have also been used to establish the intent of the perpetrator to destroy, in whole or in part, a national, ethnic, racial, or religious group of a particular region or country. It is evident in the Kayishema Trial Judgment[51] and Rwanda sexual violence, in which the women of the Tutsi population of Rwanda were targeted and raped; there are also other acts of sexual violence contributing to the destruction of the Tutsi population.

Trafficking as Enslavement and Sexual Slavery

Article 7(1)(c) of the Rome Statute and Elements of Crimes of the ICC constitute enslavement as a crime against humanity. According to the statute, enslavement is defined as an act when

> the perpetrator exercised any or all of the powers attaching to the right of ownership over one or more persons, such as by purchasing, selling, lending or bartering such a person or persons, or by imposing on them a similar deprivation of liberty. The conduct was committed as part of a widespread or systematic attack directed against a civilian population and the perpetrator knew that the conduct was part of or intended the

[50] Banks, *Sexual Violence and International Criminal Law.*
[51] *Prosecutor v. Kayishema & Ruzindana,* Case No. ICTR-95-1-T.

conduct to be part of a widespread or systematic attack directed against a civilian population.[52]

It is further implicit that such deprivation of liberty, in certain circumstances, may comprise forced labour, or otherwise degrading the status of a person to the extent of the person being described as a slave. This is broadly defined in the Supplementary Convention on the Abolition of Slavery, the Slave Trade, and Institutions and Practices, and such conduct includes trafficking in persons, especially women and children, as described in this Element of Crime.

Furthermore, enslavement also includes sexual slavery as crimes against humanity as defined in Article 7(1)(g)-2 of the Rome Statute. This article defines sexual slavery similar to that of Article 7(1)(c) of the Rome Statute, except that 'the perpetrator caused such person or persons to engage in one or more acts of a sexual nature'.

Although enslavement and sexual slavery are separate, both constitute crimes against humanity. Article 5(c) of the ICTY Statute and Article 3(c) of the ICTR Statute also define enslavement of trafficked victims as part of crimes against humanity. Enslavement includes forced labour, which could also constitute a war crime. According to ICTY, forced labour amounts to enslavement as a crime against humanity and includes the crimes of cruel and inhuman treatment, persecution, and other inhuman acts. Under the international law, forced labour is one of the contemporary forms of slavery. Accordingly, the following factors determine an act as slavery:[53]

1. The elements of control and ownership are not present.
2. There is an absence of the restriction or control of an individual's autonomy, freedom of choice, or freedom of movement; and often, in the process, some gain accrues to the perpetrator.
3. The consent or free will of the victim is absent. It is often rendered impossible or irrelevant by, for example, the threat or use of force

---

[52] ICC, 'Rome Statute', Article 7(1)(c).

[53] William Schabas, *The International Criminal Court: A Commentary on the Rome Statute* (New York: Oxford University Press, 2010), 163.

or other forms of coercion, the fear of violence, deception or false promises or the abuse of power.

4. Another major factor is the victim's position of vulnerability, detention or captivity, psychological oppression, or socio-economic conditions.

5. Exploitation is a factor.

6. The exaction of forced or compulsory labour or service, often without remuneration and often, though not necessarily, involving physical hardship, sex, prostitution and human trafficking.

It has also been noticed that slavery exists without any kind of torture or force. There are instances where many slaves are well fed, nourished, provided all forms of facilities, such as housing and clothing, but they are considered slaves since they are deprived of their physical liberty and freedom and are kept bound without any legal authority or processes. Here, it will be helpful to note how the Elements of Crimes of the Rome Statute further describes the term 'forcibly': '[It] is not restricted to physical force, but may include threat of force or coercion, such as that caused by fear of violence, duress, detention, psychological oppression or abuse of power against such person or persons or another person, or by taking advantage of a coercive environment.'[54]

The ICC Elements of Crimes defines sexual slavery as existing when a perpetrator exercises 'any or all of the powers attaching to the right of ownership over one or more persons, such as by purchasing, selling, lending or bartering such a person or persons, or by imposing on them a similar deprivation of liberty' and causes such a person 'to engage in one or more acts of a sexual nature'. Sexual slavery constitutes intentional exercise of any or all of the powers attached to the right of ownership over a person, and where the perpetrator has subjected a victim to sexual intercourse on one or more occasions.[55]

Such crimes occur in every state with the increased rate of trafficking of persons across the borders, at the country of origin, country of

---

[54] ICC, 'Rome Statute', Article 9.
[55] ICC, 'Rome Statute', Article 7(1)(g)–2.

transit, and also at the country of destination. People are trafficked from one country to another for serving as migrant labourers and slaves and eventually indulged into sexual slavery. These trafficked persons are brought mostly from South Asian countries and are trafficked to the Middle East, European countries, and the USA. The trafficked people, after being enslaved, are treated cruelly, brutally beaten up using the powers attached to the right of ownership, forcefully engaged in acts of sexual nature several times, and thus deprived of their liberty.

As per ICTY and ICTR, sexual slavery is also a form of enslavement and is not a separate offence. The second element as described in the Elements of Crime of ICC and Article 7(1)(c) defines the sexual component of the crime.

Sexual slavery is a part of human trafficking. Sexual slavery is often a result of human trafficking which normally occurs due to forced marriages, luring employment offers. The persons behind drafting the Rome Statute identified that there could be one or more perpetrators who are actively involved in sexual slavery and enslavement, who have a common goal or aim, which is conducting the organized crime of human trafficking for enslavement and sexual slavery. The perpetrators and traffickers are earning profit from this trade through such enslavement and sexual slavery.

Trafficking as Enforced Prostitution

Trafficking as Enforced Prostitution is another act comprising the Crimes against humanity of Article 7(1)(g)-3 of the Rome Statute. The Elements of Crime of the ICC and Article 7(1)(g)-3 of the Rome Statute describes trafficking as enforced prostitution and states:

1. The perpetrator caused one or more persons to engage in one or more acts of a sexual nature by force, or by threat of force or coercion, such as that caused by fear of violence, duress, detention, psychological oppression or abuse of power, against such person or persons or another person, or by taking advantage of a coercive environment or such person's or persons' incapacity to give genuine consent.

2. The perpetrator or another person obtained or expected to obtain pecuniary or other advantage in exchange for or in connection with the acts of a sexual nature
3. The conduct was committed as part of a widespread or systematic attack directed against a civilian population
4. The perpetrator knew that the conduct was part of or intended the conduct to be part of a widespread or systematic attack directed against a civilian population.[56]

The women who are trafficked in various countries across the globe are forced into prostitution and enslaved by the use of force, threat, and coercion. Enforced prostitution was made a part of the crimes in the Rome Statute as a separate crime. It was also considered as an attack or assault on the honour of a woman and an outrage on the personal dignity of a woman as per the Geneva Conventions.

Young girls and women are forced into enslaved prostitution, often coerced to serve even more than fifteen clients per day. Considering the poor economic conditions in which these women live, this crime turns into a systematic and widespread attack. Since it is often directed towards a specific group, community, religion, or ethnic tribe, enforced prostitution further justifies the statement of attack directed against a civilian population. It also justifies the statement that the perpetrator is aware of the act of the organized crime supporting the crime against humanity.

Trafficking as Other Forms of Sexual violence

Trafficking as other forms of sexual violence has been defined and described in Article 7(1)(g)-6 of the Rome Statute—Elements of Crimes of the ICC—and is mentioned under the crime against humanity:

1. The perpetrator committed an act of a sexual nature against one or more persons or caused such person or persons to engage in an act

---

[56] ICC, 'Rome Statute', Article 7(1)(g)-3.

of a sexual nature by force, or by threat of force or coercion, such as that caused by fear of violence, duress, detention, psychological oppression or abuse of power, against such person or persons or another person, or by taking advantage of a coercive environment or such person's or persons' incapacity to give genuine consent.

2. Such conduct was of a gravity comparable to the other offences in Article 7, paragraph 1 (g), of the Statute.

3. The perpetrator was aware of the factual circumstances that established the gravity of the conduct.[57]

Further, the ICTY trial chamber has recognized that 'sexual assault' is included in various provisions which have been enforced to protect human dignity, physical liberty, and integrity. It also comprises an 'outrage upon personal dignity'.[58] These aforementioned types of violence are a violation of the basic human rights. Such violations are included as crimes against humanity mentioned in the Article 5 of ICTY.

The ICTY trial chamber enumerated the elements of sexual assault as a form of persecution and considered it as a crime against humanity.[59] These elements are as follows:

- The physical perpetrator commits an act of a sexual nature on another, including requiring that person to perform such an act.
- That act infringes the victims' physical integrity or amounts to an outrage to the victim's personal dignity.
- The victim does not consent to the act.
- The physical perpetrator intentionally commits the act.
- The physical perpetrator is aware that the act occurred without the consent of the victim.

---

[57]   ICC, 'Rome Statute', Article 7(1)(g)–6.

[58]   United Nations, 'International Tribunal for the Prosecution of Persons'.

[59]   ICTY, 'Landmark Cases', available at http://www.icty.org/en/in-focus/crimes-sexual-violence/landmark-cases (accessed on 4 July 2016); ICTY, 'Kunarac et al. (IT-96-23 & 23/1)', Judgement of Trial Chamber II, available at http://www.icty.org/en/press/judgement-trial-chamber-ii-kunarac-kovac-and-vukovic-case (accessed on 30 May 2016).

Besides rape, sexual slavery, and enforced prostitution, Article 7 of the Elements of Crimes of the ICC also constitutes other forms of sexual violence such as forced pregnancy, enforced sterilization, and sexual violence.

Article 7(1)(g)-4 states the crimes against humanity of forced pregnancy as follows:[60]

- The perpetrator confined one or more women forcibly made pregnant, with the intent of affecting the ethnic composition of any population or carrying out other grave violations of international law.
- The conduct was committed as part of a widespread or systematic attack directed against a civilian population.
- The perpetrator knew that the conduct was part of or intended the conduct to be part of a widespread or systematic attack directed against a civilian population.

Article 7(1)(g)-5 describes the crime against humanity of enforced sterilization, which is stated as:[61]

- The perpetrator deprived one or more persons of biological reproductive capacity.
- The conduct was neither justified by the medical or hospital treatment of the person or persons concerned nor carried out with their genuine consent.
- The conduct was committed as part of a widespread or systematic attack directed against a civilian population.
- The perpetrator knew that the conduct was part of or intended the conduct to be part of a widespread or systematic attack directed against a civilian population.

Article 7(1)(g)-6 states the crimes against humanity of sexual violence which is described as:[62]

---

[60] ICC, 'Rome Statute', Article 7(1)(g)-4.
[61] ICC, 'Rome Statute', Article 7(1)(g)-5.
[62] ICC, 'Rome Statute', Article 7(1)(g)-6.

- The perpetrator committed an act of a sexual nature against one or more persons or caused such person or persons to engage in an act of a sexual nature by force, or by threat of force or coercion, such as that caused by fear of violence, duress, detention, psychological oppression or abuse of power, against such person or persons or another person, or by taking advantage of a coercive environment or such person's or persons' incapacity to give genuine consent.
- Such conduct was of a gravity comparable to the other offences in Article 7, paragraph 1 (g), of the Statute.
- The perpetrator was aware of the factual circumstances that established the gravity of the conduct.

Apart from the heinous sexual assault on women and girls through forced prostitution and rape, there are other forms of sexual violence, such as any kind of sexual act committed against the victims through force or coercion or threat which caused fear, detention, and psychological repression with the abuse of power in a coercive environment and without the consent of the victims. Such acts were conducted against a civilian population with an awareness of the perpetrator about the nature and magnitude of the conduct. This justifies it as a crime against humanity.

Victims of trafficking including labourers also face such sexual violence and exploitation besides women and children, especially girls. Many women of some ethnic group or tribe are forcefully made pregnant so as to exploit the ethnicity of that tribe or the group. This is a severe conduct of crime against humanity and is directed against an ethnic group and is systematic and widespread in nature.

Trafficking as Persecution

Article 7(1)(h) of the Rome Statute under the crimes against humanity of the Elements of Crimes of the ICC includes persecution as a crime against humanity; even trafficking of humans for persecution is a crime against humanity. Following are the elements according to the statute:

1. The perpetrator severely deprived, contrary to international law, one or more persons of fundamental rights.

2. The perpetrator targeted such person or persons by reason of the identity of a group or collectivity or targeted the group or collectivity as such.
3. Such targeting was based on political, racial, national, ethnic, cultural, religious, gender as defined in Article 7, paragraph 3, of the Statute, or other grounds that are universally recognized as impermissible under international law.
4. The conduct was committed in connection with any act referred to in Article 7, paragraph 1, of the Statute or any crime within the jurisdiction of the Court.
5. The conduct was committed as part of a widespread or systematic attack directed against a civilian population.
6. The perpetrator knew that the conduct was part of or intended the conduct to be part of a widespread or systematic attack directed against a civilian population.[63]

Persecution is also a crime against humanity within the jurisdiction of the ICTY and ICTR based on Article 5(h) of the ICTY Statute and Article 3(h) of the ICTR Statute.

The elements of the crime of persecution as a crime against humanity can be enumerated in short as:

- the intentional and severe deprivation of fundamental rights
- contrary to international law
- by reason of the identity of a group or collectivity
- against any identifiable group or collectivity on political, racial, national, ethnic, cultural, religious, or sexual gender or other grounds that are universally recognized as impermissible under international law

Persecution in Article 7(2)(g) of the Rome Statute Elements of Crime as Crimes against humanity is defined with an emphasis on 'the intentional and severe deprivation of fundamental rights contrary to international law by reason of the identity of the group or collectivity'.

---

[63] ICC, 'Rome Statute', Article 7(1)(h).

This means that the crime of persecution is very much intentional, which constitutes severe violation of human rights, which is clear by the fact that the victims of trafficking are deprived of their basic fundamental rights, they are exploited and abused, their movement is restricted, and they are left at the mercy of the perpetrator. The persecution lays more stress on the intent of the conduct and the nature of the discrimination which causes the individuals to be deprived of their fundamental rights. These are acts of crimes against humanity constituting violation of human rights, which is conducted with an intent against a particular group or persons, thus comprising the systematic and widespread nature of the crime against a civilian population.

The Mens Rea Element

The Rome Statute of the ICC has two aspects—*actus reus* and *mens rea*. Actus reus defines the material or the physical element and mens rea refers to the mental element for the crimes being committed, mentioned and included in the Elements of Crime. It means the intent or the knowledge of the perpetrator in committing the crime against a population.[64]

The condition for the offenders or persons accused of criminal offences must fulfil some criteria or conditions of mens rea as described in various statutes.[65] These conditions are as follows:

- Mens rea reflects the state of mind of the person who is accused of an offence. The person accused with a mind which is guilty of the offence or the crime committed is liable to be prosecuted and punished. The criminal liability of the accused must be strict.
- The essential or required mental element in prosecuting human trafficking cases is that the person should have committed the act with the intention of 'exploitation' of the victim

[64] UNODC and UN.GIFT, 'Definitions of Trafficking in Persons and Smuggling of Migrants', *Anti-Human Trafficking Manual for Criminal Justice Practitioners, Module 1*, New York, 2009.

[65] UNODC and UN.GIFT, 'Definitions of Trafficking in Persons and Smuggling of Migrants'.

The definition of exploitation in the trafficking protocol is a non-exhaustive one which states:'Exploitation shall include, at a minimum, the exploitation of the prostitution of others or other forms of sexual exploitation, forced labour or services, slavery, or practices similar to slavery, servitude or the removal of organs.'

The trafficking protocol in criminalizing the traffickers states that the domestic legislators should base their legislations on their legal framework to prosecute the traffickers and in dealing with their mens rea, that is, the intention behind committing the crime. Further, the trafficking protocol defines that the actual exploitation of human beings need not necessarily occur with the expression of intention to exploit the person. The only required condition is that the accused person has committed the crime by any of the acts as described in exploitation with an intention to exploit the person.[66]

The mental element of a crime can be established in various ways. Article 5(1) of the trafficking protocol describes the mental element. Trafficking protocol wants the countries to criminalize trafficking, referring Article 5(1), when it is committed with the intention of exploitation of persons; yet, it permits the countries to use the mens rea element in prosecuting and criminalizing the person guilty of exploitation of persons to a lesser extent of conditions such as carelessness, negligence, or willful blindness in committing the crime. Also, this should be based and subjected to the legal system of the countries at their domestic level.[67]

Article 30 of the Rome Statute deals with the aspect of mens rea but it does not deal with all its aspects. It also describes that a person committing crimes that come under Article 7 of the Rome Statute can be related to the mens rea element as well as crimes against humanity, since the crimes defined under Article 7 state clearly that the perpetrator has the intention or purpose or knowledge of the crime. The person committing such crimes with a well-thought intention should be responsible and accountable for the punishment and shall be liable

---

[66] UNODC and UN.GIFT, 'Definitions of Trafficking in Persons and Smuggling of Migrants'

[67] Duncan, 'The Hague Conference on Private International Law'.

for punishment only if the person had the intent and the knowledge of the crime.

Further, the Rome Statute of the ICC defines that a person to be punished should have the intent that the consequence of the attack or the crime will occur in ordinary course of events. The person has to have the knowledge or the awareness that such situations exist which constitutes crime against humanity.

In order to be prosecuted or punished, the perpetrator must act with the intent of commitment of the crime. The perpetrator has to commit the act of crime with the knowledge of the attack directed at the civilian population and that the action is a part of this directed attack, and is systematic and widespread.

Article 30 of the Rome Statute under the jurisdiction of the ICC describes this mental element and includes all kinds of crimes which can be constituted to be a crime against humanity. According to Article 30(1) of the Rome Statute, 'unless otherwise provided, a person shall be criminally responsible and liable for punishment for a crime within the jurisdiction of the Court only if the material elements are committed with intent and knowledge'.[68]

Article 30 is unique among international instruments. It defines the terms 'intent' and 'knowledge'. Article 30(2) and Article 30(3) of the Rome Statute further define the term as:

A person has intent where:

- In relation to conduct, that person means to engage in the conduct.
- In relation to consequences, that person means to cause that consequence or is aware that it will occur in the ordinary course of events.
- 'Knowledge' means awareness that a circumstance exists or a consequence will occur in the ordinary course of events. 'Know' and 'knowingly' shall be construed accordingly.

Article 30 of the Rome Statute further addresses the two important aspects of the mens rea element. One is the degree or extent of the mens rea which is very important is to understand the intent or the

---

[68] ICC, 'Rome Statute', Article 30(1).

knowledge. The other one is the provision which deals with the scope of the intent or the knowledge.[69]

The ICTY also describes the mens rea and states that the accused had the intent to commit the offence or crime which constitutes crimes against humanity and has the knowledge of the attack, that 'there is an attack on the civilian population and that his acts comprise part of that attack or at least that he took the risk that his acts were part of attack which may be committed with personal reasons.'[70]

In the context of human trafficking, mens rea is a very significant factor. The trafficked persons are held in captivity and slavery with a well-thought intention of exploitation and this is evident from the fact that the right of ownership is exercised on the trafficked persons and they are exploited by way of forced labour, forced prostitution, and other forms of abuses, including sexual abuses. Even the types of exploitation and crimes against humanity mentioned in Article 7 of the Rome Statute of the ICC also verify the mens rea, in which the perpetrators commit the offence of exploitation or related crimes constituting crimes against humanity with a knowledge of the nature and purpose of the crime. Thus, the accused persons or such other persons who commit the crime of human trafficking have the mens rea element in their offences.

***

Human beings are bought and sold for various reasons such as slavery and labour. This trade has flourished over the years since the so-called commodity—the human being—is reusable and the business has proved to be profitable. It has been studied and researched that human trafficking is the biggest profitable trade in the world after

[69] ICC, 'Rome Statute', article 30.

[70] *Prosecutor v. Kunarac* et al., Case No.: IT-96-23-T and IT-96-23/1-T, Judgement, 22 February 2001, paragraph 434, available at http://www.icty.org/x/cases/kunarac/acjug/en/kun-aj020612e.pdf (accessed on 30 May 2016); William Schabas, 'Mens Rea and The International Criminal Tribunal for the Former Yugoslavia', *New England Law Review* 37, no. 4 (2003): 1023–2024.

arms and drugs trade. The chapter, in its introduction, has described and discussed the nature of crimes against humanity. It has described and highlighted the different protocols and statutes which have been enacted by the United Nations and other international agencies to combat human trafficking.

Thereafter, the chapter has delved into the nature and characterization of the crime. It has highlighted the origin of the various conventions, beginning with the 1907 Hague Convention and later on its inclusion in various charters, statutes, and conventions such as Nuremberg Charter, Tokyo Charter, and statutes of the ICTY and ICTR, followed by a detailed description adopted in the Elements of Crimes of Article 7 of the Rome Statute of the ICC. These charters and statutes described in the chapter also justify the nature of conduct of acts or crime with reference to the specific clauses adopted by these charters to constitute such crimes as crimes against humanity and violation of human rights. These crimes, referred to as crimes against humanity, must ensure that these were conducted as a widespread or systematic attack directed against a civilian population and committed with the use of force or coercion.

Further, the chapter has discussed the various problems faced by all the countries across the globe, whether big or small, due to the increasing severity of human trafficking and the crimes against humanity. One of the major problems described is how human trafficking is closely related to other organized crimes such as drug and arms trafficking, as well as various terrorist activities. Further, trafficking has also been studied in relation to health problems such as HIV/AIDS, tuberculosis, and hepatitis. While these are a major concern at the international level, there are health hazards that the victims of trafficking face due to the brutality of abuses—these include mental, emotional, physical, and psychological trauma. Reasons for these problems have been seen to be non-cooperation and distrust between countries of origin and countries of destination, owing to the fear of losing the evidences or documents, fear of losing the victims, who are potential witnesses, after their return to their country of origin due to weak legislations, and lack of awareness among the law-enforcement officers, immigration officials, and other government officials. Problems faced by the nations include elevated nature of corruption and poor economic conditions, which restrict the potential investors to set up their business organizations in such countries where this is a major problem and a hindrance to development. Poor economic conditions also lead to lack of proper infrastructure for educational facilities and development activities.

This chapter thus focuses on the nuances of the crimes against humanity with reference to the Article 7 of the Rome Statute of the ICC and human trafficking. The next chapter deals with the prosecution of cases of crimes against humanity, application of the ICC in prosecuting crimes against humanity, challenges and limitations faced by the ICC in prosecuting cases of crimes against humanity, and further describes the case study on the indictment of President al-Bashir by the ICC.

5 The Feasibility of Prosecution of Crimes against Humanity by the International Criminal Court

The ICC was established with the aim to prosecute serious crimes committed against the international community, the effects of which are felt across the world. To prosecute the criminals of such crimes, the international community came together and thought of establishing a strong legal response, and thus the ICC was established. It came into force on 1 July 2002,[1] after 74 countries of the world signed the Rome Statute of the ICC; at present, 124 countries have signed it. Also known as the ICC statute, it has a universal jurisdiction over the crimes committed against the

---

[1] W.A. Schabas, *An Introduction to the International Criminal Court* (Cambridge University Press, 4th edition, 2011).

international community or citizens of any country and affects the entire world.[2] The Rome Statute, in its jurisdiction, includes crimes such as war crimes, genocide, crimes against humanity, and crimes of aggression.[3]

The most dreadful crime in the world are the war crimes, genocide, and human trafficking. Human trafficking, as it is already known, is the third largest profit-making business in the world, only after drugs and arms trafficking. To control, prevent, and counter the acts of human trafficking, the international community, with the help of the United Nations, has enforced anti-trafficking protocols and measures to combat it and laid down rules and basis for the countries to frame anti-trafficking laws at the domestic and regional levels. The United Nations enforced its most important convention—a step towards preventing and controlling trafficking of human beings—the United Nations Convention against Transnational Organized Crime, Protocol to Prevent, Suppress and Punish Trafficking in Persons, Especially Women and Children in 2003, after the ICC and the Rome Statute. The UNTOC and Palermo protocol have helped the ICC to understand, define, explain, and prosecute human trafficking cases.

The ICC may prosecute any case of crime against humanity irrespective of the amount of time passed since the crime was committed. This is in accordance with Article 29, which states that 'the crimes within the jurisdiction of the Court shall not be subject to any statute of limitations'. However, Article 24 states that 'no person shall be criminally responsible under this Statute prior to the entry into force of the Statute.'[4]

As stated before, the ICC has jurisdiction over serious crimes such as genocide, crimes against humanity, war crimes, and crimes of

---

[2] R. Chaikin, *Trafficking and the Global Sex Industry 2009* (MD Lexington Books).

[3] Hans-Peter Kaul, 'The International Criminal Court: Current Challenges and Perspectives', *Washington University Global Studies Law Review* 6 (2007): 575.

[4] Center for Study of Democracy, 'Antimafia: The Italian Experience in Fighting Organized Crime', Policy Brief No. 31, October 2011.

aggression.[5] The three important and major crimes have been very cautiously defined in the statute to avoid ambiguity or vagueness for the efficient prosecution of such cases, whereas the crime of aggression is dealt with by the court when the Assembly of States Parties agrees on the definition, elements, and conditions under which the court will exercise jurisdiction. The Rome Statute does not identify any new categories of crimes, and reflects only existing conventional and customary international law. The crimes identified and prosecuted by the ICC are briefly described as follows:

Genocide

This is a very serious form of crime and includes those crimes which are specifically listed as prohibited acts, such as killing or causing serious harm, committed with the intent to destroy, in whole or in part, a national, ethnic, racial, or religious group.

Crimes against Humanity

These include the crimes specifically listed as prohibited acts when committed as part of a widespread or systematic attack directed against any civilian population. Such crimes or acts include murder, extermination, rape, sexual slavery, and the crime of apartheid, among others.

Genocide and crimes against humanity are punishable irrespective of whether they are committed in time of 'peace' or of war.

War Crimes

War crimes include severe and grave breaches of the Geneva Conventions of 1949 and other serious violations of the laws of war, committed on a large scale in international as well as internal armed conflicts.

[5] J.N. Aston and V.N. Paranjape, 'Abolishment of Human Trafficking: A Distant Dream', *Social Science Research Network*, available at http://papers.ssrn.com/sol3/papers.cfm?abstract_id=2112455 (accessed on 28 July 2014).

The inclusion of internal conflicts is consistent with customary international law and reflects the reality that in the past fifty years, the most serious violations of human rights have occurred not in international conflicts but within the states. The definitions of the crimes in the statute are the product of years of hard work involving many delegations and their experts.

The judges of the ICC are required to strictly construe the definitions and are not to extend them by analogy. The aim is to establish objective international standards, leaving no room for arbitrary decisions. In cases of ambiguity, the definitions are to be interpreted in favour of the suspect or accused.

Application of the ICC

Among various international legal frameworks, the ICC enacted the Rome Statute to combat human trafficking and to deal with and have universal jurisdiction on the most serious crimes which are of concern to humanity. The Rome Statute also follows Article 7 of the Convention on the Abolition of Slavery, the Slave Trade, and Institutions and Practices Similar to Slavery of 1956.[6] In the convention, slavery has been defined as 'the status or condition of a person over whom any or all of the powers attaching to the right of ownership are exercised'. Article 7 of the Rome Statute was enacted with reference to 'trafficking in persons', which is considered as a crime against humanity under the enslavement provision of the statute which has been stated in Article 7(1),[7] of which the most important is Article 7(1)(a)–(k). It states that the acts to come under the crime against humanity must be 'committed as part of a widespread or systematic attack directed against any civilian population, with knowledge of the attack'.[8] Article 7 could be further explained by the following elements:

---

[6] Chaikin, *Trafficking and the Global Sex Industry 2009.*

[7] Chaikin, *Trafficking and the Global Sex Industry 2009.*

[8] International Criminal Court (ICC), 'Rome Statute of the International Criminal Court', Article 7, available at https://www.icc-cpi.int/nr/rdonlyres/ea9aeff7-5752-4f84-be94-0a655eb30e16/0/rome_statute_english.pdf (accessed on 17 May 2016).

- Perpetration of the acts being committed as mentioned in the Article 7(1)(a)–(k)
- It must constitute an attack directed against a civilian population
- It must be a widespread or systematic attack
- The perpetrator is aware and has the knowledge of the acts committed and has been a part of or intended to be a part of such attack.

In many cases of such crimes being conducted and then being prosecuted by the ICC, it has been noticed that the cases include crime against humanity as well as war crimes and thus prosecution of human trafficking in such cases is at the risk of being ignored or prosecuted under Article 7 of the Rome Statute. Thus it is very important to distinguish human trafficking and war crimes in such cases while prosecuting, and consider it under Article 7 of the Rome Statute as crimes against humanity. There are also various obstacles being faced while prosecuting cases of human trafficking, such as the jurisdiction of a country where the prosecution of the case is being undertaken and the traditional laws and values of the countries.

Acts Constituting Attack Directed against a Civilian Population

Article 7 of the Rome Statute describes the acts which must constitute an attack directed against any civilian population, which must be systematic and widespread. Such attacks mean 'a course of conduct involving the multiple commission of acts referred to in paragraph 1 against any civilian population, pursuant to or in furtherance of a State or organizational policy to commit such attack'.[9]

As defined, such attacks constitute the course of conduct referred to, such as abuse and exploitation involving multiple commissions of the acts, directed against a civilian population and is not confined to any kind of war or military attack. Further, it can be understood and observed by the fact that though such attacks are directed against civilian population, they are not against an entire population of a country

---

[9] ICC, 'Rome Statute', Article 7(1).

or a region but are conducted against individuals who belong to civilian population and, further, are conducted in cooperation with other groups of criminals such as organized crime groups.

Studies have established that any kind of intentional crime conducted in isolation against a civilian population is an outcome of terror or discrimination and persecution involving the political system of a state.[10]

The acts of human trafficking can be considered as attacks directed against any civilian population, such as trafficking of multiple persons constituting the multiple commissions as mentioned in Article 7 of the Rome Statute. Such multiple commissions can be constituted even if trafficked persons are less at a time but the crime is conducted over the years. Further, attacks also can be considered as directed against civilian population when the trafficked person, may be only one, is exploited continuously throughout the lifetime through forced labour or prostitution.

Article 7 of the Rome Statute also describes such acts as an organized crime, conducted in cooperation with various and a large number of criminal groups which work in conspiracy, and thus it can be defined as a 'joint criminal enterprise'. Such crimes are conducted by some very powerful and dominant crime groups across the borders which manage and control the entire human trafficking racket globally. All these activities of crimes are conducted intentionally in cooperation with other crime groups. Such criminal activities and conspiracies are conducted if the information about weak and vulnerable persons of one country is shared by the traffickers of that country with the traffickers of the other country—may be its neighbouring country— which could be feasible, could constitute a joint enterprise, and also can be defined as attack directed against any civilian population.

Many instances made are evidence that such attacks against civilian population are conducted, as defined as multiple commissions, by trafficking vulnerable persons from a vulnerable group, mostly including women and girls, from one country to another in an organized

[10] *Prosecutor v. Tadic*, Judgment, IT-94-1-T, 649 (ICTY Trial Chamber, 7 May 1997).

manner, selling and reselling them; also, such acts are conducted in a lesser extent but over many years.

Attacks as Widespread and Systematic in Nature

The acts of human trafficking and attacks directed against a civilian population are, generally and in most of the occasions, widespread and systematic attacks owing to the large size of the target population. They are organized strategically, and are often spread across the borders.[11] These crimes are usually large-scale in nature, with small-scale operations not identified to be as widespread owing to the reason that they are conducted through conspiracy and joint enterprise; although, now, with an increase in the number of trafficked persons/victims of trafficking over the years, it has been established to be widespread. A case in point is the trafficking of women in large numbers from North Korea to China, though more studies are required to establish it as a widespread crime, considering that conducting a study to find out the facts of trafficking in this part of the world is quite difficult due to various restrictions imposed on the information of North Korean refugees.[12]

Attacks in Furtherance to the State or Organizational Policy

The Rome Statute states that the attacks must be 'pursuant to or in furtherance of a State or organizational policy to commit such attack'. The policy as mentioned in the statute can be defined in a broad manner. Since human trafficking is an organized crime, it is executed in a planned manner and as per a policy but it is not necessary for the policy to be specified or set out in rules.

It has been noticed that the state or the country encourages such attacks against a group of persons who are vulnerable to such attacks of human trafficking and purposefully ignores or fails to take action

---

[11]   ICC, 'Rome Statute', Article 7.

[12]   J.R. Charny, *Acts of Betray: The Challenge of Protecting North Koreans in China* (UNHCR Refworld, 2009).

against the organized crime groups conducting the attacks. Such states are included as recognized countries and governments by the United Nations and are actively involved in all governmental activities and functions.

Organization, in Article 7 of the Rome Statute, refers to any such group of persons who have the capability of conducting an attack against a civilian population, which is widespread and systematic in nature. The organized crime groups prevalent in countries/states, as discussed, work in committing such attacks with the help of the government and policies of that state, which is thereby boosting their economy.

Policies which have come to the notice through various cases prosecuted by the ICC included policies such as targeting at a particular population and destroying their property or targeting a civilian population to gain control and supremacy and become dominant on that population. Thus, the trade of trafficking of human beings has mainly three policies, which are: (a) to recruit, sell, transport, harbour, or transfer humans; (b) to earn profit from the exploitation of humans; and (c) to fuel demand for the human trafficking economy.

Such attacks on civilian populations are done through human trafficking based on some policies of using the children as shields in armed conflicts, using women for sexual exploitation, exploiting women and children through forced labour, and finally, exploiting many cultural and ethnic groups or population.

It has been studied and observed that there are many states and organizations which are involved in committing the crime of human trafficking and conducting attacks on civilian population in a widespread manner, with the backing of governmental policies of that particular state. Hence, it is also seen that these states do not include policies of the United Nations and its conventions in combating the crime.

Perpetrator's Knowledge of the Attack

The Rome Statute, in its Article 7—crime against humanity—states that the perpetrator or the person committing a crime or attack aimed at civilian population in a widespread and systematic manner is aware of such an attack being conducted. The perpetrator knows that the conduct is part of or intended the conduct to be part of a widespread or systematic attack against a civilian population.

Article 7 does not require any kind of proof to establish that 'the perpetrator had knowledge of all characteristics of the attack or the precise details of the plan or policy of the State or organization'. This means that the perpetrator has been aware of the attack but might not have the knowledge of all the characteristics and precise details of the attack and the policy of the state or the organization.[13]

This has been evident from many such instances where the perpetrator was found at the scene of the crime and the political background in which the act was committed. But in some cases, it has also been noticed that the perpetrator was not aware of the consequences of the attack and the policies of the state or organizations, and has been merely a player. But since the nature of such an attack and the crime is organized and is conducted as a joint enterprise between the groups of traffickers, it is understood that the perpetrators are aware of the attack and the nature and purposes of the attack. The same can be applicable in cases of human trafficking.

Challenges and Limitations before the ICC

The ICC was established to prosecute cases which constitute crimes against humanity, as defined in Article 7 of the Rome Statute. However, for these crimes to be prosecuted by the ICC, they must qualify on the basis of the required conditions and hence, the attack has to be widespread and/or systematic in nature, has to be directed against a civilian population, and the perpetrator or the offender has to be aware or have the knowledge of the attack. Under this definition, cases of trafficking of human beings can be prosecuted since they conform to the conditions or provisions mentioned in Article 7 of the Rome Statute. Hence, the ICC can prosecute cases of trafficking in persons, sexual slavery, and forced prostitution.

---

[13] ICC, 'Rome Statute', Article 7.

Lack of a precise and accurate definition of trafficking is one of the biggest impediments in the prosecution of trafficking by the ICC.[14] The definition of trafficking given by the Palermo protocol is very precise and the ICC needs to adopt it so that the aim of establishing the Rome Statute, which is to include and expand all forms of exploitation and slavery as a consequent of trafficking, could be taken up and traffickers could be prosecuted in an effective manner.[15]

Many countries across the world have enacted various anti-trafficking laws and legislations to prosecute cases of human trafficking at the regional and domestic level. In spite of these anti-trafficking laws, various developmental activities, awareness programmes, and effective policies in countering human trafficking, it has not yet been possible to effectively prosecute and combat human trafficking. The ICC too has not yet been able to achieve success in treating the trafficking as a crime against humanity in a potential manner, despite the enforcement of the Rome Statute and its Article 7.[16] The allegations and accusations of traffickers as per the Rome Statute have not been successful to be prosecuted by the ICC so far due to the limitations of the ICC and a proper definition of trafficking. Even the ICTY and ICTR have not been successful so far in prosecuting the trafficking cases and punishing the traffickers and thereby combating the crime.[17]

There are many cases which describe the nature of the organization, the sophistication with which the traffickers carry out their activities, the different backgrounds and situations, and the extent to which they have spread across the borders and all over the world—these are the

[14] *Prosecutor v. Al Bashir*, Case No. ICC-02/05-01/09, 'Decision on the Prosecution's Application for a Warrant of Arrest against Omar Hassan Ahmad Al Bashir' I, no. 1 (4 March 2009), available at http://www.ice-cpi.int/iccdocs/doc/doc639096.pdf (accessed on 10 June 2014).

[15] B.N. Schiff, *Building the International Criminal Court* (Cambridge University Press, 1st edition, 2008).

[16] *Prosecutor v. Al Bashir*, Case No. ICC-02/05-01/09.

[17] W. Duncan, 'The Hague Conference on Private International Law and its Current Programme of Work Concerning the International Protection of Children and Other Aspects of Family Law', *Yearbook of Private International Law* II (2000): 48.

challenges of the ICC in prosecuting cases of trafficking and the cases of crimes against humanity.

Another difficulty and challenge before the ICC in prosecuting cases of trafficking is the risk of ignoring the seriousness and magnitude of human trafficking.[18] The definition of trafficking as 'trafficking in persons, in particular women and children', is clearly mentioned in Article 7(1)(c) of the Rome Statute. However, the appropriate definition of trafficking, beyond the attachment of ownership over a person or deprivations of liberty, is not lucid in the statute. The Rome Statute does not include a proper definition of 'trafficking' and hence it is a challenge before the ICC to have a potential prosecution of trafficking cases. Trafficking is considered to be modern-day slavery. The deficiency of a proper and precise definition for 'trafficking' in the Rome Statute poses a big problem because of the different definitions existing in different countries, and this has a possibility in affecting the scope of the statute to deal with and prosecute cases of trafficking. Moreover, the definition of 'enslavement' is regarded as modern-day slavery but this is not accepted legally because enslavement covers a wide range of forms which could be considered as slavery. Enslavement, as it is defined in Article 7 of the Rome Statute and also in the Convention on the Abolition of Slavery in the Elements of Crimes, is stated as 'right of ownership over a person' but poses a major question whether it is applicable to modern-day slavery.[19]

There are also cases where the crimes being conducted include crimes against humanity as well as war crimes, when brought to the ICC for prosecution. Prosecution of such cases are at the risk of being ignored or mis-prosecuted under Article 7 of the Rome Statute. Hence, there is an important and urgent need to distinguish crimes against humanity and war crimes in such cases during the prosecution and consider them under the appropriate article of the Rome Statute.

Further, it has also been noticed that the jurisdiction of the countries becomes an obstacle in the prosecution of the cases of human trafficking. The limited reach of the ICC jurisdiction and

[18]   *Prosecutor v. Al Bashir*, Case No. ICC-02/05-01/09.
[19]   Kaul, 'International Criminal Court'.

admissibility regime of the court is a challenge in itself. This is a unique combination in which a jurisdiction that is conservative in nature and a state-sovereignty–oriented system based on the principle of territoriality is combined with an admissibility regime based on the complementarity principle.[20] The complementarity principle explains the challenge of the ICC to prosecute cases unless and until the states are unwilling or fail to prosecute or are unable to have jurisdiction and prosecute the cases. It is the state sovereignty which gives the states the primary right to exercise the criminal jurisdiction and exercise its powers of prosecuting cases of human trafficking or other cases of crimes against humanity, which entails international crimes. Thus, the ICC is the last resort to prosecute cases and have jurisdiction on the crimes conducted in the state party's territory which constitute international crime, and this happens only if the country or the state fails to exercise criminal jurisdiction or is not able to investigate and prosecute the cases or is unwilling to investigate and prosecute cases.[21] It is a very complex system of the ICC. The ICC faces a dilemma also. On the one hand, if the states start prosecuting and resolving cases of trafficking and crimes against humanity in an effective manner at the national level, then the ICC will have no cases to prosecute. Whereas, on the other hand, the ICC requires successful handling of cases and prosecuting cases effectively in order to establish its worthiness and aim with which it was established.[22]

The ICC also faces challenges while prosecuting cases due to lack of effective cooperation and support from the states. Since it is dependent on the states to provide evidence and investigate in an effective manner, it finds it difficult if the state parties are not cooperating and supporting the ICC in the prosecution. The ICC neither has executive powers nor police of its own to investigate cases and thus it is fully dependent on the states. This is a weakness on the part of the ICC, which is a major challenge since the aim of the ICC has been to uphold

[20] Kaul, 'International Criminal Court'.
[21] Kaul, 'International Criminal Court'.
[22] Kaul, 'International Criminal Court'.

the states' sovereignty.[23] Hence, the ICC always requires full cooperation and support from the state parties while prosecuting cases.

Another challenge and limitation of the ICC is its restraint to carry
out investigations and collect evidences with regard to the mass crimes
committed in regions which are thousands of miles away. Thus, the
ICC faces technical and logistic difficulties of access to these regions,
since often the cases which are being prosecuted by the ICC originate
in some other country thousands of miles away (such as Uganda,
Central Africa, and the Democratic Republic of Congo). The cost of
prosecution, victim protection, residence and travelling of the victims
and the officials is also a major concern for the ICC since it faces scar-
city of financial and other resources.[24]

One more challenge faced by the ICC is the protection of the victims of trafficking while prosecuting cases of trafficking. The prosecutor and the security forces of the country need to have appropriate
security measures to provide protection to the victims and to collect
evidence from them, and provide logistics pertaining to residence and
travelling while the prosecution of the cases is going on. To provide
effective protection to the victims, the ICC needs to depend on the
states of both the countries involved in the cases to cooperate and support the ICC for efficient prosecution and judgement.

Indictment of Omar Hassan Ahmad al-Bashir, President of Sudan: A Case Study

The significance of this case in international law is that for the first
time in the history of ICC, a sitting head (president) of a state was
indicted. In the year 1989, President Omar Hassan Ahmad al-Bashir
led a military rebellion and came to power in Sudan by defeating
the former government of Sudan. In the beginning of 2003, a conflict began in the Darfur region of Sudan which was initiated by the
attack of the Sudanese Liberation Movement and the Justice and
Equality Movement at the El Fasher airport. It was to register an

---

[23] Kaul, 'International Criminal Court'.
[24] Kaul, 'International Criminal Court'.

attack against the government of Sudan. Responding to this attack, the Sudan People's Armed Forces led a counter-insurgency after which a war broke out in the region. During the war, President al-Bashir's government, with the help of its military force, attacked and destroyed hundreds of villages and dislocated over a million people. The death toll in Darfur was around 300,000, as estimated by the UN reports. Anecdotal evidence proves that a minimum of 35,000 civilians were killed between 2003 and 2004.[25] President al-Bashir's government was responsible for grave acts of crime against humanity.

The Case

Pursuant to Article 13(b) of the Rome Statute, the United Nations Security Council, on 31 March 2005, referred the Darfur situation[26] (which is a non-member state of the ICC) to the then ICC Prosecutor Luis Moreno-Ocampo.[27] Further to Article 53 of the Rome Statute, the then ICC prosecutor Moreno-Ocampo was elected to investigate the situation. Prosecutor Moreno-Ocampo did his investigation and then requested arrest warrants for six persons who were found to be involved in the Darfur situation, including President Omar Hassan Ahmad al-Bashir. Out of these six persons, five were indicted, out of which only two appeared at the Hague on their own. Prosecutor Moreno-Ocampo once again requested an arrest warrant for President al-Bashir on 14 July 2008 for committing crimes against humanity, which included genocide and war crimes. President al-Bashir was finally indicted on 4 March 2009 as an indirect perpetrator in the

---

[25] Maggie Farley, 'U.N. Puts Darfur Death Toll at 300,000', 23 April 2008, available at http://articles.latimes.com/2008/apr/23/world/fg-darfur23 (accessed on 30 May 2016); Gwen P. Barnes, 'The International Criminal Court's Ineffective Enforcement Mechanisms: The Indictment of President Omar Al Bashir', *Fordham International Law Journal* 34, no. 6 (2011): 1604–05, available at http://ir.lawnet.fordham.edu/cgi/viewcontent.cgi?article =2313&context=ilj (accessed on 30 May 2016).

[26] ICC, 'Rome Statute', Article 13(b).

[27] *Prosecutor v. Al Bashir*, Case No. ICC-02/05-01/09.

crimes. Investigations proved that there was adequate evidence that the president carried out these criminal activities and crimes against humanity using the Sudanese military and the Sudanese government. He was thus indicted for having committed five counts of crimes against humanity and two counts of war crimes[28]. It was a remarkable step taken by the ICC to issue an arrest warrant against a sitting head of a state for the first time. Finally, the ICC requested Sudan to arrest President al-Bashir on 5 March 2009 but since Sudan was not a member state of the ICC, the request was turned down. Further to Article 89(1) of the Rome Statute, the prosecutor requested the member states of the ICC to arrest the president whenever they get an opportunity to do so.[29]

Inconsistency of the ICC and the African Union Charter

The indictment of President al-Bashir by the ICC began a conflict between the ICC and the African Union. In spite of the decision taken by the African Union and the interpretation of Article 98 of the Rome Statute, on 12 July 2010, the ICC issued a second arrest warrant for President al-Bashir and he was thus indicted for the second time for three counts of genocide. These two warrants accused him for a total of ten counts of crimes, out of which five counts were of crimes against humanity, two counts of war crimes, and three counts of genocide. The ICC issued supplementary requests to Sudan and the member states of the ICC on 21 July 2010 for arresting and surrendering the president.

After receiving requests from the ICC, the African Union issued a statement with regard to the indictment of the president for genocide on 16 July 2010. It expressed concern for the new indictment as

---

[28] President al-Bashir was indicted under Article 8 for (1) intentionally directing attacks against the civilian population or against individual civilians not taking direct part in hostilities, and (2) pillaging (stating the crimes that the ICC found whereby enough evidence existed to indict President al-Bashir).

[29] *Prosecutor v. Al Bashir*, Case No. ICC-02/05-01/09.

Sudan was going through a transitional period towards a democratic and peaceful state, and if the president was to be arrested, then the situation in Sudan would worsen and a state of unrest would prevail in the region. With this concern, the African Union requested the UN Security Council to defer the prosecution of President al-Bashir, which was not accepted by the ICC.

Reaction of the Neighbouring States

The second indictment of President al-Bashir was issued by the ICC directly just before his visit to Chad, which was a member state of the ICC.[30] But Chad did not respond to ICC's request of the indictment and went ahead with the invitation to the president of Sudan for his visit. On 21 July 2010, the Sudanese president visited Chad. This visit was considered significant by the African Union because the relation between the two countries had soured during the Darfur conflict and this was a good opportunity to rebuild faith, trust, and confidence. The outcome of the visit was positive for the two countries and was welcomed by the African Union. This visit was also significant for the ICC, EU, United Nations, and many human rights organizations. The ICC requested Chad to arrest President al-Bashir but Chad refused to arrest him and the ICC failed in catching hold of him.

The ICC got another opportunity to arrest President al-Bashir when he visited Kenya on 28 August 2010, which is also a member of the ICC.[31] The president of Sudan was invited by the Kenyan government to attend a signing ceremony in honour of the new constitution of Kenya. But the ICC was unsuccessful on this occasion too, as the Kenyan government refused to arrest the president. Kenya feared of having harmful and negative implications on the peace process between Kenya and Sudan.

Furthermore, it was reported (anecdotal report) that the African Union issued instructions to all its member states not to arrest the president on request of the ICC, as a result of which these two member

---

[30] ICC, 'Rome Statute', Article 7 (signed on 20 October 1999).
[31] ICC, 'Rome Statute', Article 7 (signed on 11 August 1999).

states abided by this decision.[32] After this, the ICC filed a decision of informing the UN Security Council about the non-compliance of the member states, Chad and Kenya, with regard to the indictment of President al-Bashir, arresting and surrendering him to the ICC. This matter was referred to the UN Security Council and the Assembly of States Parties by the ICC, and they requested the United Nations to take strong immediate action against these two member states as they deemed it fit.

The African Union then responded to the ICC's decision and requested a deferral of prosecution of President al-Bashir under Article 98 of the Rome Statute.[33] It issued a press release in which it stated that it was difficult for Kenya and Chad to arrest him as these countries were neighbours of Sudan, and if they did so, then it would run a risk of disrupting peace and harmony in the African region.

The President of Kenya announced in September 2010 to hold a special summit on Sudan at the Intergovernmental Authority on Development (IGAD) in Kenya, and also decided to invite President al-Bashir for the summit. After this announcement, the ICC asked Kenya to inform if they face any problem which would prevent Kenya in arresting the Sudanese president during his second visit to Kenya. In response to this, the Attorney General of Kenya informed the ICC on 28 October 2010 that the IGAD summit will not be held in Kenya and hence the president would not visit Kenya, a step well thought by Kenya.

Gradually, it was observed that many member states were getting into the conflict of arresting the Sudanese president by warning him that he will be arrested if he visits those states. This was welcomed by the ICC

---

[32] Gwen P. Barnes, 'The International Criminal Court's Ineffective Enforcement Mechanisms: The Indictment of President Omar Al Bashir', *Fordham International Law Journal* 34, no. 6 (2011): 1607–8, available at http://ir.lawnet.fordham.edu/cgi/viewcontent.cgi?article=2313&context=ilj (accessed on 30 May 2016); Katherine Iliopoulos, 'The African Union and the ICC', Crimes of War, available at http://www.crimesofwar.org/commentary/the-african-union-and-the-icc/ (accessed on 30 May 2016).

[33] ICC, 'Rome Statute', Article 98(b).

prosecutor as a positive development in the region which would make President al-Bashir isolated. But in 2011, it was seen that the Sudanese president visited another member state of the ICC, Djibouti.[34] He visited Djibouti on 8 May 2011 in order to attend an inauguration ceremony. Further, on 7 August 2011, he again visited Chad for the second time to attend the inauguration ceremony of the head of the state of Chad, Idriss Deby. Following this, the ICC again issued a decision to the UN Security Council and Assembly of States Parties with regard to the visit of President al-Bashir to Djibouti and requested the United Nations to take necessary action. The ICC issued another decision on 18 August 2011 to the UN Security Council about the second visit of the Sudanese president to Chad and refusal of Chad to arrest him on both the occasions. Prosecutor Luis Moreno-Ocampo and Amnesty International claimed that President al-Bashir's plane could be intercepted in international airspace. Soon after this, the government of Sudan announced that the presidential plane would always be escorted by fighter jets of the Sudanese Air Force to prevent his arrest.

Weaknesses in the Rome Statute

Though the Rome Statute has been a very significant one in terms of prosecuting crimes against humanity, it is still not a perfect one. Some people call this an impotence of the ICC—it still has some loopholes and flaws. These flaws can be considered as weaknesses of the Rome Statute of the ICC.[35] These weaknesses have been evidenced from the case study of President al-Bashir's indictment.

According to the Rome Statute, indictment of an individual can be permitted if that individual[36]

---

[34] ICC, 'Rome Statute', Article 7 (signed on 7 October 1998).

[35] D. Donovan, 'International Criminal Court: Successes and Failures of the Past and Goals for the Future', Commentary, *International Policy Digest*, available at http://www.internationalpolicydigest.org/2012/03/23/international-criminal-court-successes-and-failures-of-the-past-and-goals-for-the-future/ (accessed on 12 June 2014).

[36] ICC, 'Rome Statute', Article 27.

1. is a national of a member state of the Rome Statute;
2. commits a crime in a member state; or
3. is a national of a non-member state when the Security Council of the United Nations refers the situation to the prosecutor of the ICC.

In the case of President al-Bashir's indictment, the UN Security Council referred the situation of Darfur to the then prosecutor of the ICC, Moreno-Ocampo, for committing crimes against humanity. After this, prosecutor Moreno-Ocampo indicted President al-Bashir for crimes against humanity, first for war crimes and then for genocide in Darfur. This indictment was possible only because UN Security Council referred the situation to the ICC; otherwise, it would not have been possible to indict President al-Bashir because Sudan is not a member state of the ICC and the crimes were committed in Sudan. In spite of this, the ICC was not successful in arresting the president though there were two opportunities at hand. That is when the president travelled to Kenya and Chad, which are member states, and the ICC requested both these countries to arrest the president but they refused to do so. This was because of the directions of the African Union to these countries, which are also members of the union, to refuse the indictment of the President al-Bashir by the ICC.[37]

Further, it was also observed that the Rome Statute lacks clarity in terms of immunity and thus provides the member states with flexibility to comply with the decisions of the ICC. In the case of the president, the African Union referred Article 98 of the Rome Statute, justifying its non-compliance with the ICC. As per the union's justification and Article 98 of the Rome Statute, the president has immunity and cannot be prosecuted by the ICC since he was the sitting head of a state which is also a non-member state. The Rome Statute states that there is no provision for immunity for heads of state but there is no clarity if it is applicable only to member states. On the one hand, the ICC statute states that there is no immunity to heads of state, while,

---

[37] *Prosecutor v. Al Bashir*, Case No. ICC-02/05-01/09.

on the other hand, it states that there is diplomatic immunity under Article 98(1). There is vagueness in its own provisions. Further, the Rome Statute, under Article 98(2), states that the states may not comply with the ICC's decision or requests if they have prior agreements. This article gave Kenya and Chad an opportunity to refuse the ICC's request since they already had an agreement with the African Union, being its members.

Furthermore, the Rome Statute reveals another weakness of its own by not giving clear indications of any serious consequences to be faced by the member states if they fail or refuse to comply with the decisions or directions of the ICC, or for any kind of breach of the statute. This weakness has given the member states, such as Chad and Kenya, an opportunity or choice to refuse the ICC's request. There is no clarity on consequences or explanation for breach of duty by member states except that such situations will be referred to the UN Security Council.

***

As crime against humanity is a serious crime which has had its presence felt in all the countries across the world, there is a need to have an international body or statute to address the cases of these crimes and deliver effective and efficient prosecution. Thus, the establishment of the ICC and the Rome Statute to prosecute these cases. The Rome Statute, thus ratified, had its jurisdiction over the crimes such as war crimes, genocide, crimes against humanity, and crimes of aggression and Article 7 defined the crimes against humanity. The chapter introduced the nature and operation of the ICC with reference to the Rome Statute and prosecution of cases of crimes against humanity. The chapter defined serious crimes which are dealt with by the ICC, such as genocide, war crimes, and crimes against humanity, including human trafficking. It also discussed about the importance of various protocols and conventions enforced by the United Nations for preventing trafficking, forced labour, and slavery, which forms the basis of the Rome Statute and the establishment of the ICC. The jurisdiction of the ICC and the nature of the crimes which are applicable to be prosecuted by the ICC were also discussed, specifying the type of crimes under each category of crimes against humanity.[38]

The chapter has then explained the application of Article 7 of the Rome Statute in prosecuting cases of such crimes, with a brief description of the kinds of attack to be constituted as crimes against humanity.[39] Thereafter, the chapter emphasized and explained the challenges and limitations of the ICC in prosecuting cases pertaining to crimes against humanity and specifically those of human trafficking.[40] Also suggested were the possible solutions to overcome the challenges and limitations. Further, the chapter highlighted the confusion being created between the victims of war crimes and crimes against humanity, due to which proper prosecution of such cases is ignored. Described are the reach and jurisdiction of the ICC, as well as the admissibility regime of the court and the complementarity principle of the ICC in prosecuting cases.[41]

A case study on the indictment of President Omar Hassan Ahmed al-Bashir gave a detailed description of how the UN Security Council worked towards the indictment of the sitting head of a state; in this light, the chapter has delved into the challenges and limitations of the ICC in the prosecution of crimes against humanity, and the weak points of the Rome Statute.

[38] Kaul, 'International Criminal Court'.
[39] Kaul, 'International Criminal Court'.
[40] Kaul, 'International Criminal Court'.
[41] Kaul, 'International Criminal Court'.

6 Enforcement Mechanism of the International Criminal Court

The objective of the ICC will be futile if it cannot take the perpetrators of genocide, war crimes, and other grave crimes against humanity to their logical conclusion. The consequences of the two world wars were certainly severe enough to devastate many parts of the world, and therefore, after World War II, the leaders of various nations decided to come together and officially establish an international organization to maintain consistent peace and security of the nations all over the world. While drafting the UN Charter, the drafters ensured that no individual state uses force except in situations when they need to use it for self-defence. This collective enforcement mechanism of the charter portrays the pivotal role of the UN Security Council in order to maintain consistent international peace and security.

Under international law, individual states are permitted to use measures to enforce their rights mentioned under the law. Even though there has not been any central organization to look after the security of the states and respond to the breaches of international law, the states are empowered with their rights to use force and measures in self-defence after determining the breach and its extent.[1] In the absence of a central organization controlling the states' security and maintaining peace, the entire onus of determining the breach of international law and fight for peace and security is on individual states.

The ICC was created with an aim to have a strong and independent prosecutor and a court with enforcement mechanism which was significant and legally binding. The Rome Statute of the ICC is a two-pillar system where the first pillar represents the judiciary and is thus known as the judicial pillar, and the second pillar represents enforcement and is thus known as the enforcement pillar. Both these pillars are in turn represented by the court and the states respectively and the states have a legal obligation to cooperate with the court. The legitimacy of the ICC is thus assessed by the enforcement regime of the court.[2]

The procedure and evidence of the court was made responsible for the enforcement of sentences and was hence entrusted to the presidency of the court, which is a distinct organ. The procedure and evidence, also called the 'rules', were adopted two months after the

---

[1] J.C. Barker, *Mechanisms To Create and Support Conventions, Treaties, and Other Responses*, available at http://www.eolss.net/EolssSampleChapters/C14/E1-44-01/E1-44-01-TXT-02.aspx (accessed on 10 June 2014).

[2] Judge Philippe Kirsch, President of the International Criminal Court, in his opening remarks at the Fifth Session of the Assembly of State Parties, 23 November 2006, available at http://www.icc-cpi.int/iccdocs/asp_docs/library/organs/presidency/?PK_20061123_en.pdf (accessed on 10 June 2014): 'In establishing the ICC, states set up a system designed on two pillars. The court itself is the judicial pillar. The enforcement pillar belongs to the states. In national systems, the two pillars are intertwined. Courts rely automatically on the enforcement powers of the state. In the case of ICC, the two have been separated. The Court depends upon the cooperation of the state parties. With the support and cooperation of the state parties, the Court will continue to be a strong credible judicial institution.'

statute entered into force, by the assembly of state parties. The dual-enforcement regime of the ICC is a unique system. With regard to the enforcement of sentences, in case of the ad-hoc international tribunals established by the UN Security Council, these are delegated to the judicial systems of the states which are carried out under the supervision and control of these ad-hoc tribunals. Likewise, the hybrid tribunals, such as the Special Court for Sierra Leone, maintain a balance between the enforcement of sentences of the court and state parties. Whereas, in case of the ICC, the sentenced persons are detained in the prisons of the states, and the court keeps most of the direct control on the enforcement of sentences.

The enforcement regime is based on three principles: (1) Enforcement of sentences is based on the prison facilities available in the respective state and is subjected to the laws of that state. 2) The enforcement of the sentences is supervised by the court. (3) The state where the enforcement takes place is bound by the sentence imposed by the court. Thus, this enforcement regime, which is portrayed by the relation of the state of enforcement and the sentence imposed by the court and its supervision, makes it a unique system.[3]

The enforcement of sentences of imprisonment and the role of the presidency in imposing sentences discusses the pre-enforcement requirements and procedures, and considers the particulars of the supervision by the court, the conditions of imprisonment, and the circumstances which may affect the imprisonment.[4] The state, before enforcing the sentence, has to accept its designation and the person who is convicted to a consent system as specified in the statute. This consent system specifies that the state must be featured on the list of states which are willing to enforce the sentences. Further, the states must also accept the presidency's designation of the state in a particular

---

[3] ICC, 'Rome Statute of the International Criminal Court', Part 7: Penalties, Article 77, Paragraph 1: Applicable Penalties, available at http://untreaty.un.org/cod/icc/statute/99_corr/7.htm (accessed on 2 June 2014).

[4] ICC, 'Rome Statute', Part 7: Penalties, Article 77, Paragraph 2: Applicable Penalties.

case. For instance, if the court convicted a person and enforced a sentence of imprisonment, the convicted person has to serve the sentence in the state designated by the court. The designation of the state is done by the presidency where the state is chosen from the list provided and maintained by the registrar of the court. If a state makes its willingness to accept the sentenced persons, it may attach the conditions for its acceptance to the sentences in accordance with Part 10 of the Rome Statute.[5] On the other hand, if the presidency is not in agreement with the conditions provided by the state, it may not include the state in the list, or may even ask for additional information or conditions. Besides, the state may even withdraw or amend its conditions for acceptance which is subjected to confirmation or approval by the presidency. However, the withdrawal of the state from the list does not affect the sentences which had already been accepted for enforcement prior to the withdrawal.

Regionalization of International Criminal Law

The international criminal law and its enforcement have mostly been at the international level only, which can be seen from various cases occurring internationally since 1945, when the International Military Tribunal was established at Nuremburg. For granting of jurisdiction to existing international tribunals on various international crimes occurring at various places across the world, groups of states came forward for establishing an international treaty[6] or through interstate agreement after war[7]. In recent times, it has been seen that there has been a shift of the enforcement of international criminal law towards the domestic or regional level. It is evident from the use of universal

---

[5] ICC, 'Rome Statute', Part 7: Penalties, Article 77, Paragraph 2: Applicable Penalties. Part 10: Enforcement, Article 103.

[6] ICC, 'Rome Statute of the International Criminal Court', 17 July 1998, U.N. Doc. A/CONF.183/9 (1998), reprinted in 37 I.L.M. 999

[7] See, for example, S.C. Res. 827, U.N. SCOR, 48th Sess., 3217th mtg., U.N. Doc. S/RES/827 (1993) (creating the ICTY pursuant to Chapter VII of the UN Charter).

jurisdiction and establishment of criminal courts which are semi-internationalized and are closely associated with the judicial system at the domestic level. Examples of such semi-internationalized criminal courts are the SCSL[8] and the Special Panels in East Timor.[9] At such set-up and enforcement mechanisms, the courts at the domestic level are the first to ensure the enforcement of international criminal law or the criminal justice system for crimes of international nature. But these domestic courts are supported by the ICC, which can anytime step in and take over the enforcement and prosecution on the basis of the complementarity principle of the ICC, in situations when the courts at the domestic level are unwilling or fail to act.[10]

The enforcement of international criminal law, at the national as well as international level, have various advantages and disadvantages, but the enforcement at the regional level is a beneficial one since it is at a unique position between the national and international enforcement systems. Hence, regionalization of the enforcement system could strike a balance between the advantages or benefits and disadvantages or risks between the national and international enforcement systems. Regionalization could thus become a preferable means of an enforcement system for the international criminal law in terms of political independence, costs, judicial reconstruction, and legitimacy. The current structure of international criminal law makes it easier to reap the benefits of regionalization of the enforcement of the law further.[11]

---

[8] See Agreement between the United Nations and the Government of Sierra Leone on the Establishment of a Special Court for Sierra Leone, 16 January 2002, U.N. SCOR, 57th Sess., U.N. Doc. S/2002/246, appended to Letter Dated 6 March 2002 from the Secretary-General Addressed to the President of the Security Council, app. II (2002).

[9] See *On the Establishment of Panels with Exclusive Jurisdiction over Serious Criminal Offenses*, United Nations Transnational Administration in East Timor (UNTAET) Reg. 2000/15, U.N. Doc. UNTAET/REG/2000/15 (6 June 2000).

[10] ICC, 'Rome Statute'.

[11] ICC, 'Rome Statute'.

Regionalization can be depicted in various forms, such as by the establishment of criminal courts at the regional level. But there are many options already available for regionalization of the international criminal law under the already prevailing enforcement mechanisms, which are much more flexible. These options are already cited from the Rome Statute, which states that the ICC has the option of sitting at the regional level. Further options could be the exercising of universal jurisdiction by the domestic courts or the semi-internationalized courts functioning at the domestic or regional level, drawing on procedures as well as judges of their own region. There are various alternatives or options available for the enforcement of international criminal law at the regional level, but there is also a concern about the duplication of the ICC by establishing regional criminal courts in line with the ICC, which is already supported universally. Thus, there is a need to consider various alternatives for the proper enforcement of international criminal law and the justice system for the international crimes which are being committed.

Means to Regionalize the Enforcement of International Criminal Law

The enforcement mechanism and establishment of the international criminal justice system at the regional level has a big question of implementing it in the real sense. The creation of regional courts and further enforcement of international criminal law thus needs the delegation of jurisdiction over international crimes to the regional courts by the states.[12] But the question still remains as to how to regionalize the international criminal justice system. Four specific and potential means for regionalizing it have been explained in the following subsections.

---

[12] R.E. Rauxloh, 'Regionalization of the International Criminal Court', *New Zealand Yearbook of International Law* 4 (2007), available at http://papers.ssrn.com/sol3/papers.cfm?abstract_id=1878557 (accessed on 15 June 2014).

A Regional Seat of the ICC

The first potential means of regionalizing the enforcement mechanism could be the sitting of the ICC at the regional level. Though the ICC statute is an international enforcement mechanism and its seat is at The Hague, it has a provision of sitting regionally, which is stated in Article 3 of the Rome Statute. Article 3, thus, states: '[t]he seat of the Court shall be established at The Hague in the Netherlands' but '[t]he Court may sit elsewhere, whenever it considers it desirable'.[13] Thus, the Rome Statute clearly empowers the ICC to conduct proceedings outside The Hague and also provides scope and flexibility to the court as to when it should decide to do so, and does not state when it should do so. Further, Article 38(3) of the Rome Statute states that the responsibility and the decision to sit regionally outside The Hague in any specific case, and all other logistics arrangements, need to be taken by the presidency of the court. Hence, the decision of the president of the ICC to sit regionally, preferably where the crime has been committed, is enough to permit the court to sit regionally. Further, the ICC sitting regionally would make it easier to achieve the goal of prosecuting international crimes at the regional level without any changes in the structure of the ICC. This would also help in preventing expenses on logistics and other arrangements of resources.[14]

To achieve this, there are some formalities which need to be followed. First, the court has to discuss and negotiate with a state in a particular region of crime where it aims to sit for investigating, collecting evidences, and conducting trial. The ICC also has to prepare an agreement—a temporary one though—with the state for ensuring security, safety, and sanctity of the court and the United Nations personnel during the trials and proceedings. Second, during the trials, the ICC would require and use the facilities of that state in the region, which could be done through renting or borrowing of resources.

<hr />

[13] ICC, 'Rome Statute', Article 3(3).

[14] William W. Burke-White, 'Regionalization of International Criminal Law Enforcement: A Preliminary Exploration', *Texas International Law Journal*, 38: 729.

Establishment of Regional Criminal Courts

The regionalization of international criminal justice by establishing regional criminal courts would be an excellent step towards regionalization. These courts would follow the ICC but with a territorial jurisdiction and draw upon the judges of that particular region where it is situated. These regional criminal courts would require a treaty among the states of that particular region and would also be easier to negotiate and ratify with a big consensus. Such an example could be the ICTY, which has jurisdiction of the entire territory of the former Yugoslavia, which includes Serbia, Croatia, Bosnia, and Montenegro. But the ICTY is not entirely a regional criminal court because of the fact that the judges and staff are drawn upon from the UN member states and observer states. Whereas, the regional criminal court, in its real sense, would operate only at the regional level, having judges and other personnel only from that particular region. There are many regions across the world where a strong regional enforcement mechanism exists. These regions could be best suited for the establishment of regional criminal courts. One such example could be Europe, where a very strong regional court exists in the form of European Court of Justice (ECJ) and the European Court of Human Rights (ECHR). The statute of the ECHR or the treaty of the ECJ could be slightly amended with respect to the jurisdiction over international crimes and they could operate as a good regional enforcement system for international criminal justice. On the other hand, a new regional court could be established with its jurisdiction over individuals in regions where there is a lack of strong pre-existing judicial mechanism and legal structure operating in that region—for example, the South African region.[15]

[15] United Nations Human Rights, 'Protocol to Prevent, Suppress and Punish Trafficking in Persons Especially Women and Children, supplementing the United Nations Convention against Transnational Organized Crime', Article 3, available at http://www.ohchr.org/EN/ProfessionalInterest/Pages/ProtocolTraffickingInPersons.aspx (accessed on 30 May 2016).

Exercising Universal Jurisdiction with Regional Preference

Another potential means of enforcement mechanism of international criminal justice, independent of the ICC, is with the help of exercise of universal jurisdiction at the regional level. Universal jurisdiction is generally exercised by any state in cases of serious international crimes by delegating the courts this jurisdiction. But in the case of regionalization, it can be achieved by providing jurisdictional preferences to the states of that region where the crime has actually been committed. The states of all regions across the world have a domestic legislation which allows the exercise of universal jurisdiction in prosecuting international crimes such as war crimes or crimes against humanity. There are over 120 nations that have adopted the legislation for prosecuting war crimes under the universal jurisdiction, and almost ninety-five nations have adopted legislation for prosecuting crimes against humanity. But when there are jurisdictional conflicts, no rules are observed to exercise universal jurisdiction. Jurisdictional conflicts are bound to happen because of the universal jurisdiction exercised by the state while prosecuting international crimes. Such an example of jurisdictional conflict can be cited when Augusto Pinochet was arrested in the UK in 1999. After the arrest, there was no clarity with regard to the hierarchy of the jurisdiction and about which state should be prosecuting him. The Princeton Principles on Universal Jurisdiction were used to resolve this conflict, which provided a set of criteria to determine the priority of exercising the jurisdiction by the states. Princeton Principles were an attempt by leading scholars and experts of international law in developing a set of principles guiding the exercise of universal jurisdiction.

The Princeton Principles[16] provide direction to the states in resolving jurisdictional conflicts based on an aggregate balance of

- multilateral or bilateral treaty obligations;
- place of commission of the crime;

[16] Princeton Project on Universal Jurisdiction, *The Princeton Principles on Universal Jurisdiction* (2001), 32.

- nationality connection of the alleged perpetrator to the requesting state;
- nationality connection of the victim to the requesting state;
- any other connection between the requesting state and the alleged perpetrator, the crime, or the victim;
- likelihood, good faith, and effectiveness of the prosecution in the requesting state;
- fairness and impartiality of the proceedings in the requesting state;
- convenience to the parties and witnesses, as well as the availability of evidence in the requesting state; and
- interests of justice.

The commentaries then make it clear that this list 'is not intended to be exhaustive' but is designed 'to provide states with guidelines for the resolution of conflicts'.

Establishment of Specialized Domestic Courts with Regional Judges

The fourth means of regionalization of international criminal justice system is with the help of specialized courts being set up in regions of post-conflict and transitional situations where the personnel and the resources of that region can be utilized. This is an important step towards the enforcement mechanism of international criminal law at the regional level. A specialized domestic court or semi-internationalized courts could help considerably in prosecuting international crimes in the regions of occurrence. This could be very relevant in post-conflict and transitional situations, during which neither the international tribunal nor the domestic justice system is able to deal with the intricacies and a large number of cases which are still pending.[17]

A few examples of such specialized domestic courts are those sitting in Sierra Leone (SCSL), East Timor, and Kosovo. In case of Sierra Leone and East Timor, the specialized courts are associated with the domestic courts which serve within the domestic set-up of the courts

---

[17] United Nations, *Treaty Series*, vol. 189, no. 2545.

and apply the international criminal law in an effective manner. Both these courts have a panel of judges—local as well as international—combined in a panel. Thus, it has been observed that the justice system has been very effective in this region. These courts, in order to attain regionalization status and to reduce the anomaly which is thought about them because of being part of a national judicial system, keep its impartial and regional structure by borrowing international judges from other legal systems. Thus, it keeps the sanctity of regionalization and is unbiased.[18]

An example of such kind is the existence of the agreement between the United Nations and the government of Sierra Leone on the establishment of the special court, which states that there shall be three judges who would be serving the SCSL in the trial chamber. Among these three judges, one shall be appointed by the government of Sierra Leone and rest of the two judges shall be appointed by the Secretary-General of the United Nations, after receiving nominations forwarded by the member states, in particular the states of the Economic Community of West African States and the Commonwealth, at the invitation of the Secretary-General. It has been observed that the judges of SCSL who are selected and appointed are mostly from countries such as Nigeria, Cameroon, the Gambia, the United Kingdom, and even from Sierra Leone.[19]

On the other hand, regionalization could also be achieved by the appointment of judges and personnel without any specific guidelines on appointment of judges. In case of East Timor, there are no such agreements on the selection and appointment of judges. The specialized court situated here has judges hailing from East Timor, Burundi, Portugal, and Cape Verde. Judges are appointed by the court administration and the United Nations from this region where the court sits and also from the regions where the crimes have been committed, unlike earlier times when the United Nations asked for applications from various parts of the world among the member states.

---

[18] United Nations, *Treaty Series*, vol. 189, no. 2545.

[19] ICC, 'Rome Statute', Article 3(3).

Merits of Regionalization of International Criminal Law Enforcement

Enforcement mechanism at the regional level has proven to be effective for various international legal regimes, which can be seen in the case of regional enforcement for money laundering, protection of human rights, pollution, piracy, and others. The most effective enforcement system at the regional level has been the maintenance of international security and peace by various international and regional organizations working together. The effective enforcement mechanism by the regional organizations for maintaining international peace and security is actually derived from Article 52 of the UN Charter, which states: 'nothing in the present Charter precludes the existence of regional arrangements or agencies for dealing with such matters relating to the maintenance of international peace and security as are appropriate for regional action'.[20] Thus, these effective regional enforcement mechanisms have resulted in strengthening international law.

In the recent times, when the international criminal justice system was an upcoming phenomenon, the status of international law and its enforcement focused on two major and crucial points, the first being the delegation of authority by the states to the ICC and other international tribunals for prosecuting international crimes; and the second being the delegation of authority to the national courts for the enforcement of international criminal law, which is done through the establishment of specialized international courts under the judicial system of the state and/or by exercising the universal jurisdiction. But the enforcement mechanism of the international criminal law at the international as well as the national level are often conflicting and are thus criticized for various reasons. In case of international tribunals, the costs of enforcement are very high and expensive, often unmanageable, and are physically and psychologically away from the actual region of the crime, whereas in case of courts at the national level, the costs are less because they are situated nearer the region of the crimes which are being prosecuted; but these courts lack resources to enforce and prosecute the crime. They also have

---

[20] International Court of Justice, *Charter of the United Nations*, Article 52, para 1.

the risk of unfairness, prejudice, and political manipulation. Hence the costs and benefits of international and national enforcement mechanisms are always in conflict with each other and this is seen when the benefits of regional or domestic adjudication are reaped while those of international adjudication are not received.[21]

Cost Effectiveness

The enforcement of the international criminal law and the justice system at the regional level further presents the reduced costs of legal proceedings, which is unlike the enforcement systems at the international level. The high cost of enforcement mechanisms of international criminal law at the international tribunals is a crucial impediment and thus affects the efficiency of these international tribunals. This fact can be further supported by the comments and criticism of the judges of ICTY and ICTR. As Patricia Wald, the former US judge at the ICTY says: 'United Nations is understandably anxious to bring to closure the ICTY and the tribunal for Rwanda [ICTR], which together consume almost ten percent of the total UN budget.'[22]

On the other hand, the establishment of regional courts can be capable of reducing the costs and finances of the enforcement of international criminal law, which can be made possible in ways described in the following subsections.[23]

Physical Propinquity to the Alleged Crimes

The adjudication of international criminal law at the international level has a major disadvantage in terms of the location of the courts and tribunals away from the places where the crimes have been committed.

[21] O. Bekou, *Regionalising ICC Implementing legislation: A Workable Solution for the Asia-Pacific Region?*, (Wellington: NZACL/ALCPP, 2006), available at http://www.upf.pf/IMG/pdf/rjpcrim06.pdf (accessed on 14 June 2014).

[22] P.M. Wald, 'To Establish Incredible Events by Credible Evidence: The Use of Affidavit Testimony in Yugoslavia War Crimes Tribunal Proceedings', *Harvard International Law Journal* 42 (2001): 535, 536.

[23] United Nations, *Treaty Series*, vol. 189, no. 2545.

It has been evident from many cases prosecuted at the ICTY, where it lacks the link to the cases of crimes been committed elsewhere in other countries. The ICTY had been, on many occasions, away and distant from the actual regions of crimes and very rarely have the personnel and staff of the tribunal come in contact with the region of crime. Had the tribunal been physically in touch with the local or regional justice system, the deliverance of justice and enforcement of international law would have been relevant. Same is the case with the ICC where it prosecutes cases referred from countries which are far away, while the prosecution and enforcement takes place in The Hague. This distance from the region of the alleged crimes has become a serious area of concern and has consequences in terms of judicial reconstruction and restorative justice. Furthermore, these international tribunals have had difficulties in training the domestic/national courts and their prosecutors for conducting fair trials and investigations, and many-a-times, they have been unsuccessful in properly guiding them to bring fair justice. This is mainly because of the physical distance of the regions of alleged crimes from the international tribunals.[24]

On the other hand, the regional courts have the capability of offering better and larger opportunities in terms of judicial reconstruction unlike the international tribunals, such as the ICTY, ICTR, and even the ICC. Furthermore, the semi-internationalized courts such as the SCSL and the Special Panel of East Timor have more advantage in enhancing the national justice system since they are in close proximity to the regional courts, which permits them to train the prosecutors and engage in the justice systems of those nations. Further, with the presence of these semi-internationalized courts along with the national courts, the regional courts would benefit by bringing on prosecutors and judges from those regions and train them in the enforcement and prosecution of international crimes at the regional level.[25]

<hr />

[24]   United Nations, *Treaty Series*, vol. 189, no. 2545.

[25]   United Nations Human Rights, 'Protocol to Prevent, Suppress and Punish Trafficking in Persons Especially Women and Children, supplementing the United Nations Convention against Transnational Organized Crime', Article 3.

The restorative justice is another area of concern since it has failed considerably due to the physical distance prevailing between the international courts and the actual region of alleged international crimes which are to be prosecuted to restore justice. The restorative justice aims '(1) to affirm and restore the dignity of those whose human rights have been violated; (2) to hold perpetrators accountable...; and (3) to create social conditions in which human rights will be respected.'[26]

The ICC, at The Hague, finds it difficult to conduct a prosecution and secure restorative justice while prosecuting cases of international crimes, and further, finds its scope very limited. This is due to the distance prevailing between the court and the evidence, witnesses, and the person guilty of committing the crime, which is parted by thousands of miles. One such instance can be cited from the *Kunarac* case at the ICTY—the first recorded case of rape as a crime against humanity.[27] The judgement ruled in this case had a huge benefit for the people of Foca, a small town of Southern Bosnia which witnessed this crime. Though around thirty-eight women were present in the rape camps sharing their stories and fate with ICTY, the people of this town could not personally be present to witness the proceedings and benefit from it. This is an example of the limitations of the justice system in ensuring restorative justice in a proper and efficient manner. There are many places which are devoid of technology and are isolated from this technological advancement, even in this century. This actually hampers the smooth process of restorative justice. Such isolated places are actually the regions where international crimes take place. The personal presence of the victim or the person convicted at the ICC

---

[26] Elizabeth Kiss, 'Moral Ambition within and beyond Political Constraints: Reflections on Restorative Justice', in *Truth v. Justice*, ed. Robert I. Rotberg and Dennis Thompson (Princeton University Press, 1999), 68, 79.

[27] ICTY, 'Kunarac et al. (IT-96-23 & 23/1)', Judgement of Trial Chamber II, available at http://www.icty.org/en/press/judgement-trial-chamber-ii-kunarac-kovac-and-vukovic-case (accessed on 30 May 2016); *Prosecutor v. Kunarac* et al., Case No.: IT-96-23-T and IT-96-23/1-T, Judgement, 22 February 2001, paragraph 434, available at http://www.icty.org/x/cases/kunarac/acjug/en/kun-aj020612e.pdf (accessed on 30 May 2016).

during the prosecution of cases of international crime is very crucial and also limited due to such isolation of regions and countries. Thus the enforcement of international criminal law at the regional level for conducting proceedings and prosecution provides a broader opportunity for the societies affected by international crimes. Such steps will further help these societies, from which they can benefit immensely.

Reduction of Political Manipulation

Establishing of national courts or enforcement mechanism at the national level has been mostly considered to run a risk of having political manipulation and affecting the judicial system by the governments of those nations. This political manipulation and interference by the national governments could weaken the legitimacy and effectiveness of the courts and further prevent the establishment of an international court. This would be prevalent mostly in a transitional society which faces frequent enforcement of international criminal law. An example of such an influence could be the Nuremberg Tribunal, which is often considered as a political institution. Hence, the regional courts would be a better alternative for effective enforcement of international criminal justice system. The reason behind this is that the regional courts would remain aloof from the nation's political system and the likelihood of political influence and manipulation from any specific or particular nation would be less. Thus, the regional courts would have greater legitimacy in the region where they are situated as well as in the international community. The reason behind this would be the presence of a group of state parties in a regional court, which would help in preventing the court from being influenced by the powerful nations.[28]

As mentioned, the influence and political manipulation of international and national courts at the cost of fair justice can be cited clearly from the efforts and attempts of establishing an internationalized criminal court in Cambodia for the trial of its senior leadership of the Khmer Rouge. It is clearly evident from the fact that the international

---

[28] United Nations, *Treaty Series*, vol. 189, no. 2545.

justice system in Cambodia has been captured by a political sub-group which deals all negotiations with the United Nations.

Presence of Sufficient Rich and Varied Judicial Resources

The close proximity between the regional courts, the affected community, and the reduced costs due to the establishment of these regional and national courts make this an ideal enforcement mechanism. But this needs to be counterbalanced by the advantages of international tribunals which provide availability of better judicial resources and the absence of political manipulation. In post-conflict situations, the national courts lack adequate judicial resources in prosecuting international crimes in an efficient manner. This is evident from prosecuting the suspects of genocide in Rwanda, which took place in 1994, in which more than 120,000 suspects were imprisoned. But there was limited number of resources, judges, lawyers, and other personnel, due to which the tribunal faced problems in prosecuting all the detained persons.[29]

Thus, setting up of regional courts could provide solutions to such problems of lack of resources faced by the national and international courts prosecuting international crimes. Regional courts would have the advantage of having judges with experience of the courtroom as well as training and knowledge of international law. For example, a regional court in Africa could have the advantage of getting judges and lawyers from South Africa, Nigeria, Ghana, and Ethiopia as well as from countries such as the Democratic Republic of Congo and Rwanda. Also, the administrative efficiency of the international criminal justice system can be maximized as the regional courts would have a wide range of resources across the region. There are, in fact, few nations which investigate and prosecute various international crimes at the regional level very efficiently, with an abundance of resources. Hence, the setting up of regional courts could actually minimize the expenses of administrative and judicial processes with the ability to prosecute international crimes with better resources of the region.

[29] United Nations, *Treaty Series*, vol. 189, no. 2545.

Amendment to the Rome Statute: Following from President al-Bashir's Case Study

The Rome Statute has created a lot of confusion in terms of repercussions of breach of the ICC by the member states and the immunity to indictment of the head of states if s/he is found to commit crimes which constitute crimes against humanity. Hence, there is a dire need to amend the Rome Statute.

Amendment of the Rome Statute is a comprehensive procedure. To amend the statute, it has to be proposed either by a member state, by the judges acting by an absolute majority, or by the prosecutor. These amendments, further, have to be adopted by a two-third majority during the vote of states or parties. The Assembly of State Parties will vote in the meeting on the day following the meeting for the proposal but it should take place at least three months after receiving the amendment. This Assembly of State Parties conducts a meeting once a year or whenever required by conducting special sessions. Thus, the Rome Statute has a jurisdiction which gives the ICC the power to indict a person referred to the prosecutor by the UN Security Council, but the arrest is permitted only with the help of member states or only if he travels to or is found to be in the member states.

The Rome Statute creates a great deal of confusion in indicting a head of state his/her immunity provisions under the statute and the consequences of breaches to the ICC's requests without much explanation. Hence, to clear the confusion and vagueness of the Rome Statute, there is a dire need of amendment in the statute. This confusion and weakness of the ICC has been evident in President al-Bashir's indictment by the ICC.[30]

---

[30]   G.P. Barnes, 'The International Criminal Court's Ineffective Enforcement Mechanisms: The Indictment of President Omar Al Bashir', *Fordham International Law Journal* 34, no. 6 (2011) available at http://ir.lawnet.fordham.edu/cgi/viewcontent.cgi?article=2313&context=ilj (accessed 30 May 2016).

President al-Bashir's Indictment and Reaction of the African Union

The indictment of the president faced a lot of criticism by the African Union and also globally by China and many other countries. This criticism was a result of the fear among the African Union members that there would be unrest in the region, especially in the newly formed state of Southern Sudan. This was because of the uncertainty prevailing in Sudan with regard to peace and security. A referendum to form a new state in the southern part of Sudan, which excludes Darfur, was discussed from 9 to 15 January 2011. Following this indictment, there were also concerns with regard to the country's progress and sovereignty and the African Union referred to this as an attack and harassment of Africa. But many experts across the world believe that indictment of a head of a state was a correct step by the ICC and that no state or individual is immune to indictment when it comes to serious crimes such as those against humanity. Furthermore, the African Union was not at all convinced with the ICC that it could manage a Darfur-like situation. This was because of the fact that the ICC has some limitations of conducting extensive and quick prosecution. Generally, it has been observed that the ICC prosecutes cases in a sluggish manner, and also prosecutes individuals separately with international implications. Hence, the ICC may not prosecute all individuals responsible for crimes against humanity while it may prosecute those who were not guilty.[31]

Considering all pros and cons, the African Union Peace and Security Council sent a request to the UN Security Council on 21 July 2008 to postpone the president's prosecution by twelve months, but the UN Security Council did not agree and the prosecution was carried on the then ICC Prosecutor Moreno-Ocampo. Thus, finally, the African Union decided and sent directions to its member states not to comply with ICC's request to arrest President al-Bashir.

---

[31] Barnes, 'The International Criminal Court's Ineffective Enforcement Mechanisms'.

Suggested Probable Solutions to Solve the Ambiguity of the Rome Statute

To avoid the ambiguity and to bring out a clear picture of the Rome Statute and the duty and liability, first of all Article 98 needs to be amended. Based on this Article 98 only, the African Union is excusing itself and is not complying with the ICC's decision and request. The immunity and excuses created by Article 98 need to be revised and reframed to prevent the member states from refusing and abstaining from non-cooperation with the ICC. Article 98 of the Rome Statute should be amended in such a manner that no member state has the option of refusing the ICC's decision or not cooperating with the ICC. Since Article 98(2) has created another confusion as to whom the member states should cooperate with if these states are a member of the ICC, party to the Rome Statute, and also a member of another organization, this amendment would clarify the hierarchy of the international obligations of that country.[32]

Furthermore, the Rome Statute needs to clarify the repercussions and consequences for the breach of ICC's decision and their obligations. The ICC should introduce incentives for the member states for their obligations under the Rome Statute. There could be three probable repercussions for the breach of the Rome Statute. These could be expulsion, suspension, and sanctions of the UN Security Council. For the breaches, the ICC could suspend a member state for a period of time, may be six months or a year, and see if they do not violate the Rome Statute, in which case their membership could be retained. The other probable option is expulsion of a member state but it runs a risk of losing members and jurisdiction, which will make ICC less powerful. Another repercussion for breaches is the sanction of the UN Security Council. Since it is already present in the statute, there is no need for ratification of amendment.[33]

---

[32] International Court of Justice, *Charter of the United Nations*, Article 52, para 1.

[33] International Court of Justice, *Charter of the United Nations*, Article 52, para 1.

United Nations to Introduce Convention on Prevention of Crimes against Humanity

There are many instances of crimes against humanity being committed across the world, which have affected millions of people. There are also millions of trafficked persons and smuggled migrants around the world at any given time, which also account to crimes against humanity. Trafficking in persons and smuggling of migrants are global problems and a serious threat to human dignity.

Human trafficking is an international transnational organized crime which has been given due consideration and importance in a number of international instruments so as to combat it and protect human rights and humanity. The recognition of human trafficking as a dreadful and heinous crime and as a violation of human rights has become a great area of concern all over the world. It has become the biggest threat and a great challenge for all the states all over the world. Following are some of the issues which are very conflicting and which also create confusion among the international convention and treaties and the states:

- identification of the crime including abuses covered under the treaties and conventions such as slavery, servitude, trafficking, discrimination, violence, rape, forced recruitment into armed forces, forced or exploitative labour, unlawful adoption, inheritance of women, debt bondage, forced marriage, crimes against humanity;
- span of trafficking across the world (trafficking across and within the countries);
- identification of the perpetrators which include traffickers, brothel owners, organized criminal syndicates, and individuals; and
- identification of victims such as women, children, men.

Trafficking in human beings is a crime against humanity. We know that crime against humanity is one of the three categories of crimes elaborated in the Nuremberg Charter. However, unlike genocide and war crimes, they were never set out in a comprehensive international convention. The need of the hour is to set out a Convention on Protection of Crimes against Humanity.

Setting up Article 7 of the Rome Statute of the ICC into motion and trying cases of human trafficking as a crime against humanity may also be a strong step towards curbing this menace.

It is high time that the world community takes every step to bring the perpetrators of human trafficking to justice and thereby eradicate this heinous crime against humanity from the world.

***

Desmond Tutu,[34] in his words, states that restorative justice requires 'not so much to punish as to redress or restore a balance that has been knocked askew. The justice we hope for is restorative of the dignity of the people.' Restorative justice, for attaining its goals, thus requires a close association between the court or the judiciary and the society which is affected by international crimes. This statement only further overemphasizes the need of regionalizing of international criminal justice, which is probably a very important measure for effective enforcement of international criminal law and the criminal justice system.

The entire objective of the ICC will collapse if it cannot enforce its judgement. This chapter has discussed the two main pillars of the ICC, laying stress on the enforcement pillar without which the entire exercise of setting a permanent international court in The Hague would be reduced to dust. The principally important enforcement mechanism of the ICC is to regionalize the international criminal law and the international criminal justice system as a whole, and this chapter has described the ways in which it can be done.

Further, regionalization of the enforcement mechanism of the international criminal law has been analysed. The chapter then goes on to highlight the confusion created by the consequences and repercussions of the Rome Statute while enforcing and prosecuting international crimes. It cites the example of the indictment of President al-Bashir of Sudan and suggests amendment measures to the Rome Statute in order

<hr>

[34] Desmond Tutu is a South African social rights activist and retired Anglican Bishop.

to avoid the confusion in its enforcement system. The chapter also highlights the possible solutions to the confusion of the Rome Statute.

Furthermore, the chapter concludes with the recommendation of setting up a new convention to fight against and prosecute cases of crimes against humanity, since the present conventions of the United Nations to fight crimes against humanity, including human trafficking, have proved symbolic—they have been merely representations on paper and nothing much has been done towards fighting human trafficking and considering it as a crime against humanity.

7 Conclusion and Suggestions

The judicial deliberations that have been the main subject of this book are not only a textbook example of the challenges involved in the interpretation of the Rome Statute, but the outcome is of paramount importance for the future development of international law in general and the law on crimes against humanity in particular. Anecdotal evidence has proved that trafficking in human beings has affected more victims than the Jewish Holocaust, Rwanda Genocide, the wars in Iraq, the Korean War, the Vietnam War, and both the world wars combined.[1] This data is indeed alarming. To recognize the promise of the Rome Statute and to effectively prosecute grave cases of trafficking in human beings, the court must

---

[1] Scaruffi Pierro, 'Wars and Casualties of the 20th and 21st Centuries', available at http://www.scaruffi.com/politics/massacre.html (accessed on 20 June 2014).

look outside the situations to which international law has historically been applied; otherwise, the Rome Statute will prove only symbolic, at best. The book has dealt with the need for a specialized convention on prevention of crimes against humanity, just like the genocide and war crimes convention. It has also elaborated on the need to amend various articles of the Rome Statute in order to remove ambiguity.

The book began with an introduction on human trafficking, defining ways to combat it with the help of Article 7 of the Rome Statute of the ICC. Further, the methodology and scope of the book have been described.

The next chapter focused on the extent of the human trafficking trade within and across the borders of the countries and the role played by international law and other related laws. Further, a distinction was drawn between human trafficking and human smuggling, thus highlighting the scope of sexual slavery in human trafficking. The chapter portrayed human trafficking as an organized crime, and delved into the nature of the recruitment, scams, sale, trade, and exploitation of the victims. The impact of this form of modern day slavery has been seen in terms of social, economic, and political aspects of the countries affected.

Thus, significantly, the states have an obligation under international human rights law, international labour law, and international criminal law to prevent this hideous act. The next chapter has dealt with these legal conventions, protocols, and treaties adopted and enforced by the United Nations, while studying the region-wise outlook towards them. The chapter has also highlighted the gender perspective in human trafficking and the role of women in the sexual exploitation of other women, as well as children.

In view of the protocols described in the previous chapter, the book then drew a comparative study of the United Nations Trafficking Protocol and the CoE Trafficking Convention. It laid emphasis on a strong legal response to fight human trafficking at an international level and highlighted the need for full compliance with it by all the nations. It emphasized the significance of human rights law in combating trafficking and described the aspects of human rights in the international machinery and legal instruments in preventing and combating human trafficking and exploitation. The chapter also gave an overview of the various rights provided to the trafficked victims, as stated in Article 6 of the Trafficking in Persons Protocol, which is followed by a portrayal of the victim-centred approach known as the three-P strategy of the Palermo protocol, and a brief explanation of the three-R approach.

Then, the nature and characterization of crime against humanity was explored, highlighting the inclusion of human trafficking in various charters, statutes, and conventions. The chapter then gives a detailed description of crimes against humanity as stated in Article 7 of the Rome Statute of ICC. The major charters and statutes that are adopted are studied with the aim of defining crimes against humanity, thus justifying the nature of conduct of acts or crime with reference to the specific clauses adopted by these charters to constitute such crimes as crimes against humanity and violation of human rights. The chapter discussed the problems faced by the countries across the globe due to the increasing severity of human trafficking and the crimes against humanity. In a nuanced study of the problems faced by the countries, non-cooperation and distrust has been seen in the countries supporting protocols against trafficking. In analysing the extent of the crime, the chapter has also highlighted the close relation between the major three transnational organized crimes, namely drugs trafficking, arms trafficking, and human trafficking.

This is followed by an analysis of the feasibility of the prosecution of cases of crimes against humanity by the ICC, application of the ICC, and its challenges and limitations. The chapter suggests the possible solutions to overcome these challenges and limitations. Elucidating with the case study on the indictment of the sitting head of Sudan, President Omar al-Bashir by the ICC, the chapter highlights the inconsistency of the ICC and the African Union Charter. It is followed by a discussion on the reaction of the neighbouring states of Chad and Kenya and the weaknesses found in the Rome Statute while indicting the president.

Another area that has been looked into in this book is the enforcement mechanism of the ICC and the need and necessity for it to be regionalized. The next chapter gives a description of the means of regionalization, describes the probable means, and analyses the advantages of such an enforcement. It provides a discussion on the amendment of the Rome Statute following the indictment of President al-Bashir, studying the reaction of the African Union and its member states. It also suggests probable solutions to solve the ambiguity present in the Rome Statute which surfaced during the indictment. This chapter concludes with a recommendation of introducing a Convention on Prevention of Crimes against Humanity so as to combat such international crimes.

After a comprehensive study of human trafficking and the role and importance of the Rome Statute in combating this crime against humanity, the book recommends three possible solutions.

- The ICC should prosecute cases of human trafficking as a crime against humanity by setting Article 7 of the Rome Statute in motion and trying cases of trafficking, which may be a strong step towards curbing this menace.
- There should be a regionalization of the enforcement mechanism of the ICC so as to prosecute and eradicate international crimes such as war crimes, genocide, and other crimes against humanity.
- The United Nations should introduce a special convention on crimes against humanity like it has done for genocide and war crimes; the convention should be comprehensive enough to deal with crimes against humanity, including human trafficking, in a more effective manner.

With these recommendations, the book also provides scope for further research on the enforcement mechanism of the ICC for eradicating crimes against humanity. It is now high time that the international community moves forward towards bringing the perpetrators of human trafficking to justice and thereby eradicating this heinous crime. This book also provides scope of further research on the enforcement mechanism of the ICC itself for eradicating crimes against humanity.

Appendices

Appendix I Elements of Crime: Article 7

Elements of Crime

General introduction

1. Pursuant to article 9, the following Elements of Crimes shall assist the Court in the interpretation and application of articles 6, 7 and 8, consistent with the Statute. The provisions of the Statute, including article 21 and the general principles set out in Part 3, are applicable to the Elements of Crimes.

2. As stated in article 30, unless otherwise provided, a person shall be criminally responsible and liable for punishment for a crime within the jurisdiction of the Court only if the material elements are committed with intent and knowledge. Where no reference is made in the Elements of Crimes to a mental element for any particular conduct, consequence or circumstance listed, it is understood that the relevant mental element, i.e., intent, knowledge or both, set out in article 30 applies. Exceptions to the article

30 standard, based on the Statute, including applicable law under its relevant provisions, are indicated below.

3. Existence of intent and knowledge can be inferred from relevant facts and circumstances.

4. With respect to mental elements associated with elements involving value judgement, such as those using the terms 'inhumane' or 'severe', it is not necessary that the perpetrator personally completed a particular value judgement, unless otherwise indicated.

5. Grounds for excluding criminal responsibility or the absence thereof are generally not specified in the elements of crimes listed under each crime.

6. The requirement of 'unlawfulness' found in the Statute or in other parts of international law, in particular international humanitarian law, is generally not specified in the elements of crimes.

7. The elements of crimes are generally structured in accordance with the following principles:

   (a) As the elements of crimes focus on the conduct, consequences and circumstances associated with each crime, they are generally listed in that order;

   (b) When required, a particular mental element is listed after the affected conduct, consequence or circumstance;

   (c) Contextual circumstances are listed last.

8. As used in the Elements of Crimes, the term 'perpetrator' is neutral as to guilt or innocence. The elements, including the appropriate mental elements, apply, *mutatis mutandis*, to all those whose criminal responsibility may fall under articles 25 and 28 of the Statute.

9. A particular conduct may constitute one or more crimes.

10. The use of short titles for the crimes has no legal effect.

Article 7: Crimes against humanity

Introduction

1. Since article 7 pertains to international criminal law, its provisions, consistent with article 22, must be strictly construed, taking into

account that crimes against humanity as defined in article 7 are among the most serious crimes of concern to the international community as a whole, warrant and entail individual criminal responsibility, and require conduct which is impermissible under generally applicable international law, as recognized by the principal legal systems of the world.

2. The last two elements for each crime against humanity describe the context in which the conduct must take place. These elements clarify the requisite participation in and knowledge of a widespread or systematic attack against a civilian population. However, the last element should not be interpreted as requiring proof that the perpetrator had knowledge of all characteristics of the attack or the precise details of the plan or policy of the State or organization. In the case of an emerging widespread or systematic attack against a civilian population, the intent clause of the last element indicates that this mental element is satisfied if the perpetrator intended to further such an attack.

3. 'Attack directed against a civilian population' in these context elements is understood to mean a course of conduct involving the multiple commission of acts referred to in article 7, paragraph 1, of the Statute against any civilian population, pursuant to or in furtherance of a State or organizational policy to commit such attack. The acts need not constitute a military attack. It is understood that 'policy to commit such attack' requires that the State or organization actively promote or encourage such an attack against a civilian population.

Article 7(1)(a): Crime against humanity of murder

Elements

1. The perpetrator killed one or more persons.
2. The conduct was committed as part of a widespread or systematic attack directed against a civilian population.
3. The perpetrator knew that the conduct was part of or intended the conduct to be part of a widespread or systematic attack against a civilian population.

4. A policy which has a civilian population as the object of the attack would be implemented by State or organizational action. Such a policy may, in exceptional circumstances, be implemented by a deliberate failure to take action, which is consciously aimed at encouraging such attack. The existence of such a policy cannot be inferred solely from the absence of governmental or organizational action.
5. The term 'killed' is interchangeable with the term 'caused death'. This footnote applies to all elements which use either of these concepts.

Article 7(1)(b): Crime against humanity of extermination

Elements

1. The perpetrator killed one or more persons, including by inflicting conditions of life calculated to bring about the destruction of part of a population.
2. The conduct constituted, or took place as part of, a mass killing of members of a civilian population.
3. The conduct was committed as part of a widespread or systematic attack directed against a civilian population.
4. The perpetrator knew that the conduct was part of or intended the conduct to be part of a widespread or systematic attack directed against a civilian population.

Article 7(1)(c): Crime against humanity of enslavement

Elements

1. The perpetrator exercised any or all of the powers attaching to the right of ownership over one or more persons, such as by purchasing, selling, lending or bartering such a person or persons, or by imposing on them a similar deprivation of liberty.
2. The conduct was committed as part of a widespread or systematic attack directed against a civilian population.
3. The perpetrator knew that the conduct was part of or intended the conduct to be part of a widespread or systematic attack directed against a civilian population.

4. The conduct could be committed by different methods of killing, either directly or indirectly.
5. The infliction of such conditions could include the deprivation of access to food and medicine.
6. The term 'as part of' would include the initial conduct in a mass killing.
7. It is understood that such deprivation of liberty may, in some circumstances, include exacting forced labour or otherwise reducing a person to a servile status as defined in the Supplementary Convention on the Abolition of Slavery, the Slave Trade, and Institutions and Practices Similar to Slavery of 1956. It is also understood that the conduct described in this element includes trafficking in persons, in particular women and children.

Article 7(1)(d): Crime against humanity of deportation or forcible transfer of population

Elements

1. The perpetrator deported or forcibly transferred, without grounds permitted under international law, one or more persons to another State or location, by expulsion or other coercive acts.
2. Such person or persons were lawfully present in the area from which they were so deported or transferred.
3. The perpetrator was aware of the factual circumstances that established the lawfulness of such presence.
4. The conduct was committed as part of a widespread or systematic attack directed against a civilian population.
5. The perpetrator knew that the conduct was part of or intended the conduct to be part of a widespread or systematic attack directed against a civilian population.

Article 7(1)(e): Crime against humanity of imprisonment or other severe deprivation of physical liberty

Elements

1. The perpetrator imprisoned one or more persons or otherwise severely deprived one or more persons of physical liberty.

2. The gravity of the conduct was such that it was in violation of fundamental rules of international law.
3. The perpetrator was aware of the factual circumstances that established the gravity of the conduct.
4. The conduct was committed as part of a widespread or systematic attack directed against a civilian population.
5. The perpetrator knew that the conduct was part of or intended the conduct to be part of a widespread or systematic attack directed against a civilian population.

Article 7(1)(f): Crime against humanity of torture

Elements

1. The perpetrator inflicted severe physical or mental pain or suffering upon one or more persons.
2. Such person or persons were in the custody or under the control of the perpetrator.
3. Such pain or suffering did not arise only from, and was not inherent in or incidental to, lawful sanctions.
4. The conduct was committed as part of a widespread or systematic attack directed against a civilian population.
5. The perpetrator knew that the conduct was part of or intended the conduct to be part of a widespread or systematic attack directed against a civilian population.

Article 7(1)(g)-1: Crime against humanity of rape

Elements

1. The perpetrator invaded the body of a person by conduct resulting in penetration, however slight, of any part of the body of the victim or of the perpetrator with a sexual organ, or of the anal or genital opening of the victim with any object or any other part of the body.
2. The invasion was committed by force, or by threat of force or coercion, such as that caused by fear of violence, duress, detention, psychological oppression or abuse of power, against such person or

another person, or by taking advantage of a coercive environment, or the invasion was committed against a person incapable of giving genuine consent.

3. The conduct was committed as part of a widespread or systematic attack directed against a civilian population.
4. The perpetrator knew that the conduct was part of or intended the conduct to be part of a widespread or systematic attack directed against a civilian population.

Article 7(1)(g)-2: Crime against humanity of sexual slavery

Elements

1. The perpetrator exercised any or all of the powers attaching to the right of ownership over one or more persons, such as by purchasing, selling, lending or bartering such a person or persons, or by imposing on them a similar deprivation of liberty.
2. The perpetrator caused such person or persons to engage in one or more acts of a sexual nature.
3. The conduct was committed as part of a widespread or systematic attack directed against a civilian population.
4. The perpetrator knew that the conduct was part of or intended the conduct to be part of a widespread or systematic attack directed against a civilian population.

Article 7(1)(g)-3: Crime against humanity of enforced prostitution

Elements

1. The perpetrator caused one or more persons to engage in one or more acts of a sexual nature by force, or by threat of force or coercion, such as that caused by fear of violence, duress, detention, psychological oppression or abuse of power, against such person or persons or another person, or by taking advantage of a coercive environment or such person's or persons' incapacity to give genuine consent.

2. The perpetrator or another person obtained or expected to obtain pecuniary or other advantage in exchange for or in connection with the acts of a sexual nature.
3. The conduct was committed as part of a widespread or systematic attack directed against a civilian population.
4. The perpetrator knew that the conduct was part of or intended the conduct to be part of a widespread or systematic attack directed against a civilian population.

Article 7(1)(g)-4: Crime against humanity of forced pregnancy

Elements

1. The perpetrator confined one or more women forcibly made pregnant, with the intent of affecting the ethnic composition of any population or carrying out other grave violations of international law.
2. The conduct was committed as part of a widespread or systematic attack directed against a civilian population.
3. The perpetrator knew that the conduct was part of or intended the conduct to be part of a widespread or systematic attack directed against a civilian population.

Article 7(1)(g)-5: Crime against humanity of enforced sterilization

Elements

1. The perpetrator deprived one or more persons of biological reproductive capacity.
2. The conduct was neither justified by the medical or hospital treatment of the person or persons concerned nor carried out with their genuine consent.
3. The conduct was committed as part of a widespread or systematic attack directed against a civilian population.

4. The perpetrator knew that the conduct was part of or intended the conduct to be part of a widespread or systematic attack directed against a civilian population.

Article 7(1)(g)-6: Crime against humanity of sexual violence

Elements

1. The perpetrator committed an act of a sexual nature against one or more persons or caused such person or persons to engage in an act of a sexual nature by force, or by threat of force or coercion, such as that caused by fear of violence, duress, detention, psychological oppression or abuse of power, against such person or persons or another person, or by taking advantage of a coercive environment or such person's or persons' incapacity to give genuine consent.
2. Such conduct was of a gravity comparable to the other offences in article 7, paragraph 1 (g), of the Statute.
3. The perpetrator was aware of the factual circumstances that established the gravity of the conduct.
4. The conduct was committed as part of a widespread or systematic attack directed against a civilian population.
5. The perpetrator knew that the conduct was part of or intended the conduct to be part of a widespread or systematic attack directed against a civilian population.

Article 7(1)(h): Crime against humanity of persecution

Elements

1. The perpetrator severely deprived, contrary to international law, one or more persons of fundamental rights.
2. The perpetrator targeted such person or persons by reason of the identity of a group or collectivity or targeted the group or collectivity as such.
3. Such targeting was based on political, racial, national, ethnic, cultural, religious, gender as defined in article 7, paragraph 3, of the

Statute, or other grounds that are universally recognized as impermissible under international law.

4. The conduct was committed in connection with any act referred to in article 7, paragraph 1, of the Statute or any crime within the jurisdiction of the Court.

5. The conduct was committed as part of a widespread or systematic attack directed against a civilian population.

6. The perpetrator knew that the conduct was part of or intended the conduct to be part of a widespread or systematic attack directed against a civilian population.

Article 7(1)(i): Crime against humanity of enforced disappearance of persons

Elements

1. The perpetrator:
   (a) Arrested, detained, or abducted one or more persons; or
   (b) Refused to acknowledge the arrest, detention or abduction, or to give information on the fate or whereabouts of such person or persons.

2. (a) Such arrest, detention or abduction was followed or accompanied by a refusal to acknowledge that deprivation of freedom or to give information on the fate or whereabouts of such person or persons; or
   (b) Such refusal was preceded or accompanied by that deprivation of freedom.

3. The perpetrator was aware that:
   (a) Such arrest, detention or abduction would be followed in the ordinary course of events by a refusal to acknowledge that deprivation of freedom or to give information on the fate or whereabouts of such person or persons; or
   (b) Such refusal was preceded or accompanied by that deprivation of freedom.

4. Such arrest, detention or abduction was carried out by, or with the authorization, support or acquiescence of, a State or a political organization.

5. Such refusal to acknowledge that deprivation of freedom or to give information on the fate or whereabouts of such person or persons was carried out by, or with the authorization or support of, such State or political organization.
6. The perpetrator intended to remove such person or persons from the protection of the law for a prolonged period of time.
7. The conduct was committed as part of a widespread or systematic attack directed against a civilian population.
8. The perpetrator knew that the conduct was part of or intended the conduct to be part of a widespread or systematic attack directed against a civilian population.

Article 7(1)(j): Crime against humanity of apartheid

Elements

1. The perpetrator committed an inhumane act against one or more persons.
2. Such act was an act referred to in article 7, paragraph 1, of the Statute, or was an act of a character similar to any of those acts.
3. The perpetrator was aware of the factual circumstances that established the character of the act.
4. The conduct was committed in the context of an institutionalized regime of systematic oppression and domination by one racial group over any other racial group or groups.
5. The perpetrator intended to maintain such regime by that conduct.
6. The conduct was committed as part of a widespread or systematic attack directed against a civilian population.
7. The perpetrator knew that the conduct was part of or intended the conduct to be part of a widespread or systematic attack directed against a civilian population.

Article 7(1)(k): Crime against humanity of other inhumane acts

Elements

1. The perpetrator inflicted great suffering, or serious injury to body or to mental or physical health, by means of an inhumane act.

2. Such act was of a character similar to any other act referred to in article 7, paragraph 1, of the Statute.
3. The perpetrator was aware of the factual circumstances that established the character of the act.
4. The conduct was committed as part of a widespread or systematic attack directed against a civilian population.
5. The perpetrator knew that the conduct was part of or intended the conduct to be part of a widespread or systematic attack directed against a civilian population.

Appendix II Article 7 of the Rome Statute of the International Criminal Court

Preamble

The States Parties to this Statute,

Conscious that all peoples are united by common bonds, their cultures pieced together in a shared heritage, and concerned that this delicate mosaic may be shattered at any time,

Mindful that during this century millions of children, women and men have been victims of unimaginable atrocities that deeply shock the conscience of humanity,

Recognizing that such grave crimes threaten the peace, security and well-being of the world,

Affirming that the most serious crimes of concern to the international community as a whole must not go unpunished and that their effective prosecution must be ensured by taking measures at the national level and by enhancing international cooperation,

Determined to put an end to impunity for the perpetrators of these crimes and thus to contribute to the prevention of such crimes,

Recalling that it is the duty of every State to exercise its criminal jurisdiction over those responsible for international crimes,

Reaffirming the Purposes and Principles of the Charter of the United Nations, and in particular that all States shall refrain from the threat or use of force against the territorial integrity or political independence of any State, or in any other manner inconsistent with the Purposes of the United Nations,

Emphasizing in this connection that nothing in this Statute shall be taken as authorising any State Party to intervene in an armed conflict or in the internal affairs of any State,

Determined to these ends and for the sake of present and future generations, to establish an independent permanent International Criminal Court in relationship with the United Nations system, with jurisdiction over the most serious crimes of concern to the international community as a whole,

Emphasizing that the International Criminal Court established under this Statute shall be complementary to national criminal jurisdictions,

Resolved to guarantee lasting respect for and the enforcement of international justice,

Have agreed as follows:

...

Part II: Jurisdiction, admissibility and applicable law

Article 7: Crimes against humanity

1. For the purpose of this Statute, 'crime against humanity' means any of the following acts when committed as part of a widespread or systematic attack directed against any civilian population, with knowledge of the attack:

(a) Murder;

(b) Extermination;

(c) Enslavement;

(d) Deportation or forcible transfer of population;

(e) Imprisonment or other severe deprivation of physical liberty in violation of fundamental rules of international law;

(f) Torture;

(g) Rape, sexual slavery, enforced prostitution, forced pregnancy, enforced sterilisation, or any other form of sexual violence of comparable gravity;

(h) Persecution against any identifiable group or collectivity on political, racial, national, ethnic, cultural, religious, gender as defined in paragraph 3, or other grounds that are universally recognized as impermissible under international law, in connection with any act referred to in this paragraph or any crime within the jurisdiction of the Court;

(i) Enforced disappearance of persons;

(j) The crime of apartheid;

(k) Other inhumane acts of a similar character intentionally causing great suffering, or serious injury to body or to mental or physical health.

2. For the purpose of paragraph 1:

(a) 'Attack directed against any civilian population' means a course of conduct involving the multiple commission of acts referred to in paragraph 1 against any civilian population, pursuant to or in furtherance of a State or organisational policy to commit such attack;

(b) 'Extermination' includes the intentional infliction of conditions of life, *inter alia* the deprivation of access to food and medicine, calculated to bring about the destruction of part of a population;

(c) 'Enslavement' means the exercise of any or all of the powers attaching to the right of ownership over a person and includes the exercise of such power in the course of trafficking in persons, in particular women and children;

(d) 'Deportation or forcible transfer of population' means forced displacement of the persons concerned by expulsion or other coercive acts from the area in which they are lawfully present, without grounds permitted under international law;

(e) 'Torture' means the intentional infliction of severe pain or suffering, whether physical or mental, upon a person in the custody or under the control of the accused; except that torture shall not include pain or suffering arising only from, inherent in or incidental to, lawful sanctions;

(f) 'Forced pregnancy' means the unlawful confinement of a woman forcibly made pregnant, with the intent of affecting the ethnic composition of any population or carrying out other grave violations of international law. This definition shall not in any way be interpreted as affecting national laws relating to pregnancy;

(g) 'Persecution' means the intentional and severe deprivation of fundamental rights contrary to international law by reason of the identity of the group or collectivity;

(h) 'The crime of apartheid' means inhumane acts of a character similar to those referred to in paragraph 1, committed in the context of an institutionalized regime of systematic oppression and domination by one racial group over any other racial group or groups and committed with the intention of maintaining that regime;

(i) 'Enforced disappearance of persons' means the arrest, detention or abduction of persons by, or with the authorization, support or acquiescence of, a State or a political organisation, followed by a refusal to acknowledge that deprivation of freedom or to give information on the fate or whereabouts of those persons, with the intention of removing them from the protection of the law for a prolonged period of time.

3. For the purpose of this Statute, it is understood that the term 'gender' refers to the two sexes, male and female, within the context of society. The term 'gender' does not indicate any meaning different from the above.

States Parties to the Rome Statute of the ICC[1]

124 States Parties, 32 Signatories, 42 Non-Signatories (195) as of 4 March 2016

States Parties (124)

Africa (32)

Country	Date of Ratification/Accession
Benin	22 January 2002
Botswana	8 September 2000
Burkina Faso	16 April 2004
Burundi	21 September 2004
Centr. African Rep.	3 October 2001
Cape Verde	10 October 2011
Chad	1 November 2006
Comoros	18 August 2006
Congo (Brazzaville)	3 May 2004
Dem. Rep. of Congo	11 April 2002
Djibouti	5 November 2002
Gabon	20 September 2000
Gambia	28 June 2002
Ghana	20 December 1999
Guinea	14 July 2003
Kenya	15 March 2005
Lesotho	6 September 2000
Liberia	22 September 2004
Madagascar	14 March 2008
Malawi	19 September 2002
Mali	16 August 2000
Mauritius	5 March 2002
Namibia	25 June 2002
Niger	11 April 2002

---

[1] *Ratification of the Rome Statute*, available at http://www.iccnow.org/documents/signatory_chart_Dec_2012_EN.pdf (accessed on 5 January 2012).

Nigeria	27 September 2001
Senegal	2 February 1999
Seychelles	10 August 2010
Sierra Leone	15 September 2000
South Africa	27 November 2000
Tanzania	20 August 2002
Uganda	14 June 2002
Zambia	13 November 2002

Americas (28)

Country	Date of Ratification/Accession
Antigua & Barbuda	18 June 2001
Argentina	8 February 2001
Barbados	10 December 2002
Belize	5 April 2000
Bolivia	27 June 2002
Brazil	20 June 2002
Canada	7 July 2000
Chile	29 June 2009
Colombia	5 August 2002
Costa Rica	7 June 2001
Dominica	12 February 2001
Dominican Republic	12 May 2005
Ecuador	5 February 2002
El Salvador	3 March 2016
Grenada	19 May 2011
Guatemala	2 April 2012
Guyana	24 September 2004
Honduras	1 July 2002
Mexico	28 October 2005
Panama	21 March 2002
Paraguay	14 May 2001
Peru	10 November 2001
St. Kitts & Nevis	22 August 2006
St. Lucia	18 August 2010
St. Vincent & Grenadines	3 December 2002
Suriname	15 July 2008
Trinidad & Tobago	6 April 1999
Uruguay	28 June 2002
Venezuela	7 June 2000

Asia & Pacific (17)

Country	Date of Ratification/Accession
Afghanistan	10 February 2003
Australia	1 July 2002
Bangladesh	23 March 2010
Cambodia	11 April 2002
Cook Islands	18 July 2008
Fiji	29 November 1999
Japan	17 July 2007
Maldives	21 September 2011
Marshall Islands	7 December 2000
Mongolia	11 April 2002
Nauru	12 November 2001
New Zealand	7 September 2000
The Philippines	30 August 2011
Rep. of Korea	13 November 2002
Samoa	16 September 2002
Timor Leste	6 September 2002
Vanuatu	1 February 2012

Europe (42)

Country	Date of Ratification/Accession
Albania	31 January 2003
Andorra	30 April 2001
Austria	28 December 2000
Belgium	28 June 2000
Bosnia-Herzegovina	11 April 2002
Bulgaria	11 April 2002
Croatia	21 May 2001
Cyprus	7 March 2002
Czech Republic	21 July 2009
Denmark	21 June 2001
Estonia	30 January 2002
Finland	29 December 2000
France	9 June 2000
Germany	11 December 2000
Georgia	5 September 2003
Greece	15 May 2002

Hungary	30 November 2001
Iceland	25 May 2000
Ireland	11 April 2002
Italy	26 July 1999
Latvia	28 June 2002
Liechtenstein	2 October 2001
Lithuania	12 May 2003
Luxembourg	8 September 2000
Macedonia, FYR	6 March 2002
Malta	29 November 2002
Montenegro	23 October 2006
The Netherlands	17 July 2001
Norway	16 February 2000
Poland	12 November 2001
Portugal	5 February 2002
Romania	11 April 2002
Rep. of Moldova	12 October 2010
San Marino	13 May 1999
Serbia	6 September 2001
Slovakia	11 April 2002
Slovenia	31 December 2001
Spain	24 October 2000
Sweden	28 June 2001
Switzerland	12 October 2001
Tajikistan	5 May 2000
United Kingdom	4 October 2001

Middle East and North Africa (1)

Country	Date of Ratification/Accession
Jordan	11 April 2002
Tunisia	24 June 2011

Signatories (32)

Africa (9)

Country	Date of Signature
Angola	7 October 1998
Cameroon	17 July 1998.

Eritrea	7 October 1998
Guinea-Bissau	12 September 2000
Cote d'Ivoire	30 November 1998
Mozambique	28 December 2000
Sao Tome & Principe	28 December 2000
Sudan	8 September 2000
Zimbabwe	17 July 1998

Americas (4)

Country	Date of Signature
Bahamas	29 December 2000
Haiti	26 February 1999
Jamaica	8 September 2000
United States	31 December 2000

Asia & Pacific (2)

Country	Date of Signature
Thailand	2 October 2000
Solomon Islands	3 December 1998

Europe (6)

Country	Date of Signature
Armenia	1 October 1999
Kyrgyzstan	8 December 1998
Kingdom of Monaco	18 July 1998
Russian Federation	13 September 2000
Ukraine	20 January 2000
Uzbekistan	29 December 2000

Middle East and North Africa (11)

Country	Date of Signature
Algeria	28 December 2000
Bahrain	11 December 2000
Egypt	26 December 2000
Iran (Islamic Republic of)	31 December 2000
Israel	31 December 2000
Palestine	1 April 2015

Kuwait	8 September 2000
Morocco	8 September 2000
Oman	20 December 2000
Syria	29 November 2000
United Arab Emirates	27 November 2000
Yemen	28 December 2000

Non-Signatories (44)

Africa

Equatorial Guinea
Ethiopia
Mauritania
Rwanda
Somalia
Swaziland
Togo

Americas (4)

Cuba
El Salvador
Nicaragua

Asia & Pacific (22)

Bhutan
Brunei Darussalam
China
India
Indonesia
Kiribati
Korea, Democratic People's Rep. (North
Korea)
Laos People's Democratic Republic
Malaysia
Micronesia, Federal States of
Myanmar (Burma)
Nepal

Niue
Pakistan
Palau
Papua New Guinea
Singapore
Sri Lanka
Tonga
Tuvalu
Vietnam

Europe (6)

Azerbaijan
Belarus
Holy See
Kazakhstan
Turkmenistan
Turkey

Middle East and North Africa (5)

Iraq
Lebanon
Libya
Qatar
Saudi Arabia

Appendix III   Protocol to Prevent, Suppress and Punish Trafficking in Persons, Especially Women and Children, Supplementing the United Nations Convention against Transnational Organized Crime

Preamble

The States Parties to this Protocol,

Declaring that effective action to prevent and combat trafficking in persons, especially women and children, requires a comprehensive international approach in the countries of origin, transit and destination that includes measures to prevent such trafficking, to punish the traffickers and to protect the victims of such trafficking, including by protecting their internationally recognized human rights,

Taking into account the fact that, despite the existence of a variety of international instruments containing rules and practical measures to combat the exploitation of persons, especially women and children, there is no universal instrument that addresses all aspects of trafficking in persons,

Concerned that, in the absence of such an instrument, persons who are vulnerable to trafficking will not be sufficiently protected,

Recalling General Assembly resolution 53/111 of 9 December 1998, in which the Assembly decided to establish an open-ended intergovernmental ad hoc committee for the purpose of elaborating a comprehensive international convention against transnational organized crime and of discussing the elaboration of, inter alia, an international instrument addressing trafficking in women and children,

Convinced that supplementing the United Nations Convention against Transnational Organized Crime with an international instrument for the prevention, suppression and punishment of trafficking in persons, especially women and children, will be useful in preventing and combating that crime,

Have agreed as follows:

I. General provisions

Article 1. Relation with the United Nations Convention against Transnational Organized Crime

1. This Protocol supplements the United Nations Convention against Transnational Organized Crime. It shall be interpreted together with the Convention.
2. The provisions of the Convention shall apply, mutatis mutandis, to this Protocol unless otherwise provided herein.
3. The offences established in accordance with article 5 of this Protocol shall be regarded as offences established in accordance with the Convention.

Article 2. Statement of purpose

The purposes of this Protocol are:

(a) To prevent and combat trafficking in persons, paying particular attention to women and children;

(b) To protect and assist the victims of such trafficking, with full respect for their human rights; and

(c) To promote cooperation among States Parties in order to meet those objectives.

Article 3. Use of terms

For the purposes of this Protocol:

(a) 'Trafficking in persons' shall mean the recruitment, transportation, transfer, harbouring or receipt of persons, by means of the threat or use of force or other forms of coercion, of abduction, of fraud, of deception, of the abuse of power or of a position of vulnerability or of the giving or receiving of payments or benefits to achieve the consent of a person having control over another person, for the purpose of exploitation. Exploitation shall include, at a minimum, the exploitation of the prostitution of others or other forms of sexual exploitation, forced labour or services, slavery or practices similar to slavery, servitude or the removal of organs;

(b) The consent of a victim of trafficking in persons to the intended exploitation set forth in subparagraph (a) of this article shall be irrelevant where any of the means set forth in subparagraph (a) have been used;

(c) The recruitment, transportation, transfer, harbouring or receipt of a child for the purpose of exploitation shall be considered 'trafficking in persons' even if this does not involve any of the means set forth in subparagraph (a) of this article;

(d) 'Child' shall mean any person under eighteen years of age.

Article 4. Scope of application

This Protocol shall apply, except as otherwise stated herein, to the prevention, investigation and prosecution of the offences established in accordance with article 5 of this Protocol, where those offences are transnational in nature and involve an organized criminal group, as well as to the protection of victims of such offences.

Article 5. Criminalization

1. Each State Party shall adopt such legislative and other measures as may be necessary to establish as criminal offences the conduct set forth in article 3 of this Protocol, when committed intentionally.

2. Each State Party shall also adopt such legislative and other measures as may be necessary to establish as criminal offences:

(a) Subject to the basic concepts of its legal system, attempting to commit an offence established in accordance with paragraph 1 of this article;

(b) Participating as an accomplice in an offence established in accordance with paragraph 1 of this article; and

(c) Organizing or directing other persons to commit an offence established in accordance with paragraph 1 of this article.

II. Protection of victims of trafficking in persons

Article 6. Assistance to and protection of victims of trafficking in persons

1. In appropriate cases and to the extent possible under its domestic law, each State Party shall protect the privacy and identity of victims of trafficking in persons, including, inter alia, by making legal proceedings relating to such trafficking confidential.

2. Each State Party shall ensure that its domestic legal or administrative system contains measures that provide to victims of trafficking in persons, in appropriate cases:

(a) Information on relevant court and administrative proceedings;

(b) Assistance to enable their views and concerns to be presented and considered at appropriate stages of criminal proceedings against offenders, in a manner not prejudicial to the rights of the defence.

3. Each State Party shall consider implementing measures to provide for the physical, psychological and social recovery of victims of trafficking in persons, including, in appropriate cases, in cooperation with non-governmental organizations, other relevant organizations and other elements of civil society, and, in particular, the provision of:

(a) Appropriate housing;
(b) Counselling and information, in particular as regards their legal rights, in a language that the victims of trafficking in persons can understand;
(c) Medical, psychological and material assistance; and
(d) Employment, educational and training opportunities.

4. Each State Party shall take into account, in applying the provisions of this article, the age, gender and special needs of victims of trafficking in persons, in particular the special needs of children, including appropriate housing, education and care.

5. Each State Party shall endeavour to provide for the physical safety of victims of trafficking in persons while they are within its territory.

6. Each State Party shall ensure that its domestic legal system contains measures that offer victims of trafficking in persons the possibility of obtaining compensation for damage suffered.

Article 7. Status of victims of trafficking in persons in receiving States

1. In addition to taking measures pursuant to article 6 of this Protocol, each State Party shall consider adopting legislative or other appropriate measures that permit victims of trafficking in persons to remain in its territory, temporarily or permanently, in appropriate cases.

2. In implementing the provision contained in paragraph 1 of this article, each State Party shall give appropriate consideration to humanitarian and compassionate factors.

Article 8. Repatriation of victims of trafficking in persons

1. The State Party of which a victim of trafficking in persons is a national or in which the person had the right of permanent residence at the time of entry into the territory of the receiving State Party shall facilitate and accept, with due regard for the safety of that person, the return of that person without undue or unreasonable delay.

2. When a State Party returns a victim of trafficking in persons to a State Party of which that person is a national or in which he or she had, at the time of entry into the territory of the receiving State Party, the right of permanent residence, such return shall be with due regard for the safety of that person and for the status of any legal proceedings related to the fact that the person is a victim of trafficking and shall preferably be voluntary.

3. At the request of a receiving State Party, a requested State Party shall, without undue or unreasonable delay, verify whether a person who is a victim of trafficking in persons is its national or had the right of permanent residence in its territory at the time of entry into the territory of the receiving State Party.

4. In order to facilitate the return of a victim of trafficking in persons who is without proper documentation, the State Party of which that person is a national or in which he or she had the right of permanent residence at the time of entry into the territory of the receiving State Party shall agree to issue, at the request of the receiving State Party, such travel documents or other authorisation as may be necessary to enable the person to travel to and re-enter its territory.

5. This article shall be without prejudice to any right afforded to victims of trafficking in persons by any domestic law of the receiving State Party.

6. This article shall be without prejudice to any applicable bilateral or multilateral agreement or arrangement that governs, in whole or in part, the return of victims of trafficking in persons.

III. Prevention, cooperation and other measures

Article 9. Prevention of trafficking in persons

1. States Parties shall establish comprehensive policies, programmes and other measures:
    (a) To prevent and combat trafficking in persons; and
    (b) To protect victims of trafficking in persons, especially women and children, from revictimisation.

2. States Parties shall endeavour to undertake measures such as research, information and mass media campaigns and social and economic initiatives to prevent and combat trafficking in persons.

3. Policies, programmes and other measures established in accordance with this article shall, as appropriate, include cooperation with non-governmental organizations, other relevant organizations and other elements of civil society.

4. States Parties shall take or strengthen measures, including through bilateral or multilateral cooperation, to alleviate the factors that make persons, especially women and children, vulnerable to trafficking, such as poverty, underdevelopment and lack of equal opportunity.

5. States Parties shall adopt or strengthen legislative or other measures, such as educational, social or cultural measures, including through bilateral and multilateral cooperation, to discourage the demand that fosters all forms of exploitation of persons, especially women and children, that leads to trafficking.

Article 10. Information exchange and training

1. Law enforcement, immigration or other relevant authorities of States Parties shall, as appropriate, cooperate with one another by exchanging information, in accordance with their domestic law, to enable them to determine:

   (a) Whether individuals crossing or attempting to cross an international border with travel documents belonging to other persons or without travel documents are perpetrators or victims of trafficking in persons;

   (b) The types of travel document that individuals have used or attempted to use to cross an international border for the purpose of trafficking in persons; and

   (c) The means and methods used by organised criminal groups for the purpose of trafficking in persons, including the recruitment and transportation of victims, routes and links between and among individuals and groups engaged in such trafficking, and possible measures for detecting them.

2. States Parties shall provide or strengthen training for law enforcement, immigration and other relevant officials in the prevention of trafficking in persons. The training should focus on methods used in preventing such trafficking, prosecuting the traffickers and protecting the rights of the victims, including protecting the victims from the traffickers. The training should also take into account the need to consider human rights and child- and gender-sensitive issues and it should encourage cooperation with non-governmental organizations, other relevant organizations and other elements of civil society.

3. A State Party that receives information shall comply with any request by the State Party that transmitted the information that places restrictions on its use.

Article 11. Border measures

1. Without prejudice to international commitments in relation to the free movement of people, States Parties shall strengthen, to the extent possible, such border controls as may be necessary to prevent and detect trafficking in persons.

2. Each State Party shall adopt legislative or other appropriate measures to prevent, to the extent possible, means of transport operated by commercial carriers from being used in the commission of offences established in accordance with article 5 of this Protocol.

3. Where appropriate, and without prejudice to applicable international conventions, such measures shall include establishing the obligation of commercial carriers, including any transportation company or the owner or operator of any means of transport, to ascertain that all passengers are in possession of the travel documents required for entry into the receiving State.

4. Each State Party shall take the necessary measures, in accordance with its domestic law, to provide for sanctions in cases of violation of the obligation set forth in paragraph 3 of this article.

5. Each State Party shall consider taking measures that permit, in accordance with its domestic law, the denial of entry or revocation of visas of persons implicated in the commission of offences established in accordance with this Protocol.

6. Without prejudice to article 27 of the Convention, States Parties shall consider strengthening cooperation among border control agencies by, inter alia, establishing and maintaining direct channels of communication.

Article 12. Security and control of documents

Each State Party shall take such measures as may be necessary, within available means:

(a) To ensure that travel or identity documents issued by it are of such quality that they cannot easily be misused and cannot readily be falsified or unlawfully altered, replicated or issued; and

(b) To ensure the integrity and security of travel or identity documents issued by or on behalf of the State Party and to prevent their unlawful creation, issuance and use.

Article 13. Legitimacy and validity of documents

At the request of another State Party, a State Party shall, in accordance with its domestic law, verify within a reasonable time the legitimacy and validity of travel or identity documents issued or purported to have been issued in its name and suspected of being used for trafficking in persons.

IV. Final provisions

Article 14. Saving clause

1. Nothing in this Protocol shall affect the rights, obligations and responsibilities of States and individuals under international law, including international humanitarian law and international human rights law and, in particular, where applicable, the 1951 Convention[2] and the 1967 Protocol[3] relating to the Status of Refugees and the principle of non-refoulement as contained therein.

---

[2] United Nations, *Treaty Series*, vol. 189, No. 2545.

[3] United Nations, *Treaty Series*, vol. 606, No. 8791.

2. The measures set forth in this Protocol shall be interpreted and applied in a way that is not discriminatory to persons on the ground that they are victims of trafficking in persons. The interpretation and application of those measures shall be consistent with internationally recognised principles of non-discrimination.

Article 15. Settlement of disputes

1. States Parties shall endeavour to settle disputes concerning the interpretation or application of this Protocol through negotiation.
2. Any dispute between two or more States Parties concerning the interpretation or application of this Protocol that cannot be settled through negotiation within a reasonable time shall, at the request of one of those States Parties, be submitted to arbitration. If, six months after the date of the request for arbitration, those States Parties are unable to agree on the organisation of the arbitration, any one of those States Parties may refer the dispute to the International Court of Justice by request in accordance with the Statute of the Court.
3. Each State Party may, at the time of signature, ratification, acceptance or approval of or accession to this Protocol, declare that it does not consider itself bound by paragraph 2 of this article. The other States Parties shall not be bound by paragraph 2 of this article with respect to any State Party that has made such a reservation.
4. Any State Party that has made a reservation in accordance with paragraph 3 of this article may at any time withdraw that reservation by notification to the Secretary-General of the United Nations.

Article 16. Signature, ratification, acceptance, approval and accession

1. This Protocol shall be open to all States for signature from 12 to 15 December 2000 in Palermo, Italy, and thereafter at United Nations Headquarters in New York until 12 December 2002.
2. This Protocol shall also be open for signature by regional economic integration organisations provided that at least one member State

of such organisation has signed this Protocol in accordance with paragraph 1 of this article.

3. This Protocol is subject to ratification, acceptance or approval. Instruments of ratification, acceptance or approval shall be deposited with the Secretary-General of the United Nations. A regional economic integration organisation may deposit its instrument of ratification, acceptance or approval if at least one of its member States has done likewise. In that instrument of ratification, acceptance or approval, such organisation shall declare the extent of its competence with respect to the matters governed by this Protocol. Such organisation shall also inform the depositary of any relevant modification in the extent of its competence.

4. This Protocol is open for accession by any State or any regional economic integration organisation of which at least one member State is a Party to this Protocol. Instruments of accession shall be deposited with the Secretary- General of the United Nations. At the time of its accession, a regional economic integration organisation shall declare the extent of its competence with respect to matters governed by this Protocol. Such organisation shall also inform the depositary of any relevant modification in the extent of its competence.

Article 17. Entry into force

1. This Protocol shall enter into force on the ninetieth day after the date of deposit of the fortieth instrument of ratification, acceptance, approval or accession, except that it shall not enter into force before the entry into force of the Convention. For the purpose of this paragraph, any instrument deposited by a regional economic integration organisation shall not be counted as additional to those deposited by member States of such organisation.

2. For each State or regional economic integration organisation ratifying, accepting, approving or acceding to this Protocol after the deposit of the fortieth instrument of such action, this Protocol shall enter into force on the thirtieth day after the date of deposit by such State or organisation of the relevant instrument or on the date this

Protocol enters into force pursuant to paragraph 1 of this article, whichever is the later.

Article 18. Amendment

1. After the expiry of five years from the entry into force of this Protocol, a State Party to the Protocol may propose an amendment and file it with the Secretary-General of the United Nations, who shall thereupon communicate the proposed amendment to the States Parties and to the Conference of the Parties to the Convention for the purpose of considering and deciding on the proposal. The States Parties to this Protocol meeting at the Conference of the Parties shall make every effort to achieve consensus on each amendment. If all efforts at consensus have been exhausted and no agreement has been reached, the amendment shall, as a last resort, require for its adoption a two-thirds majority vote of the States Parties to this Protocol present and voting at the meeting of the Conference of the Parties.

2. Regional economic integration organisations, in matters within their competence, shall exercise their right to vote under this article with a number of votes equal to the number of their member States that are Parties to this Protocol. Such organisations shall not exercise their right to vote if their member States exercise theirs and vice versa.

3. An amendment adopted in accordance with paragraph 1 of this article is subject to ratification, acceptance or approval by States Parties.

4. An amendment adopted in accordance with paragraph 1 of this article shall enter into force in respect of a State Party ninety days after the date of the deposit with the Secretary-General of the United Nations of an instrument of ratification, acceptance or approval of such amendment.

5. When an amendment enters into force, it shall be binding on those States Parties which have expressed their consent to be bound by it. Other States Parties shall still be bound by the provisions of this Protocol and any earlier amendments that they have ratified, accepted or approved.

Article 19. Denunciation

1. A State Party may denounce this Protocol by written notification to the Secretary-General of the United Nations. Such denunciation shall become effective one year after the date of receipt of the notification by the Secretary- General.
2. A regional economic integration organisation shall cease to be a Party to this Protocol when all of its member States have denounced it.

Article 20. Depositary and languages

1. The Secretary-General of the United Nations is designated depositary of this Protocol.
2. The original of this Protocol, of which the Arabic, Chinese, English, French, Russian and Spanish texts are equally authentic, shall be deposited with the Secretary-General of the United Nations.

In witness whereof, the undersigned plenipotentiaries, being duly authorised thereto by their respective Governments, have signed this Protocol.

Index

actus reus, definition of 170
African Union 190–95, 215–16, 222–23
al-Bashir, Ahmad Omar Hassan 188–96, 214–23
anti-trafficking 179
  laws 7, 11, 72–73, 98, 132–33
  strategies 11
Anti-Trafficking in Persons Programme 103
arbitrary deportation 144
arbitrary imprisonment 144
arms smuggling/trafficking 2, 17, 80, 146, 151–55
arms trade 154
association crimes, types of 21

attack directed against any civilian population, definition of 26, 126, 127, 135, 141, 144, 180–83, 240–41
Azerbaijan 63

Bartholet, Elizabeth 36
beatings 40, 159
bonded labourers 148
border-control measures to combat trafficking 111–13
broken in 2, 28
brothels 28, 29, 38, 45, 60n17, 73, 77, 89, 109, 146, 148, 161 (*see also* prostitution)

Bulgaria 33–34

Canada 43
Child Abuse Image Database
  (ICAID) 15
child labour 10
child trade 31–36
child traders 32, 34–35
child trafficking/children trafficking
  122 (*see also* human trafficking;
  prostitution; sexual exploitation;
  sexual servitude; sexual slavery)
  definition of 29–31
  deprived of education 36
  health-related consequences of
    44–45
  sexual slavery 29–30
  time of 30
  trading in children 31–36
CIS Co-ordination Council of
  General Prosecutors 104
civil justice system 105
Committee on the Elimination of
  Racial Discrimination against
  Women 63
common association crime 21
Convention and Protocol Relating
  to the Status of Refugees 65–66
Convention on Elimination of All
  Forms of Racial Discrimination
  against Women 63
Convention on Rights of a Child,
  on Sale of Children, and
  Child Prostitution and Child
  Pornography, Optional Protocol
  to the 62–63
Convention on the Abolition of
  Slavery, the Slave Trade, and

Institutions and Practices
  Similar to Slavery, 1956 25–26,
  52, 162, 179, 231
Convention on the Elimination of
  All Forms of Discrimination
  against Women (CEDAW),
  1979 52, 59–60
Convention on the Rights of the
  Child (CRC), 1989 60–62
Convention on the Rights of the
  Child on the Involvement of
  Children in Armed Conflict,
  Protocol to the 62
Council of Europe Convention on
  Action against Trafficking in
  Human Beings, 2008 92, 103
Council of Europe (CoE)
  Trafficking Convention 3,
  92–95, 103
crime(s)
  of aggression 8, 125, 138,
    177–78, 195
  mental element of 170
  syndicates 2, 6, 11, 20, 22, 48,
    96–97, 155, 156–57
crime of apartheid 126, 178,
  241–42
crime of persecution 169–70
  elements of 25, 133, 136–37,
    156–63, 165–167, 169–70,
    174, 186, 227
crimes against humanity 4, 8, 24,
  27, 125–27, 133–37, 159, 172,
  173–80, 184, 186, 187–89,
  190–93, 195–197, 205–14,
  217–23
  categories of 138, 178, 217
  definition of 136, 142–43

of enforced sterilization 167
of forced pregnancy 167
of sexual violence 167
cross-border trafficking of women
and children 76
CRS Report for Congress on
human trafficking 51
Czech Republic 59

deportation 14, 70, 82, 120, 126,
138–39, 141, 143–44, 149, 231,
241
Diamantopolou, Anna 22, 23n26
digital video disk (DVD) recording
38
drug addiction 49
drugs trafficking 2, 17, 32, 151–55,
157, 177, 222
association crime 21–22
and human trafficking,
comparison between 16

Economic Cooperation of West
African States Nations 37
employment laws for human
trafficking 109–11
enforced disappearance of persons
126, 241–42
enslavement 4, 8, 24, 26, 125–28,
138–44, 146, 162 (*see also* sexual
slavery)
as a crime against humanity
162
definition of 162–64, 241
Eurojust 104
European Axis Powers 138
European Convention for the
Protection of Human Rights and

Fundamental Freedoms, 1950
103
European Court of Human Rights
(ECHR) 204
European Court of Justice (ECJ)
204
European Judicial Institute 104
European Police (EUROPOL) 2,
23, 28, 104
European Union (EU) 18, 37
Europe Programme against
Corruption and Organised
Crime in South Eastern Europe
104
exploitation, definition of 171
extermination 126, 138–42,
144–45, 178, 230, 241
Extraordinary Chambers in the
Courts of Cambodia (ECCC),
Law on the Establishment of the
Article 5 of 142

forced pregnancy 142
forcibly 163, 167, 231, 234, 242

gender 13, 36, 38–39, 53, 60,
66–67, 73–74, 84, 89, 126, 169,
221, 235, 242, 254, 257
-based victimizations 39
-based violence 60
bias 68
definition of 242
dimension to distinction between
smuggling and trafficking
13–14
discrimination 36
human trafficking and 73–75
inequality 38, 75

persecution 65
sexual 171
Geneva Conventions of 1949 178
genocide 8, 125, 136, 138–40, 140,
144, 177–78, 189–90, 194–95,
197, 213, 217, 220–21, 223
Ghent system 111
global crisis (2008) 73
globalization process 17–18, 37–38,
49, 73

Hague Convention on the Civil
Aspects of International Child
Abduction, 2007 35, 136, 174
hepatitis 146, 174
HIV/AIDS 46, 146, 174
human dignity 3, 11, 50, 67, 87–89,
92, 98, 115, 129, 132, 144–46,
166, 217
human immune virus (HIV) 30, 45
human integrity 129
human mobility 151
human rights 4, 11, 13, 38, 39, 47,
49, 50, 56–57, 60, 64, 66, 67–68,
71, 81–82, 87–88, 90, 92, 98,
111, 115–17, 121–23, 128–30,
132, 136, 144, 148–51, 157, 166,
170, 174, 179, 191, 204, 208,
211, 217, 221–22, 250
international 4, 47, 128, 221
law, significance of 6, 132, 221
organizations 71, 87
protection of 67, 208
of trafficked victims 1–2, 93–94,
116–22 (see also human
trafficking)
deprivation of basic rights
25

violation of 4, 11, 38, 53, 67,
115–16, 121–22, 128, 132,
144, 145, 148, 150, 157, 166,
170, 174, 179, 217, 222
human smugglers 12–13
human smuggling 6, 9, 12, 14, 22,
37, 42, 47–48, 221
definition of 13
and human trafficking, difference
between 14
human trafficking 52, 54, 90,
153–58, 179, 222 (see also Rome
Statute of ICC)
acts of 182–83
business worth 15
causes of 36–37
challenges 6
deficiencies in laws dealing with
3, 50, 53, 66, 87–89
definition of 12, 55, 134
demographic consequences of
43–44
drugs trafficking and, comparison
between 16
as enforced prostitution 165–66
as enslavement and sexual slavery
161–64
as form of sexual violence
165–68
and gender 74–76
health-related consequences of
44–47
impact of 40, 91, 155
international legal framework
effectiveness and 101–06, 129
international problems to deal
with 145–51
law enforcement response in

Africa 80–81
European countries 81–82
Latin America and Caribbean
82–83
Middle East and Central Asia
78–80
South Asia 76–78
legal framework 2–3, 5, 42, 54,
87, 92, 97–98, 101–03, 107,
114, 129, 130, 136, 155, 171,
179
legal response, importance of
53–67, 96–101, 129–31,
176, 221
misinterpretation of terms 7
modern-day slavery 1, 11, 25,
47, 115
organized crime 20, 149–57,
165, 174, 183–85, 222–23
organized form of business 149
as persecution 168
political consequences of 42–43
prevention of, approaches
employment laws and
unemployment benefit,
effectiveness of 109–11
immigration and border-
control measures 111–13
new international treaties
113–14
prostitution, legalization of
107–08
regional treaties 114
as rape 159–61
social consequences of 40–42
statistics of 5, 83–84
threat to country's legal
framework 2, 5

as torture 157–59
torture of human beings 64
as transnational organized
crime 73, 101, 111, 121, 130,
148–50, 217
victims of 14

illegal immigration 13, 48
illicit trade/trafficking 73, 155–58
Immoral Traffic (Prevention) Act,
1956 77, 103
imprisonment 21, 57, 79, 126, 139,
143–144, 156, 159, 199–200, 213
intent 173–74
Inter-Agency Council against
Trafficking 103
Intergovernmental Authority on
Development (IGAD) 192
International Convention against
Torture, Cruel Inhuman
Degrading Treatment and
Punishment (CAT or Torture
Convention) 64
International Convention for the
Suppression of the White Slave
Traffic, 1910 54–55
International Convention on the
Protection of the Rights of All
Migrant Workers and Members
of Their Families 64–65
International Covenant on Civil and
Political Rights (ICCPR), 1966
57–58
International Covenant on
Economic, Social and Cultural
Rights (ICESCR), 1966 58–59
International Criminal Court (ICC)
3–4, 8, 91, 136

aim of 176, 198
application of 179–86
Article 4 of 8
challenges and limitations before
    184–88
complementary principle 187,
    196, 201
crimes, identification and
    prosecution 180–81
Elements of Crime of 161,
    164–67
enforcement at national and
    international level 203
enforcement regime, principles
    of 199
establishment of 20–23, 179
jurisdiction of 26–27, 178–79,
    200–02
Omar Hassan Ahmad al-Bashir
    indictment, case study
    189–190
procedure and evidence of 199
success in countering human
    trafficking 125–28
International Criminal Police
    Organization (INTERPOL)
    15–17
International Criminal Tribunal for
    Former Yugoslavia (ICTY) 4,
    26n39, 127–29, 137, 139, 144,
    159, 162, 166, 169, 173, 174–76,
    187, 204, 211–13
    Article 5(c) of 126
    Article 5 of 139–41
    Article 5(g) of 159
    Article 5(h) of 169
    jurisdiction of 26
    Kunarac case 213

powers of 141
Trial Chamber 160
International Criminal Tribunal for
    Rwanda (ICTR) 4, 140, 161,
    209
    Article 3 of 4, 140–41
    Article 3(h) of 169
international humanitarian law 11,
    47, 62, 66, 139–42, 144–45,
    228, 258
international human rights law 6,
    52, 117, 130, 222, 257
international labour law 6, 52–53,
    221
International Labour Organization
    (ILO) 17n13, 52, 83–85, 88, 90,
    92, 99, 111, 146
International Law Commission's
    Draft Code of Crimes against the
    Peace and Security of Mankind
    144
    Article 18 of 144
International Military Tribunal 127,
    137–38, 200
International Organization for
    Migration (IOM) 52, 83–84, 87,
    88, 90, 91–92, 99, 146
international treaty 200
Internet
    pornography 38, 63–64
    sale of sex over 38
Iraq war 62, 79, 220

Jewish holocaust 220
Justice and Equality Movement at El
    Fasher airport, Sudan 188

Kayishema Trial Judgment 161

knowledge 173–74
Korean war 220

labour 66
exploitation, victims of 106
forced 7, 110, 130, 132, 146, 150,
162
servitude 26–27
Laws and Customs of War on Land
of 1907 136
League of Nations 54
legal prohibition against human
trafficking 51, 88, 100
London Charter of the International
Military Tribunal 137 (*see*
Nuremberg Charter of the
International Military Tribunal)

mafia-type association crime 21–22
mens rea element
aspects of 172
conditions of 171
Mexico 45, 60, 83
Migiro, Rose 11n2
migrants/immigrants 80 (*see also*
human smuggling; human
trafficking; sexual slavery)
illegal 7, 65, 72–73, 106, 109,
130–31, 149–51, 159
labourers 164
smuggled/smuggling 14, 100,
102, 150–53, 217
smugglers of 152
victims of human trafficking 68
voluntary services of smugglers 13
women and children trafficked
as 78
workers 3, 65

migration 12, 42, 80, 128 (*see also*
human trafficking)
for employment 110
involves sexual exploitation 68
irregular 10
of labour force 107
migrant workers exploitation
during process of 64–65, 155
multinational criminal networks 6,
22, 48
murder 60, 126, 138–42, 144, 178

National Crime Records Bureau
(NCRB) 77
NHRC 77–78
non-governmental organizations
(NGOs) 55, 78, 80–83, 91, 102,
121
North Atlantic Treaty Organization
(NATO) 37
Nuremberg Charter of the
International Military Tribunal
4, 137, 174, 212
Article 6(c) of the 138–39
crimes categories 219

Office of the High Commissioner
for Human Rights (OHCHR)
52, 88, 119, 119–23
Organization for Security and
Co-operation in Europe (OSCE)
52, 88, 99
organized crime (*see also* human
trafficking)
advantage of human mobility to
smuggle humans 151–54
economic development of the
countries, impact on 155

groups 15, 49, 113
  displacement of population
    44–45
  role in trafficking 17–23
  nature of 82
  profits to the perpetrators 152
  types of 155
orphans/orphanages problems in
  Southeast Asia 36–37

Palermo Protocol 3, 24, 26, 92, 114,
  122–23, 132, 138, 152, 177, 185,
  222
persecution, trafficking as 168–70
physical abuse 40, 159
physical liberty, trafficking as
  deprivation of 156, 161
physical perpetrator 164–72
pimps 38, 60n17, 74, 108–09
Polaroid film 38
political manipulation 209, 212–13
pornography/child pornography 38,
  62–63
prevention, protection, and
  prosecution (three-P strategy) 3,
  106, 123–24
Princeton Principles on Universal
  Jurisdiction 205–07
Promotion and Protection against
  Unemployment Convention,
  1988 111
prostitute(s) 2, 28–30, 38, 55, 74,
  109–10, 150
prostitution 2, 4, 8, 10, 20, 54, 64
  (see also sexual exploitation;
  sexual slavery)
  culturally embedded tradition
    38

enforced/forced 3–4, 5, 7, 24, 26,
  49, 52, 56, 67–68, 72, 75–76,
  81–82, 91, 128–29, 131,
  135, 138, 146–47, 152–53,
  157–59, 166–67, 166–68,
  174, 185, 240
  of females under eighteen years
    2, 30
  legalization and regulating to
    combat human trafficking
    107–09
Protocol to Prevent, Suppress and
  Punish Trafficking in Persons
  (Trafficking in Persons Protocol)
  23–24, 52, 93, 99, 122, 135, 152,
  177, 250–62

rape(s) 40, 60, 109, 141–42, 144, 159
  categories of 159
  definition of 159
  gang 28
  trafficking as 160–62
red light areas 28 (see also sexual
  slavery)
refugee(s) 65–66, 70, 72, 82, 89
  definition of 66
  of human trafficking 83
  status 65, 70, 72, 82, 89, 101,
    131
regionalization of international
  criminal law 200–02
  merits of 208–12
  regional criminal courts,
    establishment of 204
  regional seat of ICC 203
  specialized domestic courts with
    regional judges, establishment
    of 206–07

universal jurisdiction with
regional preference 205–06
regional preference 205–06
rescue, rehabilitation, and
reintegration (three-R approach)
3, 4, 123, 125, 149
restorative justice 210, 211
aims of 211
failure, reasons for 193
goals, methods to attain 230
Right to Assistance 120
Right to Be Heard in Court 119
Right to Compensation for
Damages 119
Right to Information 118
Right to Legal Representation 119
Right to Privacy 118
Right to Return 121–22
Right to Safety 118
Right to Seek Residence 120
Romania 33
Rome Statute of ICC 26, 48,
125–26, 135, 138–39, 144,
149, 156–57, 169, 171–73, 200,
220–23
amendment to 214
Article 7 of 4, 9, 24–27, 49, 120,
125, 127, 133, 137, 138, 144,
149, 166–169, 171, 173–74,
175, 179–85, 195–96, 218,
221–23, 228–29
attack against civilian
population 180–84
crimes against humanity
228–29
Article 7(1) of 137, 138–39
Article 7(1)(a) of 229–30
Article 7(1)(b) of 230

Article 7(1)(c) of 24–25, 135–36,
161–62, 164, 186, 230–31
Article 7(1)(d) of 231
Article 7(1)(e) of 156, 231–32
Article 7(1)(f) of 157, 232
Article 7(1)(g) of 159
Article 7(1)(h) of 170–71,
235–36
Article 7(1)(i) of 236–37
Article 7(1)(j) of 237
Article 7(1)(g)-1 of 232–33
Article 7(1)(g)-2 162, 233
Article 7(1)(g)-3 of 233–34
Article 7(1)(g)-4 of 234
Article 7(1)(g)-5 of 234–35
Article 7(1)(g)-6 of 167, 235
Article 7(1)(k) of 237–38
Article 7(2)(c) of 135
Article 7(2)(e) of 158
Article 7(2)(g) of 169
Article 30 171–73
Article 30(1) of 172
Article 30(2) of 172
Article 30(3) of 172
Article 98 of 190
Article 98(1) of 195
Article 98(2) of 195, 216
dealing with human trafficking
3, 24–26, 50, 52, 53, 54, 56,
66–69, 69, 71, 88–90, 100,
103, 145, 148
Elements of Crime 170, 186, 227
of ICC, enforcement of 131
jurisdiction 195
origin of 136
state parties to 243–49
two-pillar system 198
weaknesses in 193–95, 222

Russia 44
Rwanda genocide/sexual violence
    160, 217

sale of a child, definition of 61–63
sex
    commercial 84
    forced 116
    -tested process 2, 28
    tourism 83
    tourists 37
    tours 38
sex trafficking 44
    causes of 49
    consequences of 49
    victims killed by clients 46
sexual
    abuse 40, 45, 61, 132, 135,
        144–46, 160, 173
    activity/ies 45, 160
    acts 4, 28
    assault 165, 168
    autonomy 160
    exploitation 54, 145
        illegal immigrants trafficking
            for 43, 106, 131
        trafficking of women and
            children for 1–2
        by women of other women
            and children 2
    favours 22
    intercourse 28, 30, 45, 163
    services 39, 41, 106, 124
    servitude 2, 4, 5, 8, 11, 30, 50, 56,
        64, 102, 130, 151
    torture 28
    violence 4, 8, 24, 26, 126, 135,
        138, 142, 160–63

sexually transmitted diseases
    (STDs) 45–46
Sexual Offences Act, 2003 103
sexual slavery 2, 4, 6, 8, 11, 26,
    64, 109, 161 (see also human
    trafficking)
    comfort stations use for facilities
        39
    definition of 163
    recruitment by false
        advertisements 2, 27–28
    trafficking 163–66
        reasons for 37–38
        scope of 15–17, 22
slave practices 4–5, 52
slavery 7, 10, 54, 56, 64, 102, 130,
    150
    factors to determine 162–63
slave trade 4, 52, 56-58, 64
Slovakia 59
Slovenia 58
Southeast European Prosecutors
    Advisory Group 104
Special Court for Sierra Leone
    (SCSL), Statute of the 141–43,
    199, 206–07
Sudanese Liberation Movement 188
Sudan People's Armed Forces 189
Sweden 109

Tokyo Charter 137, 174
    Article 5(c) of 137
torture 38, 40–41, 49, 141, 144,
    157–59
    definition of 159, 241
    trafficking as 157–59
trafficked persons/victims 6, 26–27,
    49, 54, 72, 79, 85, 101, 117–18,

120–21, 122, 133, 149, 160–61, 163, 166, 174, 182, 217 (*see also* human trafficking)

CoE Convention projection 93–97

considered as a commodity 115, 132, 146, 173

exploitation in commercial sex 75, 84–85

from South Asia 77

treatment of 162

trafficked woman, revenue earned from 18, 23, 83–84

traffickers 15, 40, 105–06, 115 (*see also* human trafficking)

assisted by families of trafficked victims 129

employed with persons for prospective victims identification 161

exploitation of traffic women and children by 31–32

hiring of employment agencies 110

misuse of weak immigration policies 112

prosecution problems 150

trafficking protocol 171

Trafficking in Persons and Transportation (Control) Act 103

trafficking in persons, definition of 1, 136

Trafficking in Persons Protocol 12–13, 93, 114, 115–117, 118–20

trafficking protocol 115, 134

criminalization of traffickers states 170

inclusion of human rights aspect 115

provisions for state parties 98

Trafficking Victims Protection Act (TVPA), 2000 103

transnational crime groups 19, 43

transnational organized crime 2, 5, 10, 74, 100, 110, 112, 123, 130–31, 147, 149 (*see also* human trafficking)

forms of 151

impact of 153

treaties at international and regional level to combat trafficking 113–15

tuberculosis 146

Tutu, Desmond 218

Ukraine 44

UN Committee on Economic, Social and Cultural Rights of 2006, Report 58–59

UN Convention on the Elimination for All Forms of Discrimination against Women (CEDAW) 1979 59–60

unemployment benefits for trafficked human 109–11

UN General Assembly 56, 59

resolution 53/111 of 1998 251

UNIFEM 77

United Nations (UN) 3, 5, 17n13, 23, 40, 53, 79, 82, 88, 91, 112, 115–16, 128, 131, 137, 144, 191, 219

abolition of slave trade and practices 4

Article 52 of Charter 208

estimation of human trafficking 53

framed international legal
framework to combat human
trafficking 92
human trafficking problem 121
enforcement action of state 123
enforcement of conventions and
protocols for 55, 99–101
United Nations Children's Fund
(UNICEF) 31, 52, 88, 99
United Nations Commissioner for
Refugees (UNHCR) 70–72
United Nations Convention against
Illicit Traffic in Narcotic Drugs
and Psychotropic Substances,
1988 153–54
United Nations Convention against
Transnational Organized Crime
(UNTOC) 23, 52, 76, 92,
98–99, 104, 114, 122, 128, 135,
152, 177, 251
United Nations Convention against
Transnational Organized Crime,
Protocol to Prevent, Suppress
and Punish Trafficking in
Persons, Especially Women and
Children, 2003 177
United Nations Convention for the
Suppression of Trafficking in
Persons and of the Exploitation
of the Prostitution of Others,
1949 52
United Nations Convention on
Prevention of Crimes against
Humanity 217–18,
United Nations Global Initiative to
Fight Human Trafficking (UN.
GIFT) 3, 52, 76, 84–86, 122,
135, 132

United Nations Human Rights
Council (UNHRC) 55, 66–67,
98
United Nations Office on Drugs
and Crime (UNODC) 3, 6, 11,
15–16, 23, 48–49, 52, 75–76,
84–86, 89, 90, 93, 98, 114, 122,
128, 132, 146, 152
United Nations Protocol against the
Smuggling of Migrants by Land,
Sea and Air 52
United Nations Protocol to Prevent,
Suppress, and Punish Trafficking
in Persons, Especially Women
and Children 52, 152, 250–62
United Nations Security Council
140, 188
United Nations Trafficking Protocol
128, 221
and CoE Trafficking Convention,
comparison between 93–97
United States Victims of Trafficking
and Violence Protection Act,
2000 103
Universal Declaration of Human
Rights (UDR), 1948 52, 57–58
UN Peacekeepers 41
UN Security Council 195–98, 203,
214–16
UN Trafficking Protocol 3
USA 43, 45
Uzbekistan 58–59

victim-blaming 41
victim-centred approach 3, 122,
132, 147, 22
victims of trafficking 66, 67–70, 76,
115 (*see also* human trafficking)

auctioned on Internet 29
broken in or sex tested 28
education level of 87
global routes of transportation
   of 22, 97
health problems faced by 144
identification of 84–85
misunderstood as illegal
   migrants 149
repatriation of 121
trafficked through abduction
   149
trauma faced by 146
witnesses for prosecuting 103
Vietnam war 220
violence 2, 28, 71

war crimes 8, 125, 137–40, 144,
   162, 177–80, 189, 217
Wenke, Daja 31–32
women 99, 122, 127, 130, 145,
   152 (*see also* human trafficking;

prostitution; sex trafficking;
   sexual slavery; transnational
   organized crime)
EUROPOL report on resale of
   28–29
as facilitators for illicit trade of
   human trafficking 73–74
images of rape on Internet 38
recruitment into sexual servitude
   slavery 2, 4
suffer from secondary
   victimization 41
trafficked 150, 157
   health-related consequences
      44–47
   importation into community
      41
   to sell their children 33
   trapped into human trafficking,
      reasons for 75
World War II 39, 197
   sexual slavery during 37

About the Author

Joshua Nathan Aston teaches Law and is Dean-Students' Welfare at Gujarat National Law University, Gandhinagar, Gujarat, India. His areas of interests are International Criminal Law, International Humanitarian Law and Human Rights Law, and Law of Contracts. He has an experience of more than six years in teaching and research. Aston holds a PhD in Law from Symbiosis International University, Pune, Maharashtra, India. He has completed his Master in International Criminal Law from the University of Sussex, Brighton, UK, wherein he also completed his Legal Secretarial Diploma from Souters Legal Training Centre, London. Besides, he did Post Graduate Diploma in Financial Management from Symbiosis Institute of Business Management, Pune—one of India's most sought after business schools. Aston has received several awards and achievements in his career, which include the Israeli Government Scholarship awarded by the Ministry of Foreign Affairs, Cultural and Scientific

Affairs Department, Government of Israel to carry out Research at Tel Aviv University, Israel for eight months. He has attended various international and national conferences and seminars including the Asia-Pacific Law Deans' Forum held in Hong Kong in 2016. He has a wide range of publications to his credit, including books, various articles, and research papers.